DOUBLE VISION

DOUBLE VISION

Moral Philosophy and Shakespearean Drama

Tzachi Zamir

PRINCETON UNIVERSITY PRESS

PRINCETON AND OXFORD

Copyright © 2007 by Princeton University Press

Requests for permission to reproduce material from this work should be sent to
Permissions, Princeton University Press

Published by Princeton University Press, 41 William Street, Princeton, New Jersey 08540

In the United Kingdom: Princeton University Press, 3 Market Place, Woodstock,

Oxfordshire OX20 1SY
All Rights Reserved

British Library Cataloging-in-Publication Data is available

Library of Congress Cataloging-in-Publication Data
Zamir, Tzachi, 1967–
Double vision : moral philosophy and Shakespearean drama / Tzachi Zamir.
p. cm.
Includes bibliographical references and index.
ISBN-13: 978-0-691-12563-3 (hardcover : alk. paper)
ISBN-10: 0-691-12563-5 (hardcover : alk. paper)
1. Shakespeare, William, 1564–1616—Criticism and interpretaion. 2. Shakespeare,
William, 1564–1616—Philosophy. 3. Philosophy in literature. 4. Literature—
Philosophy. 5. Literature—History and criticism—Theory, etc. 6. Criticism—Moral
and ethical aspects. 7. Literature and morals. I. Title.
PR3001.Z36 2007
822.3'3—dc22   2006012108

This book has been composed in Sabon

Printed on acid-free paper.∞

pup.princeton.edu

Printed in the United States of America

1 3 5 7 9 10 8 6 4 2

"HOW FINE IT WOULD BE, AGATHON," HE SAID, "IF WISDOM WERE A SORT OF THING THAT COULD FLOW OUT OF THE ONE OF US WHO IS FULLER INTO HIM WHO IS EMPTIER, BY OUR MERE CONTACT WITH EACH OTHER, AS WATER WILL FLOW THROUGH WOOL FROM THE FULLER CUP INTO THE EMPTIER. IF SUCH IS INDEED THE CASE WITH WISDOM, I SET A GREAT VALUE ON MY SITTING NEXT TO YOU."

SYMPOSIUM

Contents

Acknowledgments — ix

Introduction — xi

PART I: PHILOSOPHICAL CRITICISM IN THEORY — 1
  The Epistemological Basis of Philosophical Criticism — 3
  The Moral Basis of Philosophical Criticism — 20
  Philosophical Criticism and Contemporary Literary Studies — 44

PART II: PHILOSOPHICAL CRITICISM IN PRACTICE — 63
  A Case of Unfair Proportions — 65
  Upon One Bank and Shoal of Time — 92
  Love Stories — 112
  Making Love — 129
  On Being Too Deeply Loved — 151
  Doing Nothing — 168
  King Lear's Hidden Tragedy — 183

Appendix A:
  A Note on Lear's Motivation — 205

Appendix B:
  A Note on Shakespeare and Rhetoric — 211

Works Cited — 213

Index — 225

Acknowledgments

SOME CHAPTERS in this book were first formulated as part of a Ph.D. dissertation at Tel-Aviv University. I take this opportunity of thanking (again) my supervisor, Marcelo Dascal, for his intellectual influence and committed supervision. I am also indebted to Elizabeth Freund, Zephyra Porat, and Shirley Sharon-Zisser for their willingness to initiate a philosopher into the interests and motivations of literary critics. Eddy Zemach is among the few people who are practicing philosophers as well as literary critics, and his comments and friendship have meant a great deal to me and to the literary and theoretic orientation of that Ph.D.

The book was completed during a post-doc stay at the University of Chicago, enabled by a Rothschild fellowship and a grant by the Fulbright program. The University of Chicago is where some of the best work on philosophy and literature is done, and my firsthand acquaintance there with the people doing this work was the best intellectual gift I could have received. I am grateful to both foundations for making the stay possible.

Faculty members at the University of Chicago have been very generous in communicating their comments on shorter and longer portions of this book. I am obliged for such important input to David Bevington, Wayne Booth, Daniel Brudney, Bradin Cormack, Robert Pippin, and Richard Posner. I have also benefited from eavesdropping on seminars given by David Bevington, Joshua Scodel, Martha Nussbaum, and Richard Strier, as well as a workshop on Shakespeare and law, jointly taught by Martha Nussbaum and Richard Posner. My debts to Nussbaum are great and of several kinds: the initial impact of her writings has inspired me to take up this project in the first place. Yet, more than a formative influence, readers who are familiar with Nussbaum's writings will easily note the tight and ongoing dialogue that this book conducts with her thoughts. Finally, her comments on the entire manuscript have substantially transformed it at a crucial stage.

Chapters in this book have been published in previous forms in various journals. An earlier version of chapter one appeared under the title "An Epistemological Basis for Linking Philosophy and Literature," and appeared in *Metaphilosophy* 33 (3), April 2002, pp. 321–36. Earlier versions of chapters four and five appeared in *New Literary History* ["A Case of Unfair Proportions: Philosophy in Literature," (3), 1998, pp.

501–20, and "Upon One Bank and Shoal of Time," (3), 2000, pp. 529–51]. Earlier versions of chapters six and seven appeared in *Literature and Aesthetics* ["Love Stories: A Reading of *Romeo and Juliet*," 1999, pp. 71–98, and "Mature Love: A Reading of *Antony and Cleopatra*," 11, 2001, pp. 119–48]. An earlier version of chapter eight originally appeared in *Mosaic: A Journal for the Interdisciplinary Study of Literature* 35 (3) September 2002, pp. 167–82). An earlier version of chapter nine appeared in *Partial Answers: Journal of Literature and the History of Ideas* ["On Being Too Deeply Loved," 2 (2), June 2004, pp. 1–26]. I would like to thank these journals for permission to revise and incorporate this material here.

Introduction

Hatred, it seems, cannot be bought. They try, several times, doubling and tripling the money owed. But he persists in refusing. No amount of money will buy Shylock. In this he stands alone. Within all other relationships around him, emotions are inseparable from financial gain: Portia and Jessica are rich—not merely fair—a fact that never escapes their lovers or their own perceptions of these lovers. Male friendship too—the idealized commitments between Bassanio and Antonio—is contaminated by financial dependency. Hatred alone achieves purity in the moral cosmos of *The Merchant of Venice*, the only emotion that will remain distinct from prudence, the one emotion that they will insist on not understanding (Bassanio: "Do all men kill the things they do not love?" Shylock: "Hates any man the thing he would not kill?"). Knowingly going to trial with a "losing suit"—and suppose that the law authorizes him to kill Antonio, what then?—turns this trial into a presentation of something that Venice is unwilling to hear (Duke: "Upon my power, I may dismiss this court!"). Shylock, the dramatized oxymoron of a money-shunning Jew, will soon disappear, to everyone's relief, including our own. But not before he registers a complaint that he refuses to express directly ("I will not answer that!"; "I am not bound to please thee with my answers!").

What is Shylock's complaint? Law is conceived in *The Merchant of Venice* as more than means for adjudicating between conflicting claims or enforcing norms. Like theologized money ("my Christian ducats"), law is a vehicle for communication between a Jewish outside and a Christian nexus. Shylock's deployment of law thus parallels similar attempts by marginalized characters to trespass into formally impenetrable power structures (a disguised woman attempting to infiltrate the masculine world of law; another woman trying to use money so as to buy her way out of Judaism). The confrontation between Shylock and Portia within the context of the law thereby presents two symbolic outsiders who turn the law into a means of contact: Shylock directly and Portia through disguising herself as a man, thus gaining momentary power and agency, and breaking out of the passive role of an exquisite trophy in which she is cast at the beginning of the action. The outcome, read politically, is unsurprising: the play allows for a successful penetration into power only indirectly, momentarily, under camouflage, whereas when it is explicit and unveiled ("The Jew") it will be annihilated financially and spiritually.

INTRODUCTION

Within this legal context, Shylock will put himself on record. His resistance is subtle, since law itself seems to be presented in the play as a majestic force that will not be manipulated, and one that would ultimately cohere with justice by managing to block a fiendish plea. Law appears to be a legitimating marvel: it includes religious values—the numerous appeals to Christian-colored virtues such as valuing mercy over justice, the latter being a mere cardinal virtue to which the morality of "the Jew" is limited. But when religion cannot suffice, law generates a technical vocabulary of its own that guarantees that justice will be done. *The Merchant of Venice* thus plays up the anxiety of a rupture formed between law and justice, but also appears to reinforce a vision in which both happily seem to overlap. What Shylock can hope to create, is a momentary gap between Venice's self-image and its fantasies of moral coherence ("I stand for judgment. Answer: Shall I have it?"). Wanting to be a Jessica in the beginning of the action and to merge happily with his surrounding (why else would he lend out money gratis to Antonio when he has no reason to think that Antonio will be unable to return the debt?), he finally moves into acceptance of his alienation, and a desire to place a wedge between various constituents that form Venice's pride. He succeeds and their jubilance over Portia's technical solution in effect reduces them into relieved sophists. His hatred will be contained and then dismissed, but it will not go away. For it is precisely through the monstrosity of his suit, its horrid colorfulness and self-destructive irrationality, that Shylock will force his story to be told and retold, read and acted. Over and over, the play will generate the spectacle of distilled hatred, an alien's hatred, whetting his knife with his scales in hand, being the villainous dog they always said he was. Unlike Jessica, whom we tend to recall only upon rereading the play, Shylock will never elope: he is in our minds for good.

It is at this point that questions about general meanings—philosophical questions—become unavoidable. Villainy, justice, mercy, suffering—notions that surface in any detailed response to the play—demand clarification. How to strip away the hypocritical from the genuine, and how to assess the merit of that which presents itself as the genuine? Do we learn anything from this play about the mechanics of alienation and response to it? And if we do, can such knowledge be reapplied? Such concerns constitute much of our response to the play. They always did. Yet it is precisely here that various approaches within contemporary literary studies and within philosophy are prompted to hold up "No Entry" signs. Philosophically attuned criticism, it seems, ignores weighty

INTRODUCTION

considerations. When it does not imply aesthetic or political naiveté, philosophical reflection on literary works is simply useless: an unnecessary detour that appeals to the bookish, but is pointless for those who seek philosophical understanding.

This book is about philosophy and literature. If its philosophical argument is correct, it is also about epistemology and moral philosophy. If its literary readings are persuasive, it is also about the value of literature. The primary ground for choosing Shakespeare is the gratifying insights that his writings yield when brought into close dialogue with philosophical concerns. Showing that these insights are not divorced from the plays' literary merits but rather constitute them is one of the principal aims of this book. The secondary reason for choosing Shakespeare is that his work exemplifies literary excellence. The uncontested aesthetic value of his plays enables investigation into what makes up that value without the need to prove first that it exists.

After years of relative neglect, debates about the relations between philosophy and literature were reopened in the 1980s, most notably in the work of Martha Nussbaum and Stanley Cavell. Many have formulated excellent critiques of these pioneering works. Aesthetes worry that philosophical readings are reductive and ignore literary merits. Others dislike the way philosophical interpretations plead for one cause or another, thereby obliterating the borders between philosophy and education. Many distrust the chiseling out of general meanings from their material, ideological, or historical context. Such critiques require a fundamental reworking of the underlying premises and interpretive procedures through which the general (or the potentially reapplicable) is to be derived from a literary work. This book attempts to set a theoretical framework for philosophically oriented literary criticism, one that responds to the concerns of both literary critics and philosophers. It also unfolds a thesis regarding the question of method in philosophy.

The introductory chapters address the two very different disciplinary frameworks and motivations of philosophy and literature. I argue that an integrated "philosophical criticism"—my label for philosophical readings of literary works—can substantially compensate for some limitations of nonliterary philosophical argumentation. Philosophical criticism can also answer some institutional, professional, and personal worries that are now voiced with greater urgency as the turn toward a cultural focus in literary criticism is being reassessed. Readers who come to this book primarily as "philosophers" or as "Shakespeareans" will

INTRODUCTION

probably find it more rewarding to access its general argument through the parts that directly address their different professional agendas as I conceive of them—and to a certain extent simplify them—in these introductory essays. Separate access routes need not, I hope, hide from view deeper impasses in the philosophy-literature question that arise when disciplinary concerns are jointly considered. For example, explaining the cognitive gains of literary as opposed to non-literary articulations of the same philosophical insight will typically draw the philosophical critic into a roughly formalist stance. Irreducible "aesthetic experience" will strongly suggest itself. Culturally oriented Shakespeareans will worry that this solution is conceptually artificial and politically naive.

Making sense of philosophical insight as part of reading literature need not ignore the concerns of many contemporary culturally oriented literary critics. The introductory parts of this book outline and defend a theoretical possibility that seeks to further these critics' cause. The readings that follow the introduction exemplify this possibility and show how philosophical criticism can draw out rewarding and unfamiliar aspects of well-known plays. It is not my aim in the studies of the various plays simply to make the same theoretical points in different settings, varying my arguments only insofar as I apply them to *Othello* instead of *Richard III*. Instead, I try to highlight different aspects of the overarching theory so as to open up the fuller potential of this kind of criticism. The theoretical overlap that remains is intended to emphasize the shared core of the readings and to promote the metaphilosophical argument of the book as a whole regarding intellectual attunement and the meaning of understanding.

Philosophically oriented Shakespeare criticism in the past tended to look for signs of a philosophical thesis within the plays. Recent work has wisely given up this attempt. And yet, this book has a close affinity with the older, philosophically disposed Shakespeareans. A return to the ancients is hardly my aim. Yet, stripped of some inadequate trappings, the best moral critics of the late nineteenth century, as well as some of the great critics of the twentieth century that preceded the cultural turn, still offer valuable insights in a philosophically oriented dialogue about Shakespeare. The book will hopefully unsettle simplified distinctions between timely and obsolete criticism and may thus be discomfiting to those who relate to Shakespeare through rigid agendas.

The book will avoid traditional formulations of debates over the moral dimension of Shakespeare's plays. The merit (or lack of merit) of Shakespeare's supposed indifference to morality, the forces that make up the

INTRODUCTION

ethical world he creates, the morality implicit in his characterization—all such issues will be disregarded. Shakespeare's own real or implied moral beliefs, to which all these formulations ultimately relate, will be set aside. My goal will be to communicate with the moral potential of Shakespeare's plays in a way I see as rewarding. Convergence between what I take this potential to be and what Shakespeare may have inserted into his work is by no means ruled out (I regard such convergence, if it can be demonstrated, as a strength of the reading, and I will sometimes argue for it through source-play comparisons). But such overlap is in no way essential to the validity of the readings. Elizabethan moral thought in general will also be played down. I will sometimes relate ideas to traditions of thought that may have reached Shakespeare, but I shall do so only to dispel a sense of anachronism, a suspicion that particular thoughts in such texts could not have been formulated. Causal connections between abstract theses and Shakespeare's mind will not be suggested.

Rhetoricians form the third group of readers I intend to address, particularly by exploring and furthering criticisms of the Cartesian and Ramist intellectual ideals that still dominate Anglo-American philosophy. Chapter two makes explicit the ways in which philosophical criticism takes up the call of Cicero and Quintilian for an integrative form of thought, giving this possibility substantial content. Early-modern rhetoric, with which Shakespeare was acquainted, was familiar with this integrative ideal. Justifying it philosophically requires reflecting on those older approaches in terms of a distinction—usually left unarticulated in Elizabethan rhetorical texts as well as in their Latin sources—between psychological effectiveness and argumentative justification. "Rhetoric," as this book will develop the notion, makes room for this crucial distinction, specifying relations between effectiveness and justification that will constitute my proposed account of understanding.

In what follows, I claim that by allowing the two distinct outlooks of philosophy and literature to interplay when some issues are at stake there emerges a kind of thought—a form of double vision—that opens up important modes of understanding.

PART I

PHILOSOPHICAL CRITICISM

IN THEORY

The Epistemological Basis of Philosophical Criticism

A CUCKOLDED MAN yells at his unfaithful wife. She has just written a letter to her lover, which her husband has intercepted. The betrayed husband describes his own experience through a metaphor of authorship:

> Thou trothless and unjust, what lines are these?
> Am I grown old, or is thy lust grown young,
> Or hath my love been so obscured in thee
> That others need to comment on my text?
> Is all my love forgot which held thee dear,
> Ay, dearer than the apple of mine eye?
> Is Guise's glory but a cloudy mist,
> In sight and judgment of thy lustful eye?
> (*The Massacre at Paris*, xv.23–30)

Imaging his wife as his text (which is only one of several possible readings of the line), turning her from possession into intellectual property, serves to color the meaning of gendered ownership. She becomes words—his words, his lines, his precious production. This constitutes not only an intriguing form of objectification but also of articulating erotic bonding. The beloved, likened to one's expressed language, is being fantasized as the lover's externalized and objectified thought, which is also disturbingly out of control. Beyond ownership or love, figuring cuckoldry in terms of a commented text imports texts into the world of erotic ownership. The alarming perception of one's text being modified by another, noting its loose and prostitute-like nature, says something about the meaning of writing. Metatheatrical awareness deepens this dimension of the metaphor: *this* text, Marlowe's text, being sold to others to be changed and acted by them—Marlowe himself turning, as it were, into a cuckold forced to watch.

By saying that moments such as these exclamations of the Guise are pregnant with insights—insights about the meaning of erotic possessiveness, about relating to what one writes—we are registering an awareness of literature's capacity to awaken a realization, to inform, to create knowledge. Is this faith in literature's instructive power justified, or does this talk of insight perpetuate a misleading mirage? Does anything distinguish such knowledge, if it is one? Is it possible to strip away the literary dressing from what is credited as knowledge, or is the "medium" somehow necessary, and if so, why? Any examination of the relations between philosophy and literature requires facing these familiar questions. If the above literary excerpt informs, there must be something in the lines, in the configuration of the words, in the arrangement of the images, or the imagined or perceived vocalization of them, which is doing important and mysterious epistemic work.

Five features are needed for the epistemic (knowledge-yielding) linking of philosophy and literature.[1] A complete account regarding literature's contributions to knowledge needs to: (I) elucidate how a literary work can support a general claim; (II) show what is uniquely gained by concentrating on such support-patterns as they appear in aesthetic contexts in particular; (III) clarify whether and how features of aesthetic response are connected with knowledge; (IV) maintain a distinction between manipulation and adequate persuasion; (V) achieve I–IV without ending up with what David Novitz has called "a shamelessly functional and didactic view of literature." I shall postpone discussion of the connections between literature, epistemology, and morality until the next chapter.

Literary Language and Literary Experience

Many theories explain the ways by which literature yields knowledge. Some say that literature enables forming hypotheses, thereby creating

[1] I will not deal with conceptualizations of the philosophy/literature links that do not appeal to the knowledge-yielding aspect of literary works. I am thinking here mainly of deconstruction (which by virtue of dropping altogether the philosophy/literature distinction in favor of an all-embracing textuality, makes it impossible to investigate the relationships between philosophy and literature), but also of suggestions regarding noncognitive contributions of literature to philosophy, such as that of Cora Diamond, according to which philosophy should not be conducted as an investigation, but should rather be "an imaginative response to life" (1993, pp. 144–45). Stanley Cavell's readings of Shakespeare are in part motivated by the idea that turning existential concerns into epistemological problems is itself a form of evasion (e.g., 1987, p. 179) that philosophy has repeatedly indulged in. Cavell is focusing on skepticism, and it is difficult to know whether he means this claim to have a broader scope. I agree with Cavell that epistemological concerns do not exhaust the thoughts, anxieties, and sentiments triggered by weighty philosophical issues. But this cannot mean that the move to epistemology is itself wrong, unimportant, or forms an evasion.

beliefs—albeit not necessarily justified ones.[2] Others argue that reading a literary work creates coherence in our beliefs by revealing possible discrepancies between our general convictions and detailed contexts.[3] A third view is that a literary work can advance knowledge by functioning like an example[4] or a prolonged thought-experiment[5] in which conceptual insights are gained through engaging with the rich and complex contexts of lifelike occurrences. Others maintain that literature establishes knowledge not of the actual but of the possible.[6] For the purpose of investigating the relevance of literature to philosophy such suggestions cannot suffice. At best, such accounts will show philosophers that rigorous philosophical reflection requires examples, thought-experiments, or a delineation of the possible, not that it needs literature. In order to convince philosophers that they need "literary" examples, or "literary" thought-experiments, it is necessary to delineate an epistemological gain stemming either from features peculiar to literary language or from the experience that literature creates.

The first option, appealing to aspects particular to literary language for the purpose of advancing knowledge, will fail. Oppositions that were employed in the past to articulate the distinctiveness of literary discourse (figurative/literal, particular/general, emotions/thoughts) are no longer generally accepted. One cannot then claim that emotional appeals, particular descriptions, or figurative constructions make for distinct, irreducible, and nonparaphrasable forms of knowing. A further obstacle is that, again, all these aspects are not essentially related to literature. An elaborate case for the importance of figurative language, for example, will merely succeed in proving to philosophers that they require figurative statements, not the rich, involving experience of the literary work.[7] This

---

[2] For variations of this idea, see Beardsley (1958, pp. 429–30), Hospers (1960, p. 45), Mew (1973), McCormick (1983), Novitz (1987, pp. 131–32), and Putnam (1976).

[3] Richard Rorty (1985) links literature and knowledge through coherence, as do David Novitz (1987, p. 135), Nussbaum (1990, p. 389), and Diamond (1993, esp. p. 151).

[4] For different variations of literature as example or counterexample, see Sirridge (1975), Pollard (1977), Nussbaum (1986, p. 32; 1990, pp. 45–49, 87–93), Eldridge (1989, pp. 19–21), and Carroll (1998, pp. 142–46).

[5] Zemach (1997, pp. 198–200).

[6] This idea does not begin with the various contemporary counterfactual accounts of literature but rather goes back to Aristotle's *Poetics*, ch. 9. For some other modern examples, see D. Walsh (1943), H. Putnam (1976), and some of T. S. Eliot's ideas in "Poetry and Propaganda."

[7] Such an account may, however, be incorporated into the analysis of the existence of "literary aspects" of philosophy—that is, when a philosopher employs such means, this might suggest that he has reached the limits of philosophical discourse. The neo-Platonic

rather underrated objection is also fatal to other suggestions as to how and why literature is philosophically relevant. Consider the suggestion that literature formulates in words what has hitherto been unexpressed or not fully described. Poetic articulation can thereby form or re-form a philosophical position.[8] But descriptions of this sort require nothing as intense as involvement with literature. Citing or paraphrasing the appropriate sentences is enough. Appeals to literature's particularity lead to the same objection.[9] Particular descriptions presuppose general assumptions. A uniquely particular mode of thought is thus an illusion. Besides that, particularity is not unique to literature.

Literary experience is our second option. Colin Falck writes that literature operates through tapping into "preconscious moods," thereby circumventing a more aware experience. Martha Nussbaum characterizes literary experience as one in which certain emotions are drawn out, emotions that constitute specific beliefs that cannot otherwise surface.[10] Neoromantic accounts of reading experience stress the role of the imagination in belief formation. If the imagination plays a constitutive role in belief formation, we need to involve ourselves with the imaginative realm (literature).[11] Empathic beliefs are another popular suggestion: literary reading experiences involve knowledge of what it will be like to "live through" the situation portrayed. Shared by all these suggestions is the

---

tradition of interpreting Plato's myths as expressing the ineffable is a well-known example. See also De Man's (1978) reading of Locke.

[8] Lamarque and Olsen (1994) present a variation on this theme: ". . . [literature] . . . develops themes that are only vaguely felt or formulated in daily life and gives them a local habitation and a name" (p. 452). (Lamarque and Olsen reject the philosophical use of literature. Nevertheless, their suggestion can easily be enlisted in a defense of philosophical analysis of literature through the route that I am exploring here.) Keats presents another example of literature as articulation: ". . . Poetry . . . should strike the Reader as a wording of his highest thoughts." See his letter to John Taylor, 27 February 1818, in D. Bush, ed. (1959, p. 267).

[9] Phillips (1982, p. 29), Diamond (1993, p. 149), Eldridge (1989, p. 4, 19–21), and Nussbaum (1990, pp. 37–40) all appeal to literature's focus on particulars and aim to connect this with knowledge. In Shakespeare criticism, this idea goes back to Richard G. Moulton's *The Moral System of Shakespeare: A Popular Illustration of Fiction as the Experimental Side of Philosophy* (1903).

[10] Falck (1989, pp. 56–59); Nussbaum (1990, pp. 40–42, 282); for another formulation of emotional knowledge, see Reid's (1961) development of the idea of "cognitive feeling."

[11] Novitz (1987) and Falck (1989) both attempt to defend reformulations of romantic epistemologies along these lines by stressing the imaginative. On the cognitive relevancy of the imagination, see also Nussbaum (1990, pp. 75–82) and Currie (1998).

objective to connect qualitative features of the literary reading experience (not the makeup of literary language) with cognition.

Qualitative uniqueness, however, cannot suffice. Claims do not turn into justified beliefs merely by being contemplated in an involved and emotionally attuned state. Powerful discovery never constitutes justification.[12] The same holds for empathy. Knowing what it can be like to have a particular belief or what can make someone have that belief is not a justification for the belief itself. In fact, a recurring objection to claims on behalf of literature's moral import highlights the threat that empathy poses to a just moral assessment—the danger of developing a selective sense of justice.[13] Empathic knowledge thus seems helpful only if literature's contribution to knowledge resides in the insights gained from it regarding processes of belief formation. But if *justified* beliefs are being sought, being empathic or nonempathic to the positions discussed is clearly insufficient.

Qualitatively oriented explanations, therefore, all relate to types of belief formation, to the unique ways in which literature creates beliefs, not to the assessment of those beliefs (whether or not these are the beliefs one ought to have). Formation and assessment of beliefs can be combined, and Nussbaum attempts to integrate them by asserting that some beliefs could not be assessed at all if one did not employ emotional, empathic, or imaginative processes that enable one to form them in the first place. Nussbaum's integration of formation and assessment is sound, but can be synthesized into a broader account, which I will now outline.

Literary Arguments

I propose a conception of rational justification that can accommodate the idea of literature as knowledge yielding. I begin with theories of argumentation that employ more than deductive or inductive inference patterns as rational means of establishing propositions. Aristotle's account of examples and enthymemes in his *Rhetoric* remains the fountainhead for such theories (although the idea is older). Aristotle argued that in some domains, what we take to be a credible source of knowledge is the reapplying of a principle that was successfully applied in another known case.

---

[12] Along these lines is Hilary Putnam's (1976) partial rejection of the idea of knowledge through literature.

[13] For such criticism, see Posner (1997) and Statman (2002).

Examples of this kind do not make for inductive inferences, but only for a "kind of induction" (I.ii.13).[14] The notion of induction does not include learning from the local incidents that make up our lives and from which we reasonably establish many of our attitudes. Learning in such ways is a noninductive yet rational reapplication of a principle that emerged in a similar context. The principle in question is not a categorical "For all cases of type X, Y is the case" but is a particular affirmative or negative judgment of the form: "For some cases of X, Y is the case".[15]

At first, employing Aristotle's analysis in the context of the philosophy-literature question seems to simply lead back to the idea mentioned earlier: a view of the process of learning from fictional happenings as analogous to that of learning from examples. But Aristotle's rhetorical analysis allows for relocating the literature-as-example idea from being only a suggestion linking aesthetics with cognition to an argumentational move justified through rhetorical theory. This is *not* a terminological shift. Such relocation explains not only the plausibility of the move from one case to the other but also delineates the contingent logical status of some of the philosophical beliefs with which literature deals. For Aristotle, the need for rhetoric arises when discussing assumptions and beliefs that can be other than they are—claims that can be derived from premises that are usually not necessary but are "for the most part only generally true" (I.ii.14). Aristotle was of the opinion that most of our judgments are of such a contingent nature.

Placing literary examples, thought-experiments, arguments by analogy, or coherence-establishing mechanisms within the framework of a rhetorical theory of rationality makes it possible to deal with objections regarding the nonvalid nature of such kinds of argumentation. Drawing

---

[14] Readers of Nussbaum's account of Aristotelian practical reasoning (1990, pp. 54–106), or Stuart Hampshire's (1983, pp. 10–69), could easily see how the following sketch of Aristotle's rhetorical views could be neatly integrated with his ideas concerning ethical method. I shall later specify some of the gains of adding the rhetorical emphasis in relation to the philosophy-literature question.

[15] The distinction between particular and categorical propositions, coupled with the claim that literary examples support the former, strikes me as a more defendable position than the abductive/paraductive distinction employed by Warner (1989, pp. 345–54) in order to legitimate the inference from examples. Moving from "case to case," as paraductive reasoning supposes, cannot really circumvent assuming the existence of a mediating particular judgment that legitimates such reasoning. Peircean abduction is one way in which such a particular statement can be grounded, but it is not the only route of this kind [Abduction is the idea that P is observed, but if Q was true, P would be a matter of course: ergo, there is reason to believe that Q].

an inference from an example is not valid in the traditional sense: the impossibility of accepting a conjunction of the premises coupled with a negation of the conclusion.[16] Accepting the need for nonvalid yet rational argumentation of this kind stems from the recognition that many of the beliefs relevant to philosophical reasoning are, for the most part, contingent. Identifying justification with logical necessity is an obvious fallacy. But when this mistake is recognized, the question then becomes how to argue for claims that are contingent in the sense of an inability to derive them formally or necessarily from other assumptions. Establishing nonarbitrary first truths leads to the same problem.[17] Opting to choose argumentational principles that cannot accommodate such beliefs is to endorse a limited mode of philosophizing. Broadening the intellectual range to which philosophical methodology should be sensitive involves accepting means of argumentation that do not conclusively demonstrate a claim, but rather make it plausible, by supporting it to a certain degree. The connections surveyed above, which link the literary context and the beliefs it supports through identifying it with an example, with a delineation of the possible, etc., are such means.[18]

Locating these moves within the context of a modern reconstruction of rhetorical theory or some other approach of informal reasoning enables the normative argument on behalf of literary belief formation to emerge: if we wish to sustain the belief that some domains of human experience can be rationally discussed and understood, and if we drop the idea that rationality in these domains can always take the shape of valid reasoning, then we *should* accept as sound (though not as conclusive proof) the patterns of nondeductive reasoning that close engagement with literature can suggest. Forgoing the demand for validity need not

---

[16] There are also no inductive relationships between a statement of the type "Prince Mishkin brings out the best in those around him" and the general statement "Seeing the best in others brings out the best in them." Novitz (1980) tried to defend a version of such inductivism, but later abandoned it (1987). I shall not repeat the arguments against such implication. For these, see especially Sirridge (1975) and McCormick (1983).

[17] Aristotle sees the need for nonvalid practical reasoning regarding first-truths in his ethical work (Nussbaum, 1990, p. 75). The idea that philosophy needs literature for establishing first-truths has been suggested by Jesse Kalin (1976), most explicitly in his (1978).

[18] Some (e.g., Mason, 1989, or Warner, 1989) would perhaps go further, saying that most of philosophy is like that anyway and that when one is cured of the illusion of quasi-geometrical reasoning one is able to see just how frequently philosophical moves are actually rhetorical. I think we can have a more discriminating view, one that accommodates the possibility for rigorous arguments and yet sees these as a very limited sphere within the philosophical domain.

imply dismissing rationality. As long as we maintain the identification of argumentation with a set of legitimate means for making beliefs plausible (rather than means for conclusive proof), literature can well be a form of argument. And since "rhetoric" does not here merely denote belief-formation but is a framework for the justification of beliefs, the beliefs that emerge are candidates for what one *ought* to accept. "Candidates" is my preferred term, since being presented with a good argument—literary or nonliterary—does not automatically guarantee actual acceptance. That can only emerge after considering other, possibly opposing, good arguments.[19]

Linking philosophy and literature is thus not some closed endpoint but rather a method, a mode of philosophizing not necessarily limited to moral questions but potentially applicable whenever contingent claims or first truths need to be supported. Such broadening of the scope of linking philosophy and literature is one advantage of basing the conception not only on Aristotle's ethical writings, emphasized in Martha Nussbaum's neo-Aristotelian conceptualization, but also on his rhetoric. We can delineate four other gains. First, such a framework makes it possible to recognize that the patterns of argumentation so far suggested in the literature—examples, analogies, thought-experiments—are mostly nonvalid moves in the traditional sense. Second, it is possible to justify such moves as part of a theory of rationality. Third, recognizing the nature of the beliefs discussed in this way means that the claims in question are either contingent or first truths, or relate to some other content that can only be given limited support. Finally, we can specify an important *limitation* of this sort of inquiry: it is *not* philosophically justified when nonrhetorical means are available.[20]

---

[19] Jonathan Kertzer's *Poetic Argument* (1989) is one attempt to identify literature with argument. But Kertzer's suggestion avoids the question of normative vs. descriptive belief-formation that is so crucial for philosophical application, as does Zahava Karl McKeon's *Novels and Arguments* (1982), which also employs a notion of argument that encompasses any communicative act (pp. 24–25). A beginning along the lines above can be found in Martin Warner's essay "Literature, Truth, and Logic" (1999), which continues important earlier work of his on the ideal of geometrical reasoning within philosophy (in his *Philosophical Finesse*, 1989). The most elaborate position regarding the rhetorical interconnections between logos and pathos within the context of literature is that of Wayne Booth (both in *Modern Dogma and the Rhetoric of Assent* and in *The Company We Keep*).

[20] These remarks do not exhaust the differences between Nussbaum's approach and the one developed here. I discuss the difficulties I see in Nussbaum's position in detail in my forthcoming essay, "Literature as Aristotelian Moral Philosophy," to be published in a volume devoted to Martha Nussbaum in The Library of Living Philosophers series.

The Epistemological Role(s) of Literary Experiences

Yet it is possible to engage in rational nonvalid argument in numerous nonliterary ways. So far, the need for such argumentation merely shows that philosophers require nondeductive patterns of argument, not literature as such. Tying literature to rhetoric in this way explains the links between philosophical readings of literary works and legitimate belief assessment. The aesthetic context itself is still an unnecessary addition. How, then, does the experience of *literature in particular* add to the nonvalid yet rational move that is being made when we are learning from a literary text?

The answer to this has two dimensions. The simpler of these involves the contribution of the suggestive capacities of literature.[21] "Literary argumentation" is not merely legitimate nonvalid reasoning but, rather, reasoning conducted in a state of mind—which reading literature itself creates—in which contingent claims and nonvalid moves can be sympathetically entertained. Suspending disbelief (which is one aspect of the state of mind that good literature sometimes creates) can help us bridge (or ignore) the gap between justification and the nonnecessary conclusion we are expected to draw. Claims about love or parenting, presented later in this book, do not lend themselves to rigorous justification. Avoiding such domains is surely an option, while philosophizing about them invites suggestiveness. Proposing this is not dangerous, since advocating suggestiveness is not the same as introducing manipulation into philosophy. On its own, an involved, responsive state is neither rational nor irrational. Although it can function as illegitimate, manipulative brainwashing, it can also manifest a rational willingness to reconfigure perception so that contingent insights can be contemplated. The question of whether a specific process is one or the other cannot be decided without examining the specific context. Sifting such appeals to context will be taken up in the next chapter.[22]

---

[21] Yehoshua (2001) recently talks of the suggestive capacities of literature (though the older reference to the "willing suspension of disbelief" may already be alluding to literature's suasive abilities). The idea can be tracked back to Plato's attack on the poets.

[22] There are various restrictions that can be applied so that "the appeal to context" does not preempt the approach into one that cannot distinguish between appeals to context that should be accepted and those that are to be rejected. More than an issue of setting criteria of relevance that could function as a normative guide to successful sifting of appeals to context, the broader problem is how to devise an error theory for reasoning not predicated on validity but on the particular coordinates of the situation. Only an error theory could

But experience in general, and the experience of reading literature in particular, is connected with knowledge in deeper ways than that. Experience is unique in that there is an irreducible gap between what we experience and what we manage to communicate through a description of that experience. Many ordinary examples verify this (e.g., trying to describe a majestic landscape to someone who has not seen it). The indescribable, nonparaphrasable aspect is a form of knowing ("You have to see it to know what I am talking about"). This kind of gap or demand for actually experiencing something does not exist in the case of argumentational justification: if I grasp an argument, there is nothing additional I need to do in order to know what is being communicated. Literature creates experiences that empower and support particular beliefs, and the details and variations of this process will be shown later in the readings.

"Support" requires explication. Literary experiences do not constitute *reasons* for accepting certain implications, as false beliefs can be embedded in very powerful reading experiences. But literary experiences do have a positive (though not indefeasible) connection with knowledge. I will now characterize this positive connection in four ways. First, to miss such experiences while contemplating some beliefs can itself be a form of error. Returning to the example of natural scenery, think of an obtuse entrepreneur who, on the basis of the repeated testimony of others, genuinely believes that a certain landscape is beautiful and awe inspiring, yet follows a course of action that destroys it. Indifference to beauty can surely be at work. There may also be other overriding reasons against preserving the landscape. But sometimes one suspects a more cognitive error: a lack of understanding that could not be remedied by being exposed to more propositions, but might be corrected by being exposed to the beauty of the landscape. Some will maintain that this experience constitutes a *reason* to avoid destroying the landscape. I have no quarrel with that, since this already discloses an outlook that respects experiences as distinct anchors of knowledge. My grounds for avoiding calling this experience a "reason" is my desire to accommodate a deeper epistemological function that is at work here. For even if our environmentally obtuse person holds to the same propositional content before and after he was exposed to the landscape (and in this sense he did not acquire a new "reason" against destroying the landscape), there may still be a

---

postulate a meaningful difference between reasoning and rational reasoning that I take to be a defining distinction of philosophical method and of a credible notion of philosophical argumentation. The issue is taken up in the next chapter.

difference in knowledge between the two states, a difference that need not boil down to anything he says or does.

Missing certain experiences can lead to or itself be a form of error or misunderstanding. This is the first characterization of the positive connection between experience and knowledge. A second way to characterize this linkage is to specify various changes in what the entrepreneur would now say or do in order to explain the different kinds of knowing. Knowledge is sometimes reducible to actual or potential behavior. Thus, conduct that has changed does not merely describe manifestations of knowledge, but modifications in the knowledge itself.[23] The third characterization of the epistemic difference that results from the experience of seeing the landscape is metaphorical: the entrepreneur now knows the same content in a "deeper" or more "powerful" or "vivid" way. Disappointing as such metaphors are, they are still informative and inescapable when one tries to characterize the intrinsic dimension of transformations in epistemic 'leveling,' to use another metaphor. Powerful and deep conveying of false beliefs is a possibility that complicates matters. But this danger does not alter the positive contribution such depth makes to the epistemic status of *justified* beliefs. There is nothing incoherent about a property that can entrench false beliefs and also deepen justified ones. Fourth, such experiences can be thought of as enabling conditions. Light, for example, enables clear vision, even though it is not itself a reason for believing anything particular about what is seen. Many things can still go wrong after one turns on a light. Enabling conditions promote knowledge, but do not thereby constitute reasons.

"Emotional involvement," "empathic involvement," "enhanced perceptiveness of the particular," "conveying" as opposed to "describing," "showing" as opposed to "telling"—such constructions and oppositions that explain the unique sort of communication and intellectual experience that some literature enables are all informative. But they are also far too general, and can therefore be used only as terms that signify rich domains that need to be carefully charted.[24] If one wants a general term

---

[23] I disagree with those who believe that *all* knowledge is reducible to behavior. But I see no substantial argument between my position and that which subscribes to the more extreme view.

[24] The formulation of the describing/conveying opposition in Shakespearean commentary goes back at least to William Richardson in *A Philosophical Analysis and Illustration of Some of Shakespeare's Remarkable Characters* (London, 1774; rpt. New York, 1966). The telling/showing opposition along with the preference for the latter is explicit in *The Rape of Lucrece*: "To see sad sights moves more than hear them told, / For then the eye

here, "experience" is the least misleading and the one that focuses most clearly on the important aspect they all share: the describable and at the same time nonparaphrasable component that is being related to knowledge.

If my goal here was to present a theory of literature, it would have been necessary now to inquire what distinguishes the experiences literature provides from other experiences (and, more specifically, whether anything distinguishes literary experiences from other aesthetic experiences). I would also have to argue against those who reject the idea of aesthetic experience, claiming that no successful demarcation exists between these experiences and others. Important as such questions are, pursuing them for our concerns is not mandatory and is probably detrimental, as saying anything more specific about literature here would only pare down the possible consensus. Even if "aesthetic experience" is a myth, and nothing distinguishes literary from nonliterary experiences, this does not prevent regarding the knowledge that literature yields as a form of experiential knowing.

The Structuralization of Knowledge

My argument so far is this: if the literary text and its reading are persuasive, a claim is not only communicated but also justified. Rhetorical, invalid rational reasoning and the role of experience form the two constituents of such justification. These constituents interlock: invalid-yet-rational reasoning is *embedded* within an experience, an experience that both accommodates the move psychologically and supports the belief epistemically by becoming what may be called a "ground" for it. This does not imply that upon reading the work one also immediately accepts what it may "argue" for. Even in conventional philosophy the existence of a justification does not entail acceptance.[25] Justification—turning a claim into a truth claim, a candidate for truth—differs from verification—accepting a claim

---

interprets to the ear / The heavy motion that it doth behold . . ." (lines 1324–26). John Roe (in The New Cambridge Shakespeare edition of *The Poems* [Cambridge, 1992], p. 206) relates these lines to Sidney and follows Malone in tracing the tradition of preferring the visual back to Horace's *Art of Poetry*.

[25] Lamarque and Olsen draw a relevant distinction here, in claiming that "thematic statements . . . can be assigned significance and thus be understood without being construed as asserted" (1994, p. 328, 384).

as true—and it is the former process that literature facilitates. At the same time, if nonliterary evidence and counterarguments to the "literary argument" have been assessed and found to be corroborating the truth claim being advanced, the (mere) truth-claim can turn into a justified true belief.

These then, are the steps leading from literature to truth and knowledge. But since virtually all work on literature and philosophy (this book included) deals with moral philosophy rather than other branches of philosophy, "justification," as I have been unpacking it, should be understood as being broader in application than just relating to truth. "Truth" is a rather strained and usually redundant notion within ethics. Truth enters ethics when assessing the morally relevant facts (obvious as well as tacit facts). But the moral reasoning conducted in relation to these facts is typically not assessed in terms of it being true or false. Consequentialism, for instance, is not assessed as a true or a false theory in ethics, but as being plausible or implausible, comprehensive or limited, workable or superficial, etc. We justify certain moral outlooks, and this implies that there is something that we wish to get right, but the moral stance we accept does not become true. Rather, we adopt a moral stance because it makes sense/ is rewarding/ is conducive to happiness/ accommodates general fairness/ encapsulates sensitivities we care about—it is under one of these senses (or something like them) in which we take a moral stance to be "right." And so literary justification, while it may lead to truth as I have been arguing above, is primarily attuned to different modes of acceptance of the plausibility of claims.

Literary works make plausible certain beliefs and also support them through the experiences they create. In focusing on such moments, the following readings in this book unfold a multilayered concept of understanding. Charting various interrelations between beliefs and the carefully constructed experiences in which these are embedded exposes modalities of philosophical understanding and philosophical insight. I speak of *philosophical* understanding and insight, as the beliefs and the processes of belief-formation I shall be dealing with all relate to general and defining aspects of life and to living a life well.

Epistemological cartography of this sort makes for this book's metaphilosophical argument: particularizing epistemological processes into numerous relationships between complex experiences and specific claims—more specifically: connecting particular projections, expectations, blind spots, points of alienation, moments of involved attentiveness, aporias, and dismissals, with the claims specific readers make in such contexts, suggests a conception of human understanding. This conception can be an alternative to the one presupposed in most current Anglo-American philosophizing, in which truth claims and argumentation are all that matter.[26] The alternative could show that contemporary philosophical method is not only stylistically dry—and, it is important to note, "dryness" can be merely a "stylistic" fault only relative to a certain, no doubt dominant, conception of understanding and philosophical communication—but it presupposes a misguided view concerning human understanding and what it should ideally include. Human understanding, when functioning at its best, is not limited to accepting only what can be conclusively verified empirically or deductively. It also embraces suggestive processes that embed contingent beliefs in experiences that give them sharpness and force. But if this is so, then philosophy as it is practiced, taught, and published in some quarters perpetuates a misconception as to the nature of rationality.

A philosophical reading of literature has an epistemological basis in two ways: in being knowledge yielding, and in being itself an inquiry into the structuralization of knowledge. By "structuralization" I refer to the manner by which the same propositional content can be entertained on different levels. Epistemic structuralization also presupposes a difference between knowing and not knowing (as well as a manner of error) that does not consist in the beliefs entertained but rather depends on undergoing (or missing) certain experiences. It is in this sense that the relations between philosophy and literature are epistemological rather than moral: it is less the moral (paraphrasable) content being justified, and more the manner of contemplation, support, and acceptance of this content that constitute literature's unique contributions to philosophical reflection. And so, while the following readings will deal with attitudes and problems typically classified as moral, my primary concern is with the experience in which moral content is embedded; the argumentative move that underlies this experience and supports a moral claim; the

---

[26] The contemporary state of philosophy sometimes masks the fact that many philosophers have rejected the idea that only arguments matter. For connections between style and implicit epistemology in Plato, see my "The Face of Truth" (1999); for such connections in Nietzsche, see my "Seeing Truths" (1998). The same connections between epistemological and rhetorical concerns also animate therapeutic visions of philosophy. I am thinking here of the way in which arguments are subordinated to ethical therapeutic goals in Hellenistic thought as shown in Nussbaum (1994). The medical analogy, so central to Epicureans, Skeptics, and Stoics, implies that, just like a physician in relation to a patient's body, philosophers must always note the makeup of the recipient's mind rather than limit themselves to cerebral discourse.

manner by which experiences transform the qualitative dimension of beliefs or what it might mean to hold a belief; the way by which all this sets in motion rich forms of reasoning. In short, my concern will be epistemological.

Since these literary experiences can be described (though not paraphrased), I am not now attempting to resurrect discredited modes of private knowing. At the same time, the emphasis on a process one has to undergo personally does diverge from the linkage between public verification and knowledge, a linking that is such a dominant strand of modernist epistemology. In the next chapter, I will suggest what went wrong in the modern account of rationality, specifically in its rejection of rhetoric.

Method

Talk of experience brings up questions of method. How do we find out what these experiences are? The following readings will deal with this difficulty in various ways. One possibility is to note the mode in which a literary work operates on the reader (in this case, me). For example, in the essay on *Macbeth*, I argue that the play creates a growing disconnection from the valueless world of its hero, while establishing a preference for values that other characters exhibit. I allude to other interpreters who responded similarly to the work (though repeatability is not necessary). Another way is to note the work's effect on another interpreter. Here, for example, is Wilson Knight writing on *Julius Caesar*: "There is an almost brutal enjoyment evident in our imagery of slaughter, wounds, and blood: yet is it so flamed with imagination's joy that there is no sense of disgust."[27] Knight is telling us how some aspect of that play makes him feel. Some may object that such methods are subjective. But interpretations are not only "reports" of experiences—though they can be partly that too. In the context of interpretive discourse, Knight's use of "our" is never simply descriptive. If Knight supposed that the highly complex reaction he is describing is what we feel anyway, it makes no sense for him to argue for it or for us to read his interpretation. Interpretive remarks such as Knight's or mine are rather *suggestions* as to how one should relate to a text in the most fruitful way. This is why the subjective nature of such remarks is unimportant: since interpretations are invitations to structure one's experience in a certain way

[27] *The Imperial Theme*, Methuen & Co., London, 1945, p. 45.

(rather than descriptions of experiences the work universally creates), it hardly matters that the interpreter is the only person who has, up to this point, reacted to the work in such a way. Invitations are never evaluated in terms of being subjective or not, but according to whether or not they lead to a worthwhile way to spend one's time. Whatever constitutes a worthwhile interpretation—that is, a fruitful mode of relating to a work—is a complicated issue involving many considerations. But subjectivity is not one of them, and so that worry can be laid to rest (though this way of thinking about interpretation also shows why interpreters should avoid producing invitations that no one else can accept).[28]

To return to my main point, while interpretive discourse regarding aesthetic experiences is never simply descriptive, interpreters making such remarks as to their own responses are still committed to the idea that the text has created such experiences in them. For example, it would count against Knight's interpretation if it were revealed that he himself never really felt the sort of "brutal enjoyment" he is describing. Interpreters can surely misdescribe their experiences, and this complicates matters. But the fact that interpreters can be wrong about these experiences does not prevent the possibility of them being right about them. By appealing to vulnerable observations of reading experiences, or by preferring one set of observations to another, a philosophical use of literature is not worse off than a scientist appealing to what she sees, or a historian relying on firsthand reports of some events rather than others, or a judge putting his trust in one testimony over another. I will also add that experiences need not be ones in which beliefs are simply created, but may also involve missing certain connections. The chapter on *Romeo and Juliet* discusses the significance of readers forgetting (and interpreters dismissing the fact) that Romeo is in love with another woman at the beginning of the play.

Philosophical Criticism and Didactic Criticism

The centrality of experience enables literature to be philosophically relevant without being instrumentalized—a threat that has led to

---

[28] While I do not mean to compare this to other suggestions within reader-response theory, readers may wish to read this method against other modes of analyzing response in Shakespeare, such as that of E.A.J. Honigmann (1976), who tries to avoid subjectivism by noting the way Shakespeare attempts to create specific responses.

controversies over endangering the autonomy of art by turning literature into a form of moral philosophy.[29] Philosophers of literature need not employ a didactic concept of literature (though, in the context of early modern literature, it has often been suggested—e.g., by Dickey, 1966, pp. 12–19—that avoiding the didactic dimension of texts is itself a vulgarization of them). We read literature much for the same reason that we engage in art in general: it provides us with unique experiences that can be described but never fully conveyed through paraphrase. Some of these experiences can and should be investigated as part of the sort of descriptive epistemology I outlined above. Such investigation does not instrumentalize literature. Rather, it is an inquiry into what makes our experiences with literature unique. And this can be done, I will try to show, without postulating a generalized notion of aesthetic experience or harping too much on its conventional constituents (beauty or disinterest). Instead, it can be done by concentrating on particular experiences with powerful literary moments and the way these interrelate with specific beliefs.

❏

We now have our five-stage explanation. A fictional context provides knowledge through argumentational routes that several theorists have proposed. My addition to existing suggestions was to incorporate them into a broad context of rational justification. Theorists have delineated several unique aspects of aesthetic response. My proposed contribution to these suggestions was to connect them with the state in which contingent claims and first truths need to be contemplated, and to add the connections between such experiences and knowledge. Finally, inquiring into the ways claims emerge as part of an aesthetic response does not instrumentalize aesthetic creations. Rather, such investigation is an inquiry into our unique reactions to literature.

[29] Novitz (1987, p. 12), perhaps because he wants to allow literature to be knowledge yielding, finds it necessary to argue against aesthetically oriented views of literature. As does Nussbaum (1998) in her reply to Richard Posner (1997, 1998), who criticized her approach as involving such an instrumentalization of literature. On the issue of instrumentalization, see too the exchange between Wayne C. Booth and Richard Posner in *Philosophy and Literature* (1998), as well as Booth's contribution to ethical criticism in the special issue of *Style* (1998) devoted to the morality-literature connections, as well as *The Company we Keep*.

The Moral Basis of Philosophical Criticism

Orgoglio is too big to wield a mace, so he uses a knotty oak that he has torn out of the earth. His height threatens the sky, and under his feet the ground "groans" for "dread." He is about to dispatch the knight who now lies helpless before him. A witch, who has tempted the knight away from his rightful mistress, now begs the giant to imprison and enslave the knight rather than kill him. She promises to be his lover. The giant agrees, and the imprisoned knight will remain a captive until he will be rescued by a prince.

The tale is a moral allegory: the knight stands for holiness, threatened and overpowered by pride (the giant, whose name means pride in Italian). The knight's fall occurs when he has been disconnected from true religion (his rightful mistress), enfeebled through prolonged connection with lust and idleness (the witch). The knight can only be saved by a nonhuman agent, the prince (Christ). Pride, the consistent enemy of holiness or moral perfection, is most dangerously aroused precisely through being moral. The too easy slippage within a moral life from self-commending for one's own goodness to smugness and pride is captured through the awakened hideous giant, which one cannot hope to face without the assistance of strong attachment to the right religion (and even then one cannot do without God's direct intervention). The allegory thus captures human weakness, as well as its ability to be helped, and all this in terms of connection and disconnection from various empowering and debilitating forces.

The older vindications of literature, attributing to it the capacity to teach and delight, mobilize moralistic literature such as this snippet from Spenser's *The Faerie Queene* (I, vii). As lively as such tales are, the post-Kantian formalist bias against didactic art has now hardened into a critical instinct, making it very difficult for us to relate to moralistic literature through the prism by which it requires to be processed. Arguments ensue as to whether interpretive vulgarity lies in the moralization of literature, or rather in condescendingly ignoring the goal of authors to morally edify their readers, as if Spenser or Milton were childishly unaware of what they were supposed to be doing. Unlike Spenser or Milton, Shakespeare was not out to improve his projected audience. Yet this need not imply that his plays lack the capacity to facilitate moral reflection of a unique and important kind, precisely because they awaken and rely on an epistemology that is mobilized by didactic literature as well.

My emphasis in the previous chapter on epistemology and logic is not meant to dismiss important connections between literature and ethics, but rather to set relations of conceptual priority: I take the relations between philosophy and literature to be epistemic, not moral, but I also see these epistemological connections as carrying crucial moral implications. It is these implications that I wish to take up now. The foremost aim of this chapter is to show that it is best to view the diversified contributions into the literature-morality question not primarily as claims about ethics but as five different yet compatible proposals regarding fruitful connections among ethics, rhetoric, and literature. Seeing things in this way, I argue, focalizes the larger argument and historical continuity to which the philosophy-literature question is related. I then address three problems in this direction. The first relates to justifying the idea that an appeal to "one's whole being" rather than to one's capacities for argumentation is an advantage in moral philosophy. The second concerns explicating moral growth through literature in the absence of the Idealistic and theological frameworks that accounted for such growth in the past. The third pertains to distinguishing between reasoning and reasoning rationally when one admits the suggestive capacities of literature into an inquiry aimed at enhanced moral understanding.

Literature, Rhetoric, and Morality

Authors have conceptualized the moral contributions of literature in numerous ways. Some emphasized the contributions of thinking through particularized examples rather than through rules (Eldridge, 1989). Others saw literature as exemplifying Aristotelian moral philosophy (Nussbaum, 1990), or as either clarifying one's moral commitments (Carroll, 1998), or as exciting and stimulating them (Harbage, 1947). Still others concentrated on the viability of ethical criticism of literary works (Booth, 1988). Many connected the emotional and imaginative aspects of thinking through literature with a neoromanticism of one sort or another (Novitz, 1987; Falck, 1989; Diamond, 1991). Broadly speaking, such theories come in two versions. Milder defenses regarding the moral contributions of literature argue for aspects of moral understanding that literature enhances (empathy, detailed perception, emotional and imaginative participation, particularized understanding of lifelike moral deliberation). Stronger defenses regard moral criticism of literary works as a possible replacement for moral theory. In both versions, these approaches challenge moral method. The claim is that traditional, rule-governed reasoning in ethics either should include elements it has hitherto ignored or needs to be replaced altogether.[1]

The argument for literature as a form of moral reflection is accordingly compelling and multifaceted: morally oriented philosophical reflection on literature addresses the actual springs of moral activity; it sets in motion intellectual processes that are essential to understanding important features of morally complex situations; it creates a mode of response involving rich experience rather than superficial cleverness; it can implant enriching voices, thereby creating the various colliding forces that constitute rationality on some issues; and it can accommodate nonvalid yet rational moves on which moral philosophy depends. These individual motivations can be accepted in part, as a whole, or they can be combined in various ways, though I like to think of them as five kinds of abstract relations among literature, rhetoric, and moral philosophy that form the conceptual heart of various ways of approaching literature as a form of moral reflection.

It is usually wise to avoid talking about connections between abstract fields. My reason for risking such talk is not only because it brings out a shared conceptual framework that underlies many distinct contributions to the literature-morality question but also because it points our attention to a larger historical continuity that underlies some of the tensions involved. Not that my objective is historical. Rather, it seems to me that we risk losing sight of the more far-reaching consequences of the literature-morality debate if we misperceive the way some of the new debates recycle very old polemics that were set in different disciplinary trappings in the past.[2]

More specifically, the emphasis on rhetoric enables perceiving the connections between new claims advocating literature's moral contributions and the claims for legitimacy of the older tradition that housed these

[1] For a delineation regarding who is who in these camps, see Nussbaum (2000).

[2] "Different disciplinary trappings" is somewhat misleading, as it appears to presuppose that "literature"—a term of the late Middle Ages—was clearly marked off from "rhetoric" in the debates over the value of rhetoric in ancient Greece and Rome. But I do mean to capture through it the very similar disciplinary issues that are and were addressed when people discuss philosophy and literature or philosophy and rhetoric.

claims in the past. Rhetoricians have, for example, repeatedly accused philosophers of detachment from effective reasoning patterns, and of perverting understanding through separating expression from thought.[3] Favorable accounts of rhetoric have also often argued that rationality should not be identified with validity or certainty.[4] In some sense, it seems, arguments over the legitimacy of literature from the standpoint of moral philosophy rehash the old Socratic-Aristotelian question as to whether rhetoric is a counterpart of dialectic or of, strangely enough, cooking.

Here, then, are the five kinds of relations I have in mind:

1. In bringing out in its readers forms of evaluation and assessment that we actually employ in life, literature stands a better chance of reaching and affecting the springs of moral activity. Rhetoric, literature,

---

[3] Both criticisms go back at least to the great Latin rhetoricians (and, in the context of the following chapters, were taken up by influential English intellectual authorities in Shakespeare's England). Cicero in *On Invention* spoke against the supposedly wise who argue in ways that move no one. He also attacked what he saw as an absurd separation between teachers of thought and teachers of discourse (*The Orator*, III, 16). The focus on rhetoric in the writings of Renaissance humanists involved a hearty endorsement of this critique: "Ye know not what hurt ye do to learning that care not for words but for matter and so make a divorce between the tongue and the heart. For mark all ages . . . and ye shall surely find that when apt and good words began to be neglected . . . then also began ill deeds to spring . . ." (Roger Ascham, *The Schoolmaster*, cited in I. Rivers, 1994, p. 137). Quintilian (*Institutio*, XII.ii.9) and Petrarch (*On His Own Ignorance and That of Many Others*) both demanded a communicative style in morals that can actually touch people rather than achieve only philosophical logic chopping. All say that philosophers avoid the motivational level of moral beliefs on which the rhetorician focuses. The employment of this argument as furthering the case for the moral import of literature was already familiar to early-modern thinkers. In his *Apologie for Poetrie* (1595), Philip Sidney ridicules the impotence of philosophical fine distinctions when moral motivation is concerned: "For the Philosopher, setting down with thorny argument the bare rule, is so hard of utterance, and so misty to be conceived, that one that hath no other guide but him shall wade in him till he be old before he shall find sufficient cause to be honest . . ." (rpt. 1941, 16). Careful perusal of Sidney's *Apology* would show that the importing of arguments on behalf of rhetoric's moral and cognitive import into defenses of literature, a move which I argue above to be at the heart of the literary turn today, already takes place in early-modern England.

[4] Apart from Aristotle's account of examples and *enthymemes* in *Rhetoric*, or of Chaim Perelman's rejection of Cartesian certainty as a regulative philosophical ideal in *The Realm of Rhetoric* (both mentioned in the previous chapter), I am thinking of Wayne Booth's case (in *Modern Dogma and the Rhetoric of Assent*) for a philosophy of "good reasons" rather than one predicated on modern dogmas that import scientific models of reasoning into moral discourse.

and moral philosophy are thus linked by identifying literature with an attunement to actual, nonidealized modalities of belief-formation supplemented by a roughly Humean account of moral motivation.[5]

2. Claims regarding the moral contributions of literature constitute an epistemic rehabilitation of elements that were repeatedly perceived as noncognitive ("merely rhetorical") dispensable additions to rigorous argumentation. Literature's capacity to trigger the imagination and/or the emotions creates sensitive judgments and an enhanced sense of what matters. Literary works turn into valuable aids in moral philosophy through this rehabilitation.

3. One is able to assert the same propositions in two states, one of which constitutes superficial agreement, while the other designates actual working beliefs. Consequently, there exists a difference between knowing and not knowing that cannot be reduced to a difference in asserted statements. A moral philosophy that respects such differences in the level of depth at which beliefs are received and entertained can usefully invoke the rhetorical capacities of literature. The difference between this and the first route is the emphasis on understanding rather than motivation.[6] The difference between this and the second route is in terms of the distinction between contexts of discovery and contexts of justification: the second route argues that elements that have previously been regarded as discovery are in fact aspects of justification. This third proposal asserts that it is a mistake to regard discovery as irrelevant to rational belief-formation.

4. Some issues (including much moral philosophy) do not admit of demonstrative reasoning, yet involve rational thought. Literature's nonvalid yet knowledge-yielding contributions exemplify what rational, nondeductive reasoning could mean. This route was pursued in the previous chapter.

5. Developing moral reasoning and deliberation involves refining and adding new considerations to the ones that form it. A richer interplay than has previously existed is thus set in motion. Such interplay (and not necessarily the prescriptions that it yields) is what, to a large extent, constitutes moral reasoning. This is an old idea in rhetorical

---

[5] Humean accounts argue that cognizing what one ought to be doing is never enough for the purpose of forming genuine moral motivation.

[6] Sidney's *Apology for Poetry* includes this cognitive side of the argument for the moral contribution of literature, speaking of the "true lively knowledge" that poetry gives relative to the bony language of philosophy (1941, 17).

thought on morality.[7] Developing moral reasoning (or, in some interpretations, developing "character") requires the rhetorical capacities of literary works that are able to implant believable, enduring, "talking" voices as part of the company one keeps.

This similarity between new claims on behalf of literature's moral importance and very old claims concerning rhetorical moral reasoning has significant implications. I am claiming that when the philosophy-literature question is perceived as primarily epistemological and not moral, there emerges a larger connecting framework that underlies many contributions to the morality-literature question. This rhetorical outlook has various manifestations (five of which I have sketched), which can be connected in various ways. But it is a distinct and comprehensive outlook that has haunted philosophy from its inception, rather than some limited corrective to contemporary moral reasoning that happened to emerge in the last two decades. What is at stake is not merely how literature contributes to moral understanding and action but the possibility and desirability of "rigorous" thinking when one puts one's life through an intellectual prism; or the possibility and desirability of penetrating beyond appearances; or the possibility and desirability of tapping into claims whose truth value is supposed to reside not in actual or potential agreement but in some transhuman relation; or the possibility and desirability of isolating a mode of credible thought that hovers above other mental processes that are castigated and reduced to the level of mere persuasion-enhancing (rather than genuinely justificatory) devices.

The standard charge against rhetorical outlooks ever since Socrates is that they promote hopeless relativism and antirationalism. Yet the previous remarks state programmatically (and the following readings try to show in practice) that distrust of some of the fundamental presumptions of philosophy presents an alternative view of reasoning rather than general skepticism. Such a view of rationality can obviously be related to various contemporary models of conversationalist reasoning or the reduction of "Truth" to practices of justification. But it seems to me to be more to the point to confront three challenges that a rhetorical

---

[7] Such a view of moral reasoning can be traced back to the Protagorean *Disoi Logoi*—the need to bring out the many sides of an issue—or even earlier to Isocrates (who, in *Against the Sophists*, praises Homer for presenting his gods as arguing about some issues, thus showing that even an ideal state of knowing involves conflicting perspectives rather than systematic unequivocal knowing).

outlook of this sort faces in the specific context of relating literature to morality.

On *David*

Here is a moment in Stanley Cavell's reading of *King Lear*:

> [One of *King Lear*'s themes] is that our actions have consequences which outrun our best, and worst, intentions. The drama of *King Lear* not merely embodies this theme, it comments on it, even deepens it. For what it shows is that the *reason* consequences furiously hunt us down is not merely that we are half blind, and unfortunate, but that we go on doing the thing which produced these consequences in the first place. What we need is not rebirth, or salvation, but the courage, or plain prudence, to see and to stop. To abdicate. But what do we need in order to do that? It would be salvation. (1987, p. 81)

Cavell's educationally pitched conclusion, utilizes notions of literary depth coupled with an unmistakable instructive appeal marked by shifting to the first person plural. I will use such phrases myself, but such language needs to be justified.

Are deep appeals advantageous in moral philosophy? To see that "depth" is not an evident advantage, consider the distinction between philosophy and education. Both domains treat morality in very different ways. It is, for example, reasonable to claim that creating "deep" moral beliefs—deep in the sense of appealing to the hearer's whole sense of life—is surely important when one is trying to create moral agents. Yet the task of moral philosophy is different. Moral philosophers find, explain, and justify the values and considerations that moral agents should accept. Educators implant the findings of moral philosophers in profound and motivating ways in the minds of actual hearers. Blurring the distinctions between explanation and implementation simply leads to ineffective education as well as to bad philosophy. When philosophers encounter such language, they get the uncomfortable sense that they are being educated. On the other hand, conceptual clarifications and subtle justifications that prevent powerful rhetorical embedding of moral dispositions hinder the educator's task.

Dismissing the sharp opposition between philosophy as inquiry and philosophy as education is one possible reply to this problem. I shall

Figure 1. Michelangelo's David © 1990, Photo Scala, Florence, courtesy of the Ministero Beni e Att. Culturali, Florence, Accademia.

begin by avoiding this direction. An answer respecting the distinction between the different tasks should begin by clarifying what it is that literature is supposed to teach. It then needs to show that what is being taught is of fundamental importance to the understanding of values and is not limited to the communication of those values.

I begin with the old idea that literature can capture the paradigmatic forms of phenomena, distilling a fragment of experience. To use a familiar example from art (which holds for many literary moments too), consider the face of Michelangelo's *David*: The artist created an expression that is completely concentrated in the details of the eyes, brows, forehead, and the curve of the right nostril. David is looking up at something frightening. The brows converge. They thus capture a realization of the frightening nature of David's enemy in all his gigantic size and strength that only now dawns on him. The moment is precisely one in which his verbal agreement to do something that no one else was willing to do turns into the cold horror of reality. Yet, the details of his expression, especially the relaxed body and (again) the brows that are slightly pressed together, also convey the sense that he is determined to confront his adversary and his fear. Michelangelo's *David* thereby embodies the moment of courage as a state of overcoming extreme fear. The face is even divided in the middle (try looking at each side of the face separately): the right half conveys extreme fear, while the left expresses determined resolution.

In a way that I will have to unpack in philosophically credible terms, the statue forms a visual characterization of courage. It enables the perceiver to experience, not merely intellectually, what courage is (but it is an informative experience—we understand something—which is why it makes sense to call it a characterization). The statue creates an intimacy not limited simply to contemplating what it conveys. After all, we did not need Michelangelo to tell us that courage is a relation to fear. Such knowing through experience is also a particular quality of understanding. Experiencing courage extends both to perceiving courage in another and sensing what courage might feel like if one performed a courageous act oneself.

When we try to get a more detailed understanding of the experiential knowing of a defining aspect (in our case, the dependency of courage on fear), we could make the mistake of reducing it to one of its components: feeling, empathic involvement, or knowing what courage is like. These are all, no doubt, modalities of experiential knowing, yet the category is broader. This is why it is misleading to speak of the form perceived as what "gives a shape" to feeling, as C. J. Ducasse does in his account of aesthetic contemplation in *The Philosophy of Art*. The opposition between feeling and thinking (or, in Ducasse's own terminology, between an objectification of feeling and an objectification of meaning) is an unnecessary limitation of the complex thought that is actually at work. In aesthetic reception the conceptual component that can be paraphrased ("courage is an overcoming of extreme fear") is embedded in a structure enabling experiencing—as opposed to merely discursively grasping—what courage is. In positioning the statue of David much higher than the viewer, and in making it larger than a normal body, the aesthetic experience is one in which the viewer looks up at human nature in one of its grander moments. But the fact that David is not presented as godlike turns him and his moment into a possibility open to all. This is not empathy or feeling but an experience of an ideal recognized as such: one *looks at* courage.

My use of an example from the plastic arts lends itself to easy application to literature that highlights peak spectacles. Theyestes or Tamora feasting without realizing what they are being served enables the spectator to perceive the moment of horrifying vengeance; Timon serving warm water to his false friends exhibits anger and disappointment; Spenser's air-made giant forming a visualization of the emptiness of pride. But spectacles are not the only means through which distilled ideals may be articulated. Hours before he is condemned and torn to pieces, Ben Johnson's Sejanus says, "My roof receives me not; 'tis air I tread: and, at each step, I feel my advanced head knock out a star in heaven," thereby giving a distinct shape to hubris. Obviously, not all literature (or art) operates in such ways. My point so far has been that *some* literature does establish such connections. We shall see that these relations between literature and the precise articulation of experience allow us to confront the questions with which we began in ways that relate to nonspectacle-oriented literature as well.

The Sense of Reality

Our question was how to justify the appeal to one's whole being as part of moral inquiry. The second question I raised was how to explicate moral growth through literature. The older theories that connected literature (or art) with moral growth explained this connection in terms of theological and/or idealistic conceptualizations. One thinks here of various iconophilic arguments in Christian aesthetic thought or of Plato's claims regarding beauty as a condition for intellectual responsiveness in the *Phaedrus*. A contemporary account should explain what may replace these older coordinates or what can be reasonably retained from them.

I began with connections among aesthetic response, self-experiences, and our sense of reality. I extended the previous chapter's proposal regarding what it is that literature is supposed to teach, by adding to it an account of aesthetic articulation. Articulation is a new shape given to an aspect of experience, a shape that begins participating in thought. Paraphrase fails to achieve this particular broadening of thought because the expansion of thought that aesthetic articulation creates is not simply quantitative. We do not merely arrive at more thoughts of the same kind that we had before. Rather, aesthetic articulation enables gaining a hold on life's essentials, maintaining connections with evasive moments that escape us as they create what is most important.

Plotinus has said that a life that includes and repeatedly communicates with these distilled patterns of experience operates at more substantial dimensions. Such a life, he maintained, was in some sense "more real." One

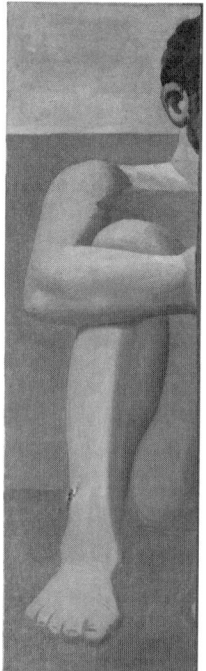

Figure 2. Picasso's *Maternity* (1921) © Succession Picasso/DACS 2005, Art Resource New York.

way to understand in modern terms the experience of added realness is to regard these defining forms as underlying numerous other experiences, and exhibiting what these mean. Compare our experience of *David* to that of the actual Hebrews who supposedly surrounded David at that moment. Let us assume that the event transpired with all the details the artist captures. For his actual contemporaries, the moment of seeing David included many other thoughts, anticipations, and fears. It immediately gave way to concentrating on the ensuing duel. Later, they may have recalled something of David's noble posture and his expression before the fight. Now compare this experience to the viewer of *David*, for whom the work of art encapsulates the moment of courage. Those who participate in the aesthetic experience are free of the all too real considerations of actual participants. They could thus absorb more of the experience of distilled courage, endowing it with greater reality than the brief moment of the historical event. To take a different example, Picasso's depictions of mothers and mothering capture something unique about maternal parenting, something

Figure 3. Picasso's *Mother and Child* and fragment from *Mother and Child* (1921) © Succession Picasso / DACS 2005. Photograph © The Art Institute of Chicago.

one hardly sees in fathers, even highly caring and affectionate ones. Such an ontological outlook obviously assumes that unlike chairs, waterfalls, and rainbows that either exist or do not, abstract entities like motherhood, compassion, or cruelty can have greater or lesser substance and presence, and that such dimensions of reality come in different degrees of sharpness. Ducasse and Nussbaum spoke of "living more" through art in the sense of art's ability to broaden our experience. We need to add to this something relating to the qualitative difference of such living. "Living through art" means maintaining and striving for contact with the distilled pictorial and discursive shapes of things. It is thus a more real life, as it seeks to maintain and develop a dimension of repeated communication with defining and regulating structures, than a life confined to some vaguely differentiated procession of random occurrences.

Marxist aestheticians will object. I am, they will say, reenacting the "tremendous cultural feat" of making fictions truer than life (e.g., Williams, 1977, p. 46). The position I am advocating participates in furthering escapism and the effacement of the complex conditions of production, as well as ignoring the history of class-dependent idealization of art (or the birth and manipulative function of the category of taste). Since the philosophical language of this book is itself "ideological," at least according to the identification of ideology with language abstracted from material conditions, a "self-contained theory" (Williams, 1977, p. 65), Marxists may well have deeper problems with my argument. I will not enter the arena of materialist/idealist polemics here (though I will do so in the next chapter), but to answer my Marxist critic I shall first say that enhanced realness through art does not compete with or replace nonaesthetic lived experiences (assuming for the moment that these are avoidable). The substantiality of one's life has several dimensions, and these are not exhausted by powerful lived experiences. Secondly, I would respond to my Marxist interlocutor by emphasizing the way literature's capacity to articulate exemplary moments extends to highlighting and capturing distinct moments of personal oppression and suffering. This is in keeping with the aims of any criticism genuinely motivated by a desire to change the state of the institutionally oppressed. Here, for example, is a chilling exchange in Toni Morrison's *Beloved*:

> "Halle and me want to be married, Mrs. Garner."
> "So I heard." She smiled. "He talked to Mr. Garner about it. Are you already expecting?"
> "No, ma'am."
> "Well, you will be. You know that, don't you?"
> "Yes, ma'am."
> "Halle's nice, Sethe. He'll be good to you."
> "But I mean we want to get married."
> "You just said so. And I said all right."
> "Is there a wedding?"
> Mrs. Garner put down her cooking spoon. Laughing a little, she touched Sethe on the head, saying, "You are one sweet child." And then no more. (p. 26)

The language of cultural materialism or Marxist critique cannot quite replace such singular moments that enforce on the reader particular sufferings and the ways they are organized within oppressive systems. My reply to my Marxist critic is then, in sum, that literature is surely politically dangerous, as it can promote smugness and curtail moral sensitivity to the culturally oppressed precisely as it commends its readers for their subtle aesthetic responsiveness. But this danger should not eliminate literature's opposite capacity—namely, forming and conveying chillingly accurate representations of suffering and abuse that are masked by culturally available discursive means. Deciding whether such moments can lead to actual social change or moral action involves the complex relations between empathy and betterment. Understanding the suffering of another is neither a necessary nor a sufficient condition for moral action. It is not a necessary condition since people can avoid creating harm without grasping what it is they are avoiding, and it is not a sufficient one since sadists can have an exceptional grasp of the suffering of their victim. Moreover, as Richard Posner claims, there are no statistics supporting the idea that professors of literature are less cruel than other people. Yet while there are no conceptual connections between empathy and action, the relation clearly (and trivially) exists on the practical level—that is, as a matter of fact much evil is done because it is not perceived as such. And it is precisely here that philosophical criticism of literary works meets and furthers the ends of contemporary political literary criticism. (More will be said regarding the political dimension of philosophical criticism in the next chapter.)

But how can we tell whether we are recognizing *correct* articulations? After all, there may well be mistaken recognition: one can forcefully articulate false or misleading ideas. How then, can we know that we should morally embrace a proposed articulation of a vague experience? The force of this (essentially Platonic) question is often underrated in accounts of aesthetic articulation. For example, it is not mentioned in Wimsatt's analysis of "the concrete universal." My own guess as to the reason for this is that people tend to accept the superficial empiricist reply to Plato according to which we simply have "an ability" (a notion that usually remains unanalyzed) enabling us to pick out correct articulating patterns (the classical empiricists' reply to Plato was to replace an ontology of forms with an ontology of abilities). The source of the superficiality of this reply is that abilities presuppose knowledge. The initial questions that led Plato to suggest innate essences in the first place will thus simply be reformulated as a need to understand the kind of knowledge that "enables picking out" these defining essentials. That is, one surely has to know something in order to be able to pick out this or that, or to see X as a correct articulation of Y, and classical empiricism left the source of this second-order knowledge mysterious (which Plato refused to do—ergo: innateness).

My own proposal is to understand the process of recognizing such forms modally. The work of literature is a *suggestion*. It sets itself as a formulation that *proposes* to make sense out of a domain of life. Neither the artist nor we have to be previously aware of the essence of courage that is being captured or expressed. We need only assume an ability to produce such suggestions and the capacity to recognize and assent to that which presents itself as exemplary. A Platonist will insist on asking what sort of knowledge we must have in order to have such capacities. Answering this need not appeal to the Platonist's own arsenal of innate essences. We can be satisfied with a more modest assumption—namely, that people try to make sense of their experiences. They therefore willingly produce, propose, and engage in (potentially refutable) organizing patterns that purport to define and capture a slice of experience.

Our problem was, first, to justify an appeal to "one's whole being" as part of philosophy rather than education. Secondly, we needed to justify the claim that such an appeal constitutes moral improvement, without the traditional coordinates that enabled speaking of literature as edifying elevation. The answer to these problems is that knowledge is structuralized. There are various levels at which beliefs can be entertained, and there are modes of misunderstanding that have nothing to do with missing certain discursive connections. The suggestive potential of literature accommodates change not primarily in the propositional content of beliefs, but in the level of their "embeddedness." (Without some error theory, this does not yet tell us which of our beliefs we should subordinate to such powers or which of them we should accept. Shakespeare's Titus publicly slaughters his raped daughter because she shames him and her presence brings him sorrow. The scene is extremely effective, and in many ages, including the Elizabethan, it would not have appeared morally outrageous to its audience. I shall address this difficulty in the next section.) This accounts for the power of literature and says something about its relation to knowledge. Art and literature give beliefs their substance. This process of substantialization constitutes growth in moral understanding and thus is part of moral philosophy rather than moral education. People who do not have a firm experiential grip on the beliefs they entertain lack understanding, not merely moral motivation. The fact that moral reflection through literature also makes a powerful educational claim adds to the need for it. This is especially so when one adopts (as I do) a more diffused view regarding the relations between moral philosophy and moral education. But this advantage should not blind us to literature's distinctly epistemic import in relation to moral understanding.

Some of our philosophical encounters with art and literature involve a recognition and contemplation of exemplary discursive and plastic shapes. The moral implications of this idea go beyond understanding or moral deliberation. They add a dimension of realness to the life of the mind, in the sense of the substantiality of the very inputs that form it. To the degree that morality not only encompasses deliberation but extends to creating character and allowing it to grow, we arrive at the most far-reaching moral contribution that art and literature can make. Art and literature not only create the conditions for moral thought but also form character, facilitating an understanding of phenomena in their distinctness, thereby enabling life to reach, at least in some moments, its fullest possibilities.

To repeat, we should not worry that this conflates philosophy and education. Those for whom such diffusion is a threat should note that, by concluding that art and literature can create conditions for moral reasoning in some domains, we remained strictly within the bounds of a narrowly conceived moral philosophy. All this is *also* self-education. Communicating such claims can *also* be an education of another. Moreover, this can *also* create realness. These added dimensions are not drawbacks but are integral to moral philosophy when it is conceived as a genuine attempt to strive for betterment.

On Error

Up to now I claimed that works of literature can function as arguments embedded in complex experiences, but this requires some explication of the possibility for error, which can distinguish between thoughts that merely arise while reading literature and those thoughts that one should accept. Without some such articulation of this distinction, the rhetorical outlook I am advocating as an important mode of moral reflection risks blurring the distinction between describing actual thought patterns and describing the thought-patterns we ought to cultivate, or between "reasoning" and "reasoning rationally," or between "psychology" and "epistemology." I will avoid arguing against these distinctions, because I wish to maintain the identification of philosophy with a normative rather than a descriptive practice. Recording effective means of persuasion cannot suffice and has to be incorporated with a procedure that can place a meaningful distinction between legitimate and objectionable derivations.

Take the example of Titus murdering his raped daughter. Only an error theory can make explicit (and add to) our ability to avoid aesthetically compelling representations of morally reprehensible acts. What accounts for our capacity to distance ourselves from what the work might be asking us to approve? Consider, too, claims such as: "Medea shows how jealousy and vindictiveness can override even the most built-in, instinctive forces" or "Hecuba and Andromache exhibit that a disaster can always turn into something worse." There is some validity to such claims, but in a philosophically acceptable frame of reference, the notions that we will need to know more of are "shows" and "exhibit." People want to say that works of literature like *Medea* or *Trojan Women* instruct us regarding concepts like hatred and disaster, and this is fine. One can, however, think of misleading, false, or unpersuasive ways of depicting hatred and disaster. We therefore need to know more about such implications from fictional occurrences to thematic concepts. More specifically, we need to know when we can accept them and when we are to dismiss them.

"The context" is sometimes relied on to decide whether such moves are to be accepted or rejected. However, this answer (the "It all depends" answer) only succeeds in refocusing the question on the notion of context (the "Depends on what?" rejoinder). Accordingly, an appeal to context will justifiably invoke a demand for criteria of relevancy for picking out pertinent aspects of contexts, or a criteria determining which contexts are legitimate for this or that derivation. Take, for instance, the idea of literary occurrences as examples. It is sometimes said that the context enables judging whether or not a literary "example" actually exemplifies. "Yet appealing to the context does not always help. For example: . . . Antigone either breaks the law of the state or breaks a higher moral commitment; Agamemnon either sacrifices an army or loses a daughter. Do these characters simply face these dilemmas in their own idiosyncratic ways, or are they doing this in some "exemplary" way (that is, in a way that carries over to similar contexts, that seems to inform in a manner that goes beyond the particularities of these characters)? What constitutes the difference between what merely occurs and the exemplary?

Or let us leave implication from examples—which, along with

enthymemes, have constituted rhetorical reasoning ever since Aristotle—and turn to an actual *enthymeme* repeatedly deployed as part of philosophical criticism of literary works: a fortiori implications. Here is Cavell on *Othello*: "If such a man as Othello is rendered impotent and murderous by aroused, or by having aroused, female sexuality—or let us say, if this man is horrified by human sexuality, in himself and in others—then no human being is free of this possibility" (1987, p. 137). One can reason validly in this way in some cases: if the Redcrosse knight is jeopardized by pride, if Guyon can be tempted to enter Mammon's cave, all of us are vulnerable. But a fortiori moves of this kind are frequently not simply valid. Cavell's use is an example: after all, lesser mortals than Othello can be *less* vulnerable to such anxieties. Consequently, one needs to employ a more context-sensitive implication. We will have to say things like "People who resemble Othello in being insecure about their identities, are more likely to have such fears when they are disoriented by the demands of a sexual partner."

Yet philosophers will have problems even with the weaker operators used above. Why is it "more likely" that such people will react in these ways? Do the critics offering such suggestions mean that they can support such propositions by statistics or by basing themselves on a psychological theory of some kind? Obviously, the critic is not appealing to anything of the sort. Such claims are rather modalities of practical reasoning. They are predicated on nothing stronger (though nothing weaker) than the author's experience and perception of life, and they appeal to a similar sense of life in the reader. Such assertions are not checked for correspondence with existing knowledge. Rather, we examine them according to their success in making sense of numerous experiences, but this still needs to be supplemented by an account that explains how we can accept a claim of this sort as an addition to understanding rather than rejecting it as an idiosyncratic imposition of the critic. We thus arrive again at the need for an error theory that can differentiate between reasoning and rational reasoning.

A (last) variation of the same problem recurs in relation to appeals to the emotions, the imagination, or one's "whole being." After acknowledging the importance of these, we need to be able to tell the difference between appeals that we should accept and those we should not. Here too a reply that depends on "the context" or appealing to the metaphor of intellectual balancing can render the entire argument specious. This would be an inevitable outcome if these suggestions boil down to an underdeveloped notion of context, or if nothing distinguishes between rational and irrational "balancing." Even if one is opposed to the idea of some transcendent frame of reference, one needs conceptual coordinates that can function as a normative guide to action.

Here are the answers that we can gather from the literature regarding such an error account. First, Rorty, Nussbaum, Novitz, and Diamond suggest that it is possible to base an error theory on coherence among one's beliefs. A new claim that is being entertained (e.g., Cavell's claim regarding the frightening nature of sexuality) should be examined in light of other factual beliefs or critical dispositions. Such coherence also restricts and balances the responses themselves, preventing us, for example, from over-sympathizing with murderers like Camus's Meursault, Sartre's Erostratus, or Shakespeare's Titus.

Another alternative is a strategy suggested by Wayne Booth, which involves examining one sort of nonvalid implication embedded within a fictional context by setting it against opposing implications that can be drawn from other literary texts. Not all works of literature pass the tests required for creating deep and lucid beliefs—most don't—but the ones that do can be played against others. Juliet speaks of her forthcoming sexual encounter with Romeo in terms of being "enjoyed." Yet an early-modern theatergoer who would relate to this as exhibiting conventional female passivity would have been "corrected" in this view by consideration of Cleopatra showing more active ways in which female sexuality can be channeled. People may sympathize with the way Romeo's passion overrides all other considerations. But a Titania, a Phaedra, or a Tarquin will remind them that the same power that can cause overwhelming love can create the sort of blindness that leads to falling in love with an ass, with one's stepson, or can set in motion the underlying mechanisms of rape.

Finally, many will probably claim that some modalities of knowledge do not admit of an error "theory" and at the same time are not accepted uncritically. We cannot always specify the conditions under which we should withdraw our assent to some beliefs. Yet we still argue (and seem to do so rationally) regarding these. Fortunately or not, this embarrassing state is experienced regarding some of the things we are most anxious to get right.

I take these answers to be satisfactory in preventing the conclusion that the direction we are here examining will inevitably fail to supply substantial coordinates that could function as an error theory. But I also wish to propose one addition to them.

On Marriage

An aging academic sits down to write a marriage proposal. He produces this:

> My dear Miss Brooke,—I have your guardian's permission to address you on a subject than which I have none more at heart. I am not, I trust, mistaken in the recognition of some deeper correspondence than that of date in the fact that a consciousness of need in my own life had arisen contemporaneously with the possibility of my becoming acquainted with you. For in the first hour of meeting you, I had an impression of your eminent and perhaps exclusive fitness to supply that need (connected, I may say, with such activity of the affections as even the preoccupations of a work too special to be abdicated could not uninterruptedly dissimulate); and each succeeding opportunity for observation has given the impression an added depth by convincing me more emphatically of that fitness which I had preconceived, and thus evoking more decisively those affections to which I have but now referred . . . I have discerned in you an elevation of thought and a capability of devotedness which I had hitherto not conceived to be compatible either with the early bloom of youth or with those graces of sex that may be said at once to win and to confer distinction when combined, as they notably are in you, with the mental qualities above indicated. It was, I confess, beyond my hope to meet with this rare combination of elements both solid and attractive, adapted to supply aid in graver labours and to cast a charm over vacant hours . . . (Bk. 1, ch. 5)

The alarming sense of Casaubon's emotional deadness—looking more for a research assistant than for a wife: the utmost he allows himself to say, erotically speaking, is that Dorothea has managed to interrupt his lofty work-related thoughts—is coupled with his inability to break free from the conventions of treatise prose. The numerous qualifying clauses crammed into the sentences: the footnote-like phrased "mental qualities above indicated"; the professional caution implied by the "perhaps" in "perhaps exclusive fitness"; the dry and solemn tone; the air of responsibility transmitted through preference for the scientific language of "observation" and consequent verification; the superfluous negatives and double negatives—all lead us to heartily agree with James Chettam's (rather uncivil) exclamation of horror upon hearing of Dorothea's agreement to marry Casaubon:

> "What do you mean, Mrs Cadwallader?" said Sir James . . . "What has happened to Miss Brooke? Pray speak out."
>
> "Very well. She is engaged to be married." Mrs Cadwallader paused a few moments, observing the deeply-hurt expression in her friend's face, which he was trying to conceal by a nervous smile, while he whipped his boot; but she soon added, "Engaged to Casaubon."
>
> Sir James let his whip fall and stooped to pick it up. Perhaps his face had never before gathered so much concentrated disgust as when he turned to Mrs Cadwallader and repeated, "Casaubon?"
>
> "Even so. You know my errand now."
>
> "Good God! It is horrible! He is no better than a mummy!" (Bk. 1, ch. 6)

Unlike the previous suggestions, which provide means for evaluating the *content* of claims, an account of error can also proceed in a different way. Suppose that a critic attempts to pinpoint the precise perception of erotic limitation that feeds our comic reaction to these moments in *Middlemarch*, saying something like the following: "Casaubon's expressive rigidity registers the degree of affective ossification that he has reached. It is from living matter as dead as this that a proposal based upon nothing more than a correspondence between needs and their satisfaction can in fact arise. While it would be anachronistic to object to the business-like tone of the proposal, or to its author's self-centeredness, Eliot's placing of this lifeless offer in the midst of more intense erotic worlds, cannot fail in striking us as a critique. The comic effect is a form of distancing from erotic outlooks that reduce the object to its projected ability to fit neatly into one's own life-plan."

The previous suggestions regarding sifting between adequate and inadequate derivations would concern themselves with examining the critic's move from the particularities of *Middlemarch* to love. Yet "rationality," in relation to subjects such as love (or, for that matter, parenting, facing failure, losing a friend, confronting one's fears—issues that recur in literary works), amounts to more than holding on to the right content-claims, even if we are sure what these are. Rationality in relation to love involves the participation of all kinds of plastic and literary articulations. This interplay itself can be more or less rational, not only when measured against possible independent standards but by being richer or poorer, by lacking or having certain important voices that we may take the critic to be drawing out of the work. It is important to have Casaubon's love letter not because he presents right or wrong ideas about love but because the letter embodies vividly a possible stance to marriage, connecting it with a more general view of life. This stance is not merely a bizarre logical possibility, since it interestingly overlaps with erotic perceptions that are less ludicrous. Casaubon is, for example, offering Dorothea participation in what he values most: he is offering her a life that he likes and that, as far as he perceives things, constitutes an opportunity for her.

Thoughts about love and its expression that include Casaubon's letter are richer than thoughts that lack it. Such epistemic enrichment through literature was by no means unfamiliar to early-modern defenders of drama.[8] The problem with "enrichment" is that it is a dangerous normative guide since we want to avoid a quantitative outlook according to which the addition of any voice is an automatic improvement. On the other hand, enrichment is a useful metaphor by which to register growth, since richness never simply designates mere quantitative addition but growth in something that is itself deemed valuable. It is the critic's job to reveal (or create) that value. This can be done by showing that Casaubon's stance is right or wrong, or that it is comic when viewed from the supposedly right erotic outlook. But less ambitiously than these, the value may reside in the powerful articulation of an outlook on love and marriage, which is what Casaubon's is. Such articulations form and become thought. Here it is important to distinguish between those voices that are valuable to have, and those that encapsulate values that one takes to be correct. It is morally valuable to have voices such as Gonerill's when relating to one's parents, since Gonerill captures the way in which an understandable need to set limits for an aging and uncompromising parent can turn into moral blindness. Voices such as Edgar's and Cordelia's demonstrate the possibility of forgiving a parent as well

---

[8] "If we present a foreign history, the subject is so intended, that in the lives of Romans, Grecians, or others, either the virtues of our countrymen are extolled, or their vices reproved; as thus, by the example of Caesar to stir soldiers to valor and magnanimity; by the fall of Pompey that no man trust in his own strength; we present Alexander killing his friend in his rage, to reprove rashness; Mydas, choked with his gold, to tax covetousness; Nero against tyranny; Sardanapalus against luxury; Ninus against ambition, with infinite others, by sundry instances either animating men to noble attempts, or attacking the consciences of the spectators, finding themselves touched in presenting the vices of others." Thomas Heywood, *An Apology for Actors*, 1612, p. 53.

as the incapacity to tell the parent that he is loved. Voices such as Racine's Hyppolytus exhibit the way kindness to a parent can be ultimately destructive. All of these are morally valuable as constituents of thought regarding filial obligation. All should interplay and constitute rational moral thinking about relating to a parent. None should simply be followed.

Of course, there are always voices that seem ineffectual or damaging. Judging whether a particular voice is enriching is an open question and leads to the sort of arguments that constitute much interpretive discourse. Is Marlowe's Edward II a silly weakling, or does he exhibit a courageous modality of fighting to maintain his homosexual identity in impossible circumstances? Is Barabas no more than a heartless, money-grubbing villain who unscrupulously kills his own daughter, or does the Jew of Malta bring into play a pattern of resistance to repeatedly expose his oppressor's hypocrisy? Does Dr. Faustus embody a detailed formulation of a mistake that he is always aware of as he is making that mistake, or does his character reveal a general predicament in which only moments of willing blindness contain the possibility of living intensely? We argue about the content of these "voices" and their value, and any reasonable theory of interpretation must not exclude such arguments. My point here is that an error theory can relate not only to the content of voices but to their existence: sometimes, reasoning that lacks certain voices is flawed.

Positing enrichment of this kind as a moral contribution of literature runs the risk of confusing the rationality of the deliberative situation and the rationality of the decision itself. Two people who are both aware of the same voices may still act differently or wrongly. But, then again, strong capacities for argumentation can also be misapplied or lead different people to different conclusions, and yet it still makes sense to say that people should have those capacities and that rationality partly *means* having these capacities. Moreover, admitting that the existence of such voices still leaves some openness means no more than that a discourse combining a philosophical, poetic, and rhetorical outlook is not a comprehensive approach in ethics, and therefore it needs to be supplemented by other forms of reasoning.

Such limiting of scope allows us to see another contribution literature makes to moral understanding and moral reasoning. One moral justification of literature is that its suggestive capacities enable voices to emerge and interplay at the most fundamental levels of thought. These constitute rational reasoning not in the sense of ensuring correct action but in *creating adequate conditions* for deliberation. Unlike the moral advantages I surveyed previously, the voices formed do not necessarily capture defining structures or "moments." They are required so as to give shape to the possibilities that some states or relations open up. Unlike *David*'s relation to courage, there is nothing exemplary or defining in Casaubon's marriage proposal, but in giving vivid shape to this possibility, George Eliot enriches our thoughts about love. The critic's remark about the letter should not then be assessed only in terms of whether or not they disclose a truth about love but also in terms of articulating erotic impotence, an articulation that is itself a valuable addition to our thoughts, even if we cannot determine its truth. Literature's moral contributions thus also pertain to its capacity to create forms that constitute richer thinking regarding some issues. Such an approach moralizes literature, but does not reduce it into didactic statements.

Philosophical Criticism and Contemporary Literary Studies

P<small>HILOSOPHICAL CRITICISM</small>, I claimed, brings together several strands of thought: the antirationalism of Hamann and his romantic and existentialist offshoots; the neoromanticism of Diamond, Novitz, Falck, and Nussbaum; the new rhetorics of Perelman, Burke, and Booth. All of these have challenged major conceptual distinctions (form/content, emotive/cognitive, suasion/justification) that underlie the separation of "philosophy" from "rhetoric" that has been a part of philosophical theory and practice since Ramus. Reflection through literature thus presents an alternative to the false rigor of analytical philosophy without adopting the deadening skepticism that underlies so much postmodern thought. This may explain why it is winning increasingly more adherents within philosophy.[1]

Within literary criticism things are less rosy. Foucault, Marx, Heidegger, and Derrida still supply most of its conceptual coordinates. Yet, when it comes to philosophical criticism of the type produced by Nussbaum or Cavell—criticism that reflects through literary works on themes such as love, or nihilism, or self-knowledge—many literary critics (I have been told) sense that there is an anachronism here. The feeling is that

---

[1] Here is, for example, Martha Nussbaum's (2000) assessment of the growing popularity of this approach:

> By now, things have to some extent changed. It would be totally commonplace to find discussions of the literary aspects of historical philosophers on the program of an APA meeting, and even more commonplace to find discussions of love, anger, moral perception, and other themes that reflection about fiction might well enhance. Explicit discussion of literary authors as diverse as Sophocles and Coetzee, Wordsworth and Dostoyevsky, Henry James and Knut Hamsun, might easily be found on the program of any mainstream meeting in the area of philosophical ethics. And at least many of the leading moral philosophers would be willing to state that such works make a valuable contribution to philosophical understanding. It is a sign of the times that we discovered recently, in my own Philosophy Department, that our graduate offering for next year contained courses on both Kierkegaard and Proust, as well as one on Seneca's letters, but no course devoted to a traditional mainstream topic in ethical theory.

philosophical criticism appears to operate within the conceptual parameters of the New Criticism and the Arnoldian humanism and romanticism that underlie it. The charge is that philosophical criticism has not seriously dealt with the numerous challenges to formalism within literary studies. It thus replays the "Old Criticism" practiced before the cultural turn in literary studies, and it does this without addressing the reasons that have led literary critics to avoid thematic reflection through poetry. To put the case more bluntly, philosophical criticism appears to recycle the romantic propensity to perceive the world through emotional and imaginative prisms. Its emphasis on particulars seems to reinvent the "concrete universals" of Ransom and Wimsatt, and it sets the "depth" achieved by reflection through literary works in contrast to the "coldness" of abstract philosophical thought, thus duplicating the opposition between scientific and poetic discourse that figured in the metacritical writings of Richards, Ransom, and Brooks.

The fact that the theoretical frontiers of the literary studies done fifty years ago are currently being heralded as important novelties in contemporary philosophy may flatter literary critics, but it will not get them interested in such work. This may explain the limited impact of philosophical criticism in literary studies, in contrast to the growing excitement with which it is met in philosophy. While some literary journals have devoted special issues to ethical criticism (including *Style, Poetics Today, New Literary History*, and *Philosophy and Literature*, the latter two featuring such work on a regular basis), it is difficult to find a sustained response to this trend in literary studies. In Shakespearean criticism, for example, the philosophical work of Weitz, Beauregard, and Cavell has largely failed to enter into meaningful dialogue with contemporary work. There are well-insulated pockets of critical attention to philosophical approaches, but nothing like a genuine engagement with these ideas. The example of Cavell is particularly troubling, as his work is widely known and respected and, while he is often mentioned, there does not seem to be any evolving dialogue with his work in contemporary Shakespearean publications.

This discrepancy between philosophical enthusiasm and literary disinterest raises two questions. The first is whether philosophical criticism is still a viable textual approach in an age in which so many orientations (New Historicism, feminism, postcolonialism, cultural materialism) have shifted away from the aesthetics, politics, and interpretive assumptions of formalism and romanticism. Given the assumption that philosophical criticism is defendable, a second question is whether contemporary literary criticism stands to *gain* anything from such readings. A more forceful restatement of this same point would be that the moral interest of the readings of Booth, Diamond, or Brudney leads to the kind of character analysis practiced long ago by Bradley, Moulton, Heilman, or even Johnson and Rymer. Consequently, although philosophical interpretations in this vein may interest philosophers, they nevertheless represent nothing new for literary critics. And even more traditionally oriented critics, who refuse to take the anthropological tack, may well share this impression. Addressing these issues is the aim of this chapter.

THE CULTURAL TURN AND PHILOSOPHICAL CRITICISM

Begging Tarquine not to rape her, Shakespeare's Lucrece says this:

> My sighs like whirlwinds labour hence to heave thee.
> If ever man were moved with woman's moans,
> Be moved with my tears, my sighs, my groans;
> All which together, like a troubled ocean,
> Beat at thy rocky and wrack-threat'ning heart,
> To soften it with their continual motion;
> For stones dissolved to water do convert.
> O' if no harder than a stone thou art,
> Melt at my tears and be compassionate!
> Soft pity enters at an iron gate.
>   (*The Rape of Lucrece*, lines 586–95)

Since early-modern audiences would have conceptualized rape primarily as a property-related assault on the victim's male patron, we do not expect Lucrece's language of complaint to appeal to the sense of personal offense, to personal violation and other attributes of the experience of a raped woman today (if these latter dimensions would be touched at all). Indeed, Lucrece and Tarquine would both explicitly relate to the rape in terms of damage done to her husband. But Shakespeare's language also presses against its own cultural limitations through continuously alluding to nonlinguistic expression: Lucrece is sighing, moaning, groaning, crying. These allusions to nonlinguistic expression through language create a dimension of personal suffering, escaping the culturally available expressive forms. Shakespeare intensifies the attempt to move from language to expressive sound through his use of alliteration in these lines: the whooshing sound of the first line, in which the *h* sounds invoke the sound of wind, or the whirlwind she is referring to ("My sighs like whirlwinds labor hence to heave thee"); the density of *m* sounds as Lucrece is referring to her moaning (man, moved with woman's moans, moved, my) thus creating the sound of moaning as she is referring to moaning; the repetition of *t* sounds, when she is saying that she wants to melt Tarquine's heart. In employing *t* sounds (together, troubled, beat at, threatening heart, to soften it, continual), Lucrece is mouthing the sound that resembles most the trickling of raindrops precisely at the moment in which, on the semantic level of the aquatic figures, she intends to dissolve or melt her assailant's fierce soul. Despite the conservative moral tone of the poem as a whole, Shakespeare's language is here morally innovative precisely in its capacity to suggest dimensions of personal pain in a discursive matrix that does not yet contain such articulation. Literature can thus articulate modes of suffering that escape the limitations of culturally available expressions of complaint.[2]

Philosophical criticism is neither a theory of interpretation nor a new collection of critical tools. Therefore, it should not be set alongside, say, New Historicism or deconstruction as a competing approach. More than anything else, philosophical criticism represents an orientation and a sensitivity to the limitations of standard argumentative prose and an attunement to the way these can be overcome through reflection that is interpenetrated with literature. Once it is recognized that the antagonism between philosophical criticism and contemporary literary criticism cannot be thought of in terms of humanism vs. posthumanism, modernism vs. postmodernism, right vs. left, a promising horizon comes into view, where political and philosophical criticism overlap.[3] In its ability to dwell on particular kinds of pain, and precisely through its willingness to employ transhistorical notions of suffering and humiliation, philosophical

---

[2] "Postmodern" moral outlooks have contributed the more detailed work on the relations between damage and possibilities for the verbalization of the damage and its formulation as a complaint (J. F. Lyotard, 1988; A. Ophir, 2000). Yet I see nothing that should prevent philosophers with a non-Continental bent from accepting these insights. Hebrew readers may examine a detailed analysis of the representation of Lucrece's complaint that aims to situate literature's capacity to transcend cultural modes of complaint within contemporary discussions of the relations between law and literature (J. Shkabatur and T. Zamir, 2005). The detailed reading also addresses the arguments among Shakespeareans over the moral status of Lucrece's voice (or lack of it), and the conservative or subversive meaning of her suicide.

[3] The (possible) antagonism between philosophical criticism and contemporary literary studies should not be conceptualized as an opposition between humanism and a posthumanist hostility to the traditional apology for poetry as means for cultivating humanity

criticism is able to reveal the numerous patterns of oppression associated with modernism. And if its assumptions regarding argumentative method are accepted, philosophical criticism can amount to a critique that can add to the political effectiveness of critical discourses that focus on exposing and correcting acts of marginalization. In this, philosophical criticism is able to highlight ways in which reflection on marginalization, when done through literary works, differs importantly from other kinds of cultural critique. Philosophical criticism thus allows politically oriented literary studies to retain its uniqueness rather than dissolving into all-embracing cultural criticism. And so, while some philosophical critics perceive themselves as romantics or humanists or liberals and engage in political polemics with posthumanists, this should not blind either party to the ways in which philosophical criticism itself is only contingently related to these positions.

Here is one example of how philosophical criticism may complement and enrich political criticism. Raymond Williams wrote that good literature goes beyond the experience of its contemporary social networks. It presents an imaginative response to those networks, a response that constitutes something greater than mere reformulation (1980, pp. 24–25). *Lucrece* is an example. Many Shakespeareans would hesitate to relate to Lucrece through our vocabulary of selfhood, subjectivity, and individuality, a vocabulary that blurs differences between contemporary and early-modern articulations of personal experience (especially so for women). But if it makes sense to account for the heavy alliteration of the lines not only in terms of the creation of personal suffering but also in stating a resistance to the available modes of complaint, the poem reshapes the coordinates that governed and organized its production and

---

through the arts. Philosophical critics may well be relying on Arnoldian and formalist justifications of the humanities in their criticism of conventional argumentative philosophy. Such, for example, is the emphasis on emotional and experiential articulation as opposed to "scienticism" (the importing of scientific, problem-solving thought patterns into all aspects of life); or the emphasis on the social function of art and the empathic involvement it demands so as to forge ethical attachments; or the ability of literature to emulate the aesthetic, moral, and political functions of religion. But because their work deviates from and criticizes influential rationalist assumptions regarding argumentative "rigor," the relationship between philosophical critics and modernism is complicated. On the other hand, the relationship between poststructuralist political criticism and humanism is itself not just a story of a simple break. Rather, it has often been acknowledged that sensitivity to the numerous modes of cultural oppression that humanistic culture fostered is not only itself conceptually implicit in humanist assumptions but is also a practical consequence of that very humanist culture.

reception. Williams was responding to Lucien Goldmann's distinction between actual and possible consciousness. According to Goldmann, most sociology of literature tries to decipher actual consciousness in literary texts, but we should rather look for possible consciousness. Apart from exemplifying (surprisingly) the way radical political readings rely on the older privilege of authorial insight (the way it goes beyond the actual and penetrates to the possible—a theme going back to Aristotle's *Poetics*), Goldmann's remarks also suggest one way of integrating political and philosophical criticism. It is precisely here that one would ask Goldmann and Williams to formulate the advantages of a specifically *literary*—as opposed to a nonliterary—delineation of the imaginative response. Of course, one could deny the existence of a uniquely literary discourse. But that has not been the direction taken by the most insightful political criticism.

Before adding more substance to the possible merging of interests between political and philosophical criticism, I must examine the most influential theoretical claims in contemporary literary studies against thematic reflection through literary works. Much cultural criticism that is not explicitly political would, if pressed to justify its existence, still appeal to the kind of political motivations given by New Historicists and cultural materialists. Accordingly, I will concentrate on the latter approaches. Of these, I will refer especially to Raymond Williams, who is the most persuasive and explicit thinker in his antiphilosophical stance. Williams's influence is implicit in the work and orientation of many other theorists, even when they avoid cultural materialism. I shall not focus on familiar arguments against philosophical interpretations that do not carry much weight against the new kinds of philosophical criticism. For example, it has been argued against thematic criticism that in their search for inclusiveness, as they battle against other thematic interpretations, such readings essentially lose sight of the particularity of character and occurrence (R. Levin, 1982, pp. 26–27). But this objection cannot plausibly relate to the philosophers who are now reading literary works, since it is precisely the particularity of literature that is often defended as an advantage over reflection that is limited to general rules (Phillips, 1982, p. 29; Diamond, 1993, p. 149; Eldridge, 1989, pp. 19–21; Nussbaum, 1990, pp. 37–40). As for the threat of instrumentalizing literature, this charge too cannot be credibly leveled against readings that focus on morality as experience rather than as conceptual lessons. These in any case do not reduce the value of literary works to philosophical messages, an issue that was defended and developed in previous chapters.

Against Philosophical Criticism

Here then, are what I take to be the more weighty arguments against philosophical criticism from the standpoint of contemporary, politically and culturally oriented literary studies:

Some will argue that in its assumptions regarding the possibility of thematic dialogue with past literary works, philosophical criticism perpetuates the misconception of almost all pre-eighties interpretive practices in literary studies that posited a "continuous tradition of religious, social and aesthetic values shared by [past] poets and twentieth-century critics" (Montrose, 1989). But the very idea of "tradition," says Williams, is a mirage, in which one ignores the active selection and reselection that is what "tradition" is, and regards it "as an object, a projected reality, with which we have to come to terms on its terms, even though those terms are always and must be the valuations, the selections and omissions, of other men" (1980, p. 16). Against philosophical criticism, there now follow the familiar claims against the specific selections and biases that constitute Western tradition.

Aside from the problematic contents of the tradition being transmitted, philosophical criticism seems to advocate the older conception regarding what teaching and interpreting literature should be. Ascribing privileged status to the phenomenological insights of canonical authors invokes an interpretive stance that turns the critic into an agent rather than an interrogator of ideology. This violates the politics of a new teaching ethos that does not ignore the ideological aspects of teaching, as did older critics with their politically unreflective assumptions regarding high culture. Instead, the new ethos advocates setting in motion for students a critical sense of their own historicity and participation in ideological production and consumption, empowering those students whose identities have so often been marginalized by past explanatory schemes. Philosophical criticism is thus politically naive, which may turn the critic into a coopted ideological tool, and returns literary criticism to the state of political impotence from which it has only recently managed to emerge.

A different case against philosophical criticism relates to method. Williams sees Marxism as presenting an alternative vision of the "constitutive human process itself" to that favored by focusing on a "culture" made up of "ideas" (1977, pp. 19–20). Others say that the very distinction between notions and culture (upon which philosophical criticism seems to depend) is itself a false tool for constructing subjects (Gallagher,

1989). The problem with such insulation of a realm of philosophical ideas (not to say of *Aeternae Veritates*) is that in actuality such concepts are and always were imbued with ideological content that was repeatedly masked by adopting a supposedly objective and neutral stance. When one scrutinizes (historicizes) the workings of actual thematic categories such as, say, love, honesty, truth, loyalty, parenting, obedience, guilt, and other notions that have been reflected upon in abstraction by older critics, one finds that these cannot be understood without taking into consideration diffused conceptual and ideological networks. These networks transcend the boundaries of aesthetic or philosophical production and demand attending to complicated practices and various interests. From such a perspective, the mistake of philosophical reflection that relies on a shared dialogue with the past lies in perceiving and analyzing culture through the wrong lenses. Dynamic processes of articulation are erroneously replaced with static thematic entities that hover ahistorically above social life. The philosophical critic errs by choosing a superficial framework for analysis, which is itself the outcome of ideological forces that the critic is compelled to strengthen. The critic thereby ignores (or is simply unaware of) a superior form of understanding of the human process. (According to Williams, such an alternative framework has been introduced by Marxism, a framework that is immune from—or at least less vulnerable to—ideological "coopting" of those who aim for an adequate understanding of culture.)

From this claim concerning method emerges another objection regarding the faulty moral status of philosophical criticism. "Ideology," at least in one of its Marxist renderings, is "self-dependent theory," severed from "actual existing conditions" (Williams, 1977, p. 65). From this perspective, philosophy as such is ideology, repressing the social forces that underlie and enable abstract reflection. Philosophical criticism purports to be a contemplation of literature that attempts to generate normative as opposed to descriptive claims, in order to bring about a shaping and reshaping of the self. But since the categories involved are part of a "self-dependent theory," the procedure itself turns out to be an examination of one set of cultural representations through a collection of seemingly descriptive categories, the employment of which is morally reprehensible. Philosophical criticism thus amounts to a moral engagement with art that remains superficial at best, dishonest at worst, since it continues the insulation of the abstract from the practical that underlies various kinds of oppression. This argument against an implicit faulty morality differs from the one that focuses on the contents of the tradition to which philosophical critics appeal, since it emphasizes the ethical stakes involved in abstract reflection as such, exposing the very move to abstract thought as a way of being taken in by a powerful cultural deception.

A different target of attack will be the notion of self assumed by any interpretive procedure that, like philosophical criticism, focuses on character analysis, which is supposed to establish the notion of self-knowledge either for these critics or for their projected readers. Criticism that focuses on categories of personal experience as the basic building blocks of character analysis ignores the interpenetration of the social and the personal and misconstrues these experiences as basic in some way. It is not so much that these experiences are simply *products* of ideology (as most critics today will refuse to see social forces as exerting pressure on the individual from the outside). Determining forces are, rather, dynamic entities, forever reshaping and complicating any clear distinctions between the personal and the social. Character analysis should thus employ less naive categories of analysis than those proposed by the philosophical critic. It should replace beliefs, emotions, etc., with "structures of feeling" or some such categories of "thick" description that will enable an analysis of experience that is always attuned to the social nature of personal experience (Williams, 1977, pp. 131–33; cf. Dollimore, 1993, ch. 16).

Response

I am not primarily interested in replying to these charges but rather wish to focus on seeing the way through which philosophical criticism can accommodate and advance some of the sensitivities that these criticisms embody. Yet it is important to see the shortcomings of these arguments when they are presented as a direct critique of philosophical criticism. Beginning with "tradition," arguments over the merits and cooptive dangers of connecting with tradition can no longer proceed as they did two decades ago. We have certainly not reached a state of genuine equality, especially in my own part of the world that has not been swept by sensitivities regarding marginalization. This, as well as the discrepancy between sentiments that have been analyzed to the point of banality in the academic world (at least in the humanities) and the way in which they are still fought over outside the universities, means that we cannot yet say that political literary criticism is no longer needed. But the importance of political readings cannot reasonably imply that interpretive work that does not focus on power structures and subversion is misguided. Since philosophical criticism does not advocate an honorific stance toward tradition, I do not really see the danger of philosophical critics or their readers becoming homophobic, xenophobic, racist, or chauvinist simply by reading texts that were written from the viewpoint of such dispositions.

The criticism that denies a separation of the ideational from the material suffers from self-reflexive difficulties that prevent its own articulation (it is, after all, a highly abstract critique). Apart from that, it involves a "genetic fallacy," in which the importance of noting the various material contingencies that are related to the genesis of a philosophical position is supposed to somehow preclude an examination of the philosophical position that emerges. The former can be a fascinating project (I am thinking, for instance, of Terry Eagleton's analysis of the aesthetic, or Raymond Williams's description of the emergence of the category of taste). But we also know that the same cultural circumstances led to *conflicting* philosophical theories, and this reveals a criterion of conceptual justification that is itself only contingently related to influential social conditions. Some will claim that the very criterion for the supposedly independent examination of conflicting philosophical positions is deeply implicated in the social realm. Yet, for much philosophizing, this is a senseless claim (in what way, for example, are Hegel's critique of the Kantian *Ding an sich*, or Berkeley's critique of Locke's distinction between primary and secondary qualities "implicated" in the social realm?). Even where it does make sense, what follows from this claim is far from clear. Overdramatizations of its importance usually involve confusion between *some* influence of the social on the abstract (a thesis that no one disputes) and the *exhaustive* determination of the abstract by the social (a thesis that no one has proved).

As for the replacement of character analysis by broader frames of reference, to begin with, it is questionable whether thicker categories for articulating experience (Williams's "structures of feeling") have meaningful content that does not smuggle in the older vocabulary that governs self-talk. There is also a strong *political* reason to avoid abandoning self-talk: it has to do with suffering. Political readings march under the banner of sensitivity to modalities of personal suffering. Deconstructing boundaries of self-culture undermines this motivation, as one wants to say something about *who* it is that suffers. Power works in complicated ways, filtering into "internal" articulations and motivations, and it is thus not limited to being an external force. Yet, somewhere along the line, the very point of political readings is to give voice to those individuals who suffer, and suffer personally, from cultural hegemonies that repeatedly efface the contingency of the structures they impose. And since suffering determines so much of personal experience, the idea that character analysis is politically defective must be abandoned.

But I wish to go beyond the level of polemics or of showing that philosophical criticism is defensible. I shall therefore turn to what philosophical criticism can add to contemporary, politically oriented literary criticism. Like many others, I believe that the contemporary critical scene presents a false dichotomy between "right" and "left," "humanism" and "posthumanism," "Old Criticism" and "cultural studies," etc. The dichotomy is false because the new orientations are meaningless if they do not maintain strong links with the older frameworks.[4] I shall now articulate these tacit continuities, and then show how philosophical criticism as I characterize it can create links between the new sensitivities and these older assumptions. I will argue for continuities and gains (from the perspective of contemporary, politically oriented literary critics) that relate to ethics, truth, and aesthetics. The resulting argument will be neither reactionary, nor a simplified belief in a policy of "live and let live" that allows these orientations to carry on unimpeded. Instead, we will arrive at an articulated (rather than a programmatic) possibility of avoiding the false choice between worshiping an oppressive tradition on the one hand and adopting a "resentful" stance on the other.

Ethics

The sensitivity to the violence inherent in all acts of hegemonic reinstatement—a sentiment so obviously shared by political critics—necessarily indicates ideological preferences. Yet, while political criticism is certainly committed to specific moral hierarchies, it usually avoids artic-

---

[4] We often hear that the relations between postmodern and modern frameworks cannot be fruitfully conceived as those of discontinuity and replacement. This becomes especially obvious when attempting to integrate postmodern political sensitivities into a viable and constructive educational stance (e.g., in the work of Henry Giroux). In general, the arguments over political criticism and cultural studies sometimes suffer from superficiality, as they are not set in relation to an integrated philosophy of education, and are satisfied with educational insights, say, defamiliarization in relation to formative narratives. Important as such insights are they cannot replace a regulative view of self and a normative view of living and of happiness that justifies these insights.

ulating the conceptual stance that justifies them. In the absence of explicit argument, one can only guess that this avoidance arises from the difficulty of grounding moral commitment in a poststructuralist framework. Yet why should sensitivity to the suffering of others, for example, override a desire for unity? Fortunately, we do not ask questions of this sort anymore (at least not in most academic circles), but it should be remembered that the answers were couched in humanist terminology. When one attempts to justify the assumptions regarding minimizing suffering and maximizing freedom one rediscovers modernism with its assumptions regarding transhistorical and transcultural human needs. Regardless of the form of justification—whether it be some theory of natural rights, or contractarianism with its premises regarding largely uniform preferences on which a just social order could be constructed, or a utilitarianism with its essentialist assumptions regarding the basic need to minimize suffering, or Kantianism with its reason-based justification for avoiding instrumentalizing others—any genuine commitment to poststructuralist ideology cannot remain within the framework of discursive games and tentative convictions.

By avoiding any connections between literature and betterment—whether through Aristotelian emotional purging, or Platonic and Plotinian idealism, Heideggerian world disclosure, or Gadamerian self-completion—contemporary political approaches have not succeeded in "avoiding" theory, as some of them so eagerly wished to do, but rather they only managed to evade some crucial issues that literary critics are supposed to address. On one level, this shows that comparing, say, romanticism with New Historicism is like comparing apples and oranges. Romanticism, apart from representing a different attunement to life and a way of advocating a new kind of art, proposed existential hierarchies that aspired to a better mode of living. This enabled romantic critics to involve themselves and their readers in didactic insights as an adjunct to their readings. In contrast, influential contemporary critics, such as Stephen Greenblatt, explicitly avoid theory (by "theory" I mean answers to such questions as: Why does literature matter? What is the purpose of literary criticism? Do people gain anything from literature that they could not get elsewhere?). Avoiding these questions means that New Historicism is not a competing approach to romanticism, and one cannot be a critique of the other even if it sees itself as articulating a postromantic stance. More importantly, the disconnection from any attempt to provide existential coordinates, romantic or otherwise, undermines a genuine political endeavor.

In a similar way, Williams (who, unlike Greenblatt's implied politics, does have an explicit political agenda that connects literary criticism with an articulated moral and political stance), has limited himself to a strictly Marxist moral agenda. But the moral scope of literary works must necessarily extend beyond simply correcting inequalities. Here again, romanticism does not seem to be competing with cultural materialism, as Williams does not propose anything regarding what people should strive to be and do *after* genuine equality is attained. From a cultural materialist stance, the political damage inherent in perceiving romanticism as an obvious enemy is that the values romantics proposed could be pursued after a successful revolution or in contexts in which relative equality has been achieved. To perceive such a proposal as antagonistic leads to cultivating a political agenda that is too narrow and prevents one from constructing a meaningful alternative social and moral order. In short, radical political thought cannot dismiss the discussion of possibilities that will be open to all in the proposed just society. Romanticism, when not employed as a means of effacing material oppression, is thus conceptually continuous with cultural materialism.

Political criticism cannot meaningfully maintain its moral convictions and at the same time break with traditional ethics. More than paying lip service to conceptual continuities, the practical implication of this is that the political critic must attempt to articulate the metaphysical, ethical, and existential merits of reading literature, as these give substance to the opportunities that society *should* offer to everyone. Apart from this connection to the work done by philosophical critics, if the political critic has a genuine moral motivation (rather than excusing his or her critical preferences morally), he or she will also want to know how moralizing through literature differs from other moral activity. This is necessary even if one refuses to see a clear-cut distinction between aesthetic and nonaesthetic production. After all, a genuine anthropological interest in culture requires that one respect the differences among discourses even when they do overlap, and it is precisely these differences that philosophical criticism explains.

Truth

There are certain queer times and occasions in this strange mixed affair we call life when a man takes this whole universe for a vast practical joke, though the wit thereof he but dimly discerns, and more than suspects that the joke is at nobody's expense but his own.

(*Moby Dick*, ch. 49)

Truth presents a second connection between philosophical criticism and contemporary literary studies. Literary works are replete with sententious remarks just like this one from *Moby Dick*, which purports to disclose a truism about life. But although this remark of Melville's narrator seems true today even though it was written one hundred and fifty years ago, some contemporary literary critics would be uneasy about the remark's veracity (since that appears to presuppose a mimetic view of literature), and would also probably avoid saying that Melville is articulating a truth. Contemporary cultural criticism focuses on past-present discontinuities. The political motivation for this is that continuities tend to attach themselves to an oppressive interpretation of human nature. Lurking in the background is also a certain ennui toward the usual "histories of ideas" that have so often presented a shared idealism underlying some grand narrative. One drawback of the preference for discontinuities is that avoiding similarities and points at which different cultural moments articulate a shared structure of feeling leads to a rather insubstantial contact with the past (the essay on *King Lear* explores this topic further). But continuities raise questions of emotional, psychological, and existential *truth* that the descriptive language of cultural anthropology persistently eschews. Othello and Medea articulate something similar, as do Romeo, the Ovidian Echo, and Plato's Lysias in the first part of the *Phaedrus*. Could love or jealousy possess a shared core? Or, to use a language that does not assume a transhistorical ontological given, could the focus on discontinuities be overemphasized, given the way by which representations produced from extremely different cultural and historical contexts repeatedly overlap? This question, in either of its versions, would have been routinely answered in the affirmative by older critics who saw the whole point of literary interpretation as furthering dialogue based on such overlapping human experience. But poststructuralists avoid truth. They endorse the language of "representation," "system," "discourse," and other categories that enable circumventing the descriptive presumptions of literature. When literary works turn into "representations," it is no longer easy to explain in what sense they can be a source of "insight" or a means through which minute subtleties of thought and sentiment are "articulated" or "captured." For poststructuralists all of these terms are couched in a mimetic view of literature and should thus be avoided.

Apart from disallowing Melville's remark to be "about" that affair we call "life," a further problem that political approaches have if they advocate a thorough disconnection from all mimetic presumptions is, again, with suffering. I argued that any genuine political approach has to posit a means by which ideologies could be morally compared and assessed. Such transcultural evaluative principles (minimizing suffering and oppression, for example) need to be justified, and this prevents a radical break with the transhistorical assumptions and argumentative practices of traditional "idealistic" ethics. I am now claiming that similar considerations prevent a disconnection from the traditional mimetic view of art.[5] This time the central notion is not ethics but truth. Positing a transhistorical descriptive idea of the workings of suffering (the assumption, for instance, that hegemonic structures cause suffering through practices of oppression and effacement that, in turn, call for subversion) is a necessary descriptive requirement for any political approach. This requirement, along with the rich assumptions that could legitimize such transcultural descriptive psychosocial claims, jointly prevent a clean break with mimetic criticism.

If political criticism relies on truths rather than mere representations, if it is motivated by a desire to perceive literature as a serious means of contacting the pain of the past and of being a mediator of change in the present, it reconnects with philosophical criticism in a second way. For bringing in truth makes unavoidable questions regarding the connections between literary representations and reality, or the rationality of acting or believing on the basis of fictional "data," or the nature of rational justification involving learning from literary texts. One can think, for example, that in emphasizing the way in which rape is characterized primarily as damage to the husband of the raped woman, Shakespeare's *The Rape of Lucrece* participates and reenforces the conventional association of women as property, denying a personal dimension to their suffering. But then, after noting the various ways in which Lucrece's words spill over into nonlinguistic expression, after pondering over the significance of the silence between Lucrece and her crying maid and what this could mean in relation to the poem's possible resistance to a discursive inability to articulate the personal suffering of a woman in Elizabethan culture (precisely in its insistence on structuring a prolonged silence), we unavoidably enter into issues of truth (or, in my own version of philosophical criticism, of justification). For after reading Taylor on the self, Macpherson on possessive individualism, Greenblatt on the inadequacy

---

[5] Though here it is not clear whether political approaches are indeed detached from such a stance. Greenblatt (1988, p. 7), for example, wrote that blurring the distinction between representation and reality is a "theoretical mistake and a practical blunder", though he advocates a view in which these are not separately understood.

of psychoanalytical categories, or Ferry and Maus on inwardness, and after practicing caution against carelessly imposing our own self-categories on Renaissance texts, the question remains: can we plausibly deny Lucrece a dimension of *personal* suffering? Can we deny her a form of suffering that has nothing to do with her husband, existing in the face of a cultural discourse that cannot articulate it as *personal* pain? And if we cannot deny this, what justifies a belief in a transhistorical aspect of suffering that can be traced beyond the admittedly important differences in the experiences of raped women across times and cultures? How can the fictional portrayal of rape in *Lucrece* be the basis for such a conclusion? And how should such beliefs affect our interpretive practices? Indeed, can such beliefs be consistent with the disposition to avoid a thematic dialogue with the past? Such questions bring out the need for a form of criticism that can make sense of the way literary works can justify beliefs about nonfictional life. By explicating the connections between literature, truth, and justification, philosophical criticism can supply content to the metaphysical and argumentative assumptions upon which political approaches have always relied.

Aesthetics

The third gain I see in combining political and philosophical interests relates to aesthetics. It is here that philosophical criticism opens a new sense of literary criticism and its irreducible intellectual significance as opposed to other modes of cultural critique. While political criticism has always sought to complicate the relations between aesthetic and nonaesthetic production, it has also (at least since Lukács) avoided reductive positions. Greenblatt and Gallagher (2001, p. 9) posit an unanalyzed notion of aesthetic "power" that they deny that their work excludes. In an earlier work, Greenblatt spoke of "pleasure" as the primal function of art that should not be reduced to the social contingencies of the work or its reception (1990, pp. 9–11). Much earlier, Raymond Williams wrote of "quite physical" sensations that are the "true effects of many kinds of writing." These include "specific alterations of physical rhythms, physical organization: experiences of quickening and slowing, of expansion and intensification" (1977, p. 156), which, for him, escape the reduction of the aesthetic into ideology.

The ways in which Greenblatt, Gallagher, and Williams preserve literature's uniqueness strike me as too thin. In one way, the weakness is institutional. It involves an inability to specify an important distinguishing feature capable of preventing literature's eventual reduction into cultural studies (though institutional instability is less of a worry for political critics). But the weakness is also theoretical—a rich anthropological interest should seek a detailed understanding of the distinctiveness of cultural discourses. A loss of distinctions, or distinctions that relate only to superficial or partial characteristics, leads to poor anthropology and impoverished cultural study. George Levine's attempt to salvage such uniqueness by reclaiming aesthetic disinterest that some works momentarily enable also strikes me as too weak (Levine, 1995; 2001). Levine makes no attempt to rework and defend the older connections between beauty, truth, and betterment, a reformulation that would have given his attempt some substance. The unique value Levine would place on literature is thus ultimately limited to momentary escapism from instrumental thought. This does not get us substantially beyond the theoretical poverty of Greenblatt's "pleasure" or "power," or the disturbing way in which Williams's thoughts on literary uniqueness are limited to the physical.

In opposition to these, philosophical criticism supplies rich and elaborate content to literary criticism's uniqueness as a distinct mode of cultural inquiry. Here philosophical criticism connects with contemporary thought in literary studies, as the polemic which occupies George Levine, Michael Bèrubè, Eugene Goodheart, and others (e.g., the "new aestheticism," if it can be classed as a movement)[6] over the reduction of literature to anthropology does not relate to losing sight of literature, but rather to the possibility and desirability of articulating *the uniqueness* of the literary. Throughout this book, I argue that philosophical criticism can circumvent impasses in the arguments of moral philosophy in relation to first truths or contingent claims and other areas that resist direct argumentation. In the end, it is the specific suggestive capacities of literary discourse that allow us to approach an otherwise inaccessible part of life rationally and with wholeness. It is thus not merely "play" or "pleasure" or "power" or momentary "disinterest" that literature provides but unique and irreducible modes of thought and transformation that go to the heart of existential reflection.

Literature can no doubt be used to attain a richer anthropology. But wherever we locate its roots (myths, the birth of fiction, tragedy, music), literature—not the linguistic category of the late Middle Ages but the ancient cultural productions that the term later came to designate—has

---

[6] See *The New Aestheticism*, Joughin and Malpas, eds. (2003).

always maintained a complex relation with moral functions. Therefore, if we wish to read the emergence of literature *politically*, we need to assume that it had to take on some normative functions that could not be fulfilled by other institutions. Such politics itself was often misguided, and this surely points to the dangers of literature as well as to its advantages, yet this is no argument against the need for rhetorical forms that go deeper than other discursive appeals. Literature is sometimes a branch of moral philosophy. And when it is seen in this way, it can, in unique ways, further a detailed understanding of the suffering of the weak. It can create an experiential understanding of the workings of power and the limitations of self-articulation that power creates. It forms an understanding—that differs qualitatively from other kinds of understanding—of what it is like to occupy certain positions in oppressive systems. Reading literature in this way does not necessarily make one better, just as the ability to understand arguments does not imply that one knows how to think critically. In both, these are only a preliminary step on the way to intellectual, moral, and political growth.

Philosophical criticism investigates the rational basis that enables literature to be a viable component of moral and political thought and action. The conceptual difficulties are not simple. Empathizing with a certain attitude is no reason to think that that position is justified, just as knowing something experientially is not necessarily the kind of knowledge one ought to rely on. Fictional exemplification is precarious both in terms of distinguishing between good and bad literary examples and in perceiving how fictional examples support nonfictional conclusions. Philosophical criticism does not deal with these difficulties in the manner practiced in abstract aesthetics, but rather as an integral part of actual readings. My point is that without such inquiries it becomes impossible to explain in what sense literature can be political.

PART II

PHILOSOPHICAL CRITICISM IN PRACTICE

A Case of Unfair Proportions

THE DEGREE OF HIS ACTUAL UGLINESS is still difficult to determine. Various sources tell us that he was short, that one of his arms was smaller than the other, that his legs, too, were of unequal size, and that his shoulders were disproportionate. They say that he was not merely crook-backed but had a "mountain on his back," and that his face was ugly, that he was a crab-faced impotent who was born feet-first and toothed. The historical soundness of this description has been challenged many times.[1] But whether or not it constitutes an adequate portrait of the historical Richard III is unimportant for the purpose of a literary exploration of the psychological links between alienation and villainy, and even less so for a philosophical inquiry into a literary staging of amoral conduct chosen for its own sake. What is significant for such an undertaking is close scrutiny of the details with which a literary work configures a response that permits a uniquely powerful presentation of a conceptual claim.

The idea of philosophy as experience created through literary works has become a focal point of much discussion into the relations between philosophy and literature,[2] and in the first two chapters I tried to explain the broader basis for this tendency. Understanding is not always reducible to the paraphrasable content that is being grasped. The notion of cognitive experience, I claimed, accommodates and justifies the belief that a fuller comprehension of some beliefs requires literature. One challenge that faces proponents of connections between cognitive experience and fiction is replacing programmatic terms with detailed claims. Most of this chapter will be devoted to a detailed investigation of the characterization and motivation of Richard III. It has regrettably become a commonplace of the criticism of the play to dehumanize Richard, seeing him as no more than instancing the dramaturgic convention of the Vice, a personification of unmotivated evil. By contrast, I will argue that this

---

[1] The sources for this description of Richard are Sir Thomas More's *History of King Richard the Third*, and Shakespeare's descriptions of him in *King Henry VI, Part III*. For a critique of the historical inadequacy of this description, see Emyr Wyn Jones (1980).

[2] See Jesse Kalin (1976), Ronald Duska (1980), Martha C. Nussbaum (1990), and Frank Palmer (1992).

reduction of Richard can only be achieved by ignoring the details of Shakespeare's text. My broader theoretical aim, though, is not to show that Shakespeare anticipates post-Freudian psychology or that, as Harold Bloom says, Shakespeare is inventing the parameters of the human. It is to show one avenue by which the links between the rhetoric of literary texts and philosophical response patterns can be explored.

I chose to open this section of the book with an investigation into the most familiar experiential pattern that figures in the writing on literature and morality: the idea of empathy (the other readings in this book will cover less familiar modalities of experiential understanding). Yet I mean to explore empathic understanding in a context that has been repeatedly presented as a danger for such approaches: empathic understanding of an evil character. The danger is supposed to be that effective literary articulations of immoral choices can themselves be immoral, as they create reading experiences in which the distinction between understanding and justifying evil is blurred. This is sometimes countered by saying that aesthetic and moral concerns overlap, and so a truly evil character or a literary work that operates on a detached moral plane would usually not elicit strong empathic responses from a reader, and so the danger of destabilizing the reader's moral framework is exaggerated. I shall avoid this reply. Instead, I will allow myself to be taken in by a splendid staging of evil. One of the aims of the following reading is to show the implausibility of the said danger, even when one succumbs to the seductive powers of immoral literature.

Richard's Justification of Evil

Let us call "amoralism" the position that asserts that there are no compelling reasons for choosing moral behavior. Other terms have been used to designate this position (meta-ethical skepticism, immoralism, and so on). But for our purposes, the amoralist is someone who answers negatively the question "Should I be moral?" Amoralists can put in practice such a rejection of morality in two ways: they can ignore ethical considerations, or—more palpably—they can challenge morality through explicitly choosing immoral conduct. In Shakespeare's terms, the second option amounts to willfully choosing villainy, a theme he explores in *Richard III*.[3]

---

[3] In his typology of immoralities, Ronald D. Milo (1984) has further distinguished the second type of ethical skepticism (what he terms "wickedness") into "preferential wickedness" (the villain acknowledges his actions as wrong, but performs them because he values some

A CASE OF UNFAIR PROPORTIONS

"Exploring" a philosophical theme through literary means can mean various things. One can try to "confirm" or "refute" a position by, for example, showing how an agent who chooses it flourishes or is made to regret his choice (Cyril Tourneur's *The Atheist's Tragedy* ends with such didactic awakening on the part of its villain).[4] If he would have chosen such routes, Shakespeare could have "taken sides" in disputes concerning skepticism, a position that gained considerable strength in Renaissance theological and intellectual polemics.[5] The subtleties of Shakespearean rhetoric, however, cannot be reduced to such simple modes of contact with a conceptual position.

When the atrocity of an action is itself considered an advantage, the notion of evil suggests itself strongly. Richard's justification of his actions in the opening soliloquy is unique in that, unlike Edmond, Iago, or Macbeth, for whom villainy at least appears to start off as a form of revenge or as instrumental for future gain, Richard finds merits and pleasure in the villainous action itself and chooses it as such.[6] How exactly this is marshaled becomes apparent from a scrutiny of his opening soliloquy:

> Now is the winter of our discontent
> Made glorious summer by this son of York;
> And all the clouds that low'r'd upon our House
> In the deep bosom of the ocean buried.
> Now are our brows bound with victorious wreaths,
> Our bruised arms hung up for monuments,
> Our stern alarums chang'd to merry meetings,

---

other end over morality) and "perverse wickedness" (the agent believes his actions are actually good). Since in both variants the agent does not choose morality, this further distinction does not affect the manner in which both exemplify ethical skepticism.

[4] See also, Kalin's (1976) treatment of nihilism in John Barth.

[5] For one historical account that traces the growing popularity of skeptical thinking from Erasmus through Gianfrancesco Pico della Mirandola to Montaigne, see Brian P. Copenhaver and Charles B. Schmitt (1992). But apart from the revival of classical skepticism during Shakespeare's times (which might well be dismissed as coincidental with, but not related to, his work), a strong case for the idea that Shakespeare's plays are actually preoccupied with questions concerning skepticism has already been made by Stanley Cavell's *Disowning Knowledge*.

[6] Moulton (1885; rpt. New York, 1966, p. 93) and Rossiter (1961, p. 13) both ground the ascription of evil to Richard on this, although the fact that Richard's villainy is noninstrumental is not the only reason for regarding him as *evil*. The many direct and indirect satanic allusions to him constitute further support for the use of the extreme notion. For a survey of these, see R. Chris Hassel Jr. (1986) and Gillian M. Day (1991).

PHILOSOPHICAL CRITICISM IN PRACTICE

> Our dreadful marches to delightful measures.
> Grim-visag'd War hath smooth'd his wrinkled front:
> And now, instead of mounting barbed steeds
> To fright the souls of fearful adversaries,
> He capers nimbly in a lady's chamber,
> To the lascivious pleasing of a lute.
> But I, that am not shap'd for sportive tricks,
> Nor made to court an amorous looking-glass;
> I, that am rudely stamp'd, and want love's majesty
> To strut before a wanton ambling nymph:
> I, that am curtail'd of this fair proportion,
> Cheated of feature by dissembling nature,
> Deform'd, unfinish'd, sent before my time
> Into this breathing world, scarce half made up,
> And that so lamely and unfashionable
> That dogs bark at me as I halt by them—
> Why, I, in this weak piping time of peace,
> Have no delight to pass away the time,
> Unless to see my shadow in the sun,
> And descant on mine own deformity.
> And therefore, since I cannot prove a lover
> To entertain these fair well-spoken days,
> I am determined to prove a villain
> And hate the idle pleasures of these days.
> Plots have I laid, inductions dangerous,
> By drunken prophecies, libels, and dreams,
> To set my brother Clarence and the King
> In deadly hate the one against the other . . . [7]

We observe a tripartite breakdown: lines 1–13 inform us about the peaceful times; lines 14–31 establish the cause-and-effect nature of Richard's ugliness and his vindication of villainy; lines 32–40 inform us of the plots Richard has already laid.

Richard's justification is peculiar.[8] It is presented as an argument, the "stages" of which are as follows: (a) these are peaceful times; (b) love is most appropriate for such periods; (c) I am ugly, hence unfit for love; (d)

---

[7] All references and quotations from *Richard III* and *King Henry VI, Part III* are taken from the Arden editions except this quotation, for which—for a reason I shall give later—I preferred *The Riverside Shakespeare*.

[8] Moulton (ibid, p. 93) claimed that Richard's villainy is insufficiently motivated.

therefore, since I cannot be a lover, I will be a villain. Choosing a noninstrumental form of villainy differs from the very similar pseudoargument "he" gives in *King Henry VI, Part III* that stresses ambition as his motive.⁹ We note that the syllogistically styled justification of villainy in the latter play works only if he assumes that being a lover or a villain is an exhaustive existential alternative. But why should he believe that? What makes his "therefore" reasonable? How does villainy replace whatever is achieved by love?

Ugliness

The first-person plural ("our") is repeated six times in the first eight lines of the soliloquy. It contrasts sharply with the nine times the first-person singular forms ("I," "my," and "mine") are used in lines 13–30. This provides evidence of a strange usage: unlike the typical employment of the first-person plural, in Richard's case "our" is not used inclusively: our "glorious summer," "merry meetings," and "delightful measures," are not "mine." Richard's speech conveys a strong sense of alienation not merely by distinguishing between "I" and "them" but rather by deploying an "I"/"our" distinction. It is not simply a matter of a group of people who enjoy certain emotions that Richard cannot share but that he cannot be a part of his group. He cannot fulfill desires planted in him by his formative context because of his ugliness.¹⁰

Bernard Spivack (1958, p. 36) not only accepted Moulton's view but added that "every sensitive reader of the play" will find it so.

⁹
>   And am I then a man to be belov'd?
>   O monstrous fault to harbour such a thought!
>   Then since this earth affords no joy to me
>   But to command, to check, to o'erbear such
>   As are of better person than myself,
>   I'll make my heaven to dream upon the crown;
>   And, whiles I live, t'account this world but hell,
>   Until my misshap'd trunk that bears this head
>   Be round impaled with a glorious crown.
>   (III.ii.163-71)

¹⁰ Moulton (ibid, p. 93), Robert Ornstein (1972, p. 67), and Antony Hammond (1981, p. 105) all play down the significance of Richard's deformity and argue for the implausibility

In a space of ten lines that follow the first part (lines 14–23) Richard uses no less than nine different expressions to describe his deformity. Only one of the constructions used by Richard—"rudely stamp'd"—metaphorically refers to his ugliness. Three others designate activities he cannot perform because of it: "not shap'd for sportive tricks," "nor made to court an amorous looking glass," and "want love's majesty to strut before a wanton ambling nymph." The constructions "not shap'd for sportive tricks" [Quarto's "sharped"], "unfinish'd," "half made up," and "lamely" strongly hint at impotency.[11] The other five are synonymous with ugliness through negatives or implied negatives: "curtail'd of this fair proportion," "cheated of feature," "deform'd," "unfinish'd," and "unfashionable."

In all of these expressions, Richard is in the passive, linguistically positioned as someone for whom ugliness is not merely a state but rather the consequence of some action. The cause of the unfairness, he says, is nature, "dissembling nature." This suggests that, like Edmond and Iago, Richard's villainy is vindictive. Indeed, it is "the most replenished sweet work of Nature" that he later causes to be destroyed (IV.iii.17–19).[12] Whereas Edmond and Iago direct their revenge at a particular person, Richard's vengeance seems to be general. It is not individuated, working through a crude me/world distinction: the outer world has been the cause of his suffering; therefore, "it" has to pay.

"Dissembling nature" is a telling construction in another way. It reveals Richard's conception of beauty. Beauty is a false mask (compare I.ii.268), a cover-up of the true nature of people that needs to be camouflaged. Richard is choosing nonspecific words: "features" (beauty) are dissembling not for this or that person but for all of them. The implication of this conceptualization is that villainy creates a consistency between exteriority and character. Villainy reveals through performance the true, core content of every person, thereby turning villains like Richard

---

of regarding it as an exhaustive explanation for his motivations However, if the following analysis is correct, the text supplies enough detail concerning Richard's extreme relationship with his body in order to sufficiently explain his actions.

[11] D. Burton (1981) and E. Jones (1980) argue for this point. Impotency is already hinted at in *King Henry VI, Part III* (V.vi.81–83).

[12] The maternal associations of "nature" for Elizabethan audiences suggest that vengeance is only superficially directed at nature and is in fact aimed at nature as mother. This route has been followed in detail by many commentators who trace the relations between Richard and his mother. See the opening pages of Adelman (1992) for argument and many references to such attempts.

into messengers of truth. This challenges the Elizabethan belief in physical appearance as an outward reflection of internal constitution.[13] Such a belief is true only concerning ugliness. Beauty reflects nothing. It simply lies. Another intriguing possible implication, in the context of Richard's motivations, is that beauty contributes to forming systems of signification in which representatives—such as Richard's face and body—are ostracized precisely because they contain the threatening possibility of truth.

But since he does not develop the point, and never returns to it, such an abstract move—arguing from human nature to conduct—seems merely to function as a superficial excuse. Like many others who want to justify an immorality, Richard, too, momentarily appeals to a particular belief concerning an essentially evil human nature, which he then supposedly exemplifies by his conduct. But he is not really interested in making explicit such a general conceptual defense. The implied philosophical is only alluded to and then immediately gives way to a return of the explicitly personal: *his* preoccupation with *his* ugliness.

Dogs

The aforementioned descriptions of ugliness do not yet include the most vivid: the "barking dogs." This construction completes Richard's self-description and paves the way for lines 24–27, which are devoted to his self-hatred. The strength of this particular terminological choice lies in the way it eliminates a conventionalized conception of ugliness. The use of dogs, of inhuman entities, means that reacting to beauty and ugliness is more than conditioning to a socially constructed opposition. For Richard, to be ugly is not only to be "unfashionable" but also to not belong to the human world. Alienation is at its extreme. So is the irony of

---

[13] "Certainly there is a consent between the body and the mind; and where nature erreth in the one, she ventureth in the other," in Francis Bacon, "Of Deformity," in *The Essays* (1908, pp. 200–203). Shakespeare invokes this convention in *The Rape of Lucrece* (lines 1527–30). Relevant too is the idea that more than reflecting inner constitution through outward show, the body is in fact the form of the soul, the good soul thus forms a beautiful body: "For soul is form, and doth the body make. / Therefore wherever that thou dost behold / A comely corpse, with beauty fair endued, / Know this for certain: that the same doth hold / A beauteous soul, with fair conditions thewed, / Fit to receive the seed of virtue strewed. / For all that fair is, is by nature good; / That is a sign to know the gentle blood." Spenser's *Hymn in Honor of Beauty*, lines 133–140. Cf. Sidney's *Astrophil and Stella*, stanza 174.

the celebrative "our" of the first eight lines. He is out of time, out of fashion, spurned as a lover, and avoided not only by every person but also by any creature. But the use of dogs—specifically, the barking of dogs—means more than this, and in fact explains in a fascinating way why Richard employs such a repetitious chain of nearly synonymous adjectives to convey his motivation for his villainy.

To theorize about literary repetition is to analyze sufficiency. This is one important way in which we can see the workings of propositional content that is embedded in an experiential structure that aims to convey meaning, yet a meaning that cannot be reduced to propositional content. Deploying repetition presupposes that important components of meaning can be left out if certain information is communicated only once (in Richard's case, his claim that he is ugly). These components cannot be part of the propositional content, since in that case they would have been sufficiently conveyed merely through using it once.[14] One may obviously object that I am assuming a too narrow idea of propositional content here, and that Richard is communicating much more than his ugliness, and doing so through language. While I agree that much more than a declaration of ugliness is being communicated—indeed these additional elements are precisely what I am after—I am claiming that Richard achieves this through a *narrowing down* of language, repetition rather than opulence thus conveying not simply meaning but *an experience with meaning*.

One use of literary repetition is to convey the significance of certain information to a character. This is what partly seems to be going on in Lear's five "nevers" when he bemoans Cordelia ("Thou'lt come no more, Never, never, never, never, never."), although the force of that line has more to do with a degree of grief that reduces Lear almost to speechlessness, to an inarticulate repetition of information using a single word. Lear reaches this breakdown of elocution—identical repetition was considered by Renaissance rhetoricians to be a grave fault[15]—after realizing an aspect of his grief, he loses forever that particular kind of joy brought about by having one's child enter one's visual field.

---

[14] "Repetition is itself a mode of meaning," says Heilman (1948, pp. 9–10), and I agree (and refer interested readers to Heilman's helpful summery of literature on Shakespearean repetition leading up to the 1950s), though not with his connecting this to the symbolic. See, too, Granville-Barker (1946, pp. 282–83) in seeing a development in Shakespeare's use of repetition.

[15] "Worse than *tautologia* is *omoiologia* [identical repetition], which, as Quintilian says, has no variety to relieve the tedium and is all of one monotonous colour. Who has got

In contrast to Lear, Richard's repetition appears to mark expressive failure. He seems to fumble about, to grope for a precise formula with which to capture his ugliness and what it means for him. He is not only "rudely stamp'd" but "unfinish'd," "deform'd," or any of the other complex adjectives. It is tempting to surmise that these labels jointly succeed in forming a description of his state that satisfies him, but the uniqueness of this soliloquy will not allow us to do that. Richard's self-descriptions move from a metaphor to a bark, from a sophisticated figurative expression to a vocal reaction that is not language anymore. The process is that of a collapse of language. Literal and figurative signifiers fail for Richard, so he has to resort to nonhuman aversion.

But this is still not enough for him. The barking dogs description in line 23 is given through an aposiopesis.[16] This implies that he wants to go even further but cannot. The line is incomplete not only because—as Dolores Burton notes—the curtailed sentence imitates the incomplete work of nature but also in order to take the incapacities of description one step further. In a context of self-hatred and alienation, the bounds of copious speech are fixed by the move from the human to the nonhuman and from there to silence. Richard's soliloquy moves to its termination using words that are set on a course of an ever growing amplification of self-aversion, a process that culminates in a total disconnection from human language, a gap that parallels the state and message of the speech's alienated producer. For Richard, language can no longer capture the degree of his deformity. He is *that* ugly.

Splitting

Richard then moves to his double "delight": "spying" (or "seeing")[17] his own shadow and descanting (commenting or singing about) his own deformity. Aversion is not only a relationship between the world and a self

---

ears patient enough to put up even for a short time with a speech totally monotonous?" Erasmus, *De Copia*, tr. B. I. Knott, Book I, ch. 8, lines 10–14, in *The Collected Works of Erasmus*, 24:302. For two other sixteenth-century texts that regard repetition as a rhetorical fault, see George Gascoigne, *Certayne Notes & Instructions Concerning the Making of Verse or Ryme in English* (1575; rpt. London, 1868), p. 36, and Richard Sherry, *A Treatise of Schemes and Tropes* (1550; rpt. Gainesville, Fla., 1961), p. 33.

[16] I am following Burton (1981) in seeing an aposiopesis in line 23. Such a reading is consistent with the Riverside edition as well as many other editions that hyphenate line 23, thereby indicating an aposiopesis to the actor. The point is controversial, however. The

but between a self and his own body. Richard becomes one with society. He, too, mocks the ugly. This process of conforming to a conventional reaction allows Richard to belong. It is only then, when his body is externalized and mocked, that he experiences delight. Language moves from the passive to the active. Richard becomes an agent through self-hatred.

This split suggests further understanding of his choice of villainy, in which Shakespeare is anticipating Adlerian psychology with its emphasis on modalities of belonging.[18] As long as Richard feels one with his body, he does not belong. His ability to relate to himself like a spectator to a perceived object makes at least one part of him harmonious with his social setting. Indeed, Anne blames him for experiencing "delight" when he views his "heinous deeds" and the "pattern of [his] butcheries" (I.ii.53–54). Externalizing evil performance allows socially constructed voices to participate: ugliness is thereby overcome and the loneliness it induces is broken. Such a pattern of belonging is introduced immediately after the extreme degree of alienation implied by the aposiopesis of the previous line. Richard's descent from the human to the inhuman ends up in his totally moving out of language. His reentering language can only be achieved through self-aversion, since regaining his position within a human context requires reaffirming the hierarchies that constitute that context. Later on in his soliloquy at Bosworth Field (given below), he repeats the pattern: self-hatred through negative self-descriptors (lines 190–202) culminates in an aposiopesis (line 202) that resolves itself into a justification and reaffirmation of conventional social reaction (lines 203–4). Whether such reaffirming is actually necessary is not our question. It is sufficient that Richard chooses it, thereby betraying a psychology that connects self-aversion with hopes for belonging.

Further support for reading Richard this way is found in an observation—made by several commentators—that he repeatedly refers

---

Arden editors have hyphenated line 21 as well as line 23, thereby turning lines 22 and 23 simply into a parenthesized remark. My general point concerning the moving out of language, however, is sufficiently established by the barking dogs construction and does not depend on the existence of an aposiopesis (although it does support the idea that the trope is actually being employed).

[17] The variations between Folio and Quarto are both consistent with my reading.

[18] The label "Adlerian" is only a general pointer, and I do not mean to turn Richard into an exemplifier of that theory. For a genuine Adlerian reading of Richard III, see Charles A. Adler (1936).

to himself as an actor playing a role: that in his determination to "prove" a villain, he seems to be acting out the part.[19] He will seem a saint when in fact; he will "play" the devil. This is double-acting. He not only uses acting—seeming to be "a saint"—to achieve the villainies he performs (compare III.ii.182–85, 191–92; *King Henry VI, Part III*, I.ii.266) but his actual villainy is a performance too. He *plays* the devil (compare *King Henry VI*, V.vi.77 when Richard claims that in this world he should "play the dog"). Further on in the play, he likens himself to "the formal Vice, Iniquity" (III.i.82)—that is, he relates to himself as a dramatic exemplification of evil. That Richard's villainy is a performance is further suggested by its unmistakably exhibitionistic nature. In many of his asides and soliloquies, Richard describes his actions to the audience (I.i.32–40; I.ii.231–68; I.iii.324–38; III.i.82–83), revealing a self-proclaiming villainy that seeks to be perceived. He not only communicates his villainy to the audience but most of his victims also get to know precisely who caused their sufferings. His evil is not, therefore, merely a form of revenge set off by the psychological consequences of exclusion but a performance that is inherently tied to perception and, ultimately, to self-perception.

Indeed, it is precisely after such a performance—the successful wooing of Lady Anne—and before conducting another one—his return to her, "lamenting" after he has buried her father-in-law—that the need for self-perception arises:

> But first I'll turn yon fellow in his grave,
> And then return, lamenting, to my love.
> Shine out, fair sun, till I have bought a glass,
> That I may see my shadow as I pass.
>
> (I.ii.265–69)

[19]

> I do the wrong, and first begin to brawl:
> The secret mischiefs that I set abroach
> I lay unto the grievous charge of others.
> Clarence, whom I, indeed have cast in darkness,
> I do beweep to many simple gulls,
> Namely to Derby, Hastings, Buckingham;
> And tell them 'tis the Queen and her allies
> That stir the King against the Duke my brother.
> Now they believe it, and withal whet me
> To be reveng'd on Rivers, Dorset, Grey.
> But then I sigh, and, with a piece of Scripture,

Self-seeing, calling out to be perceived through the very faculty responsible for his exclusion is Richard's victory over dissembling nature. This victory is orchestrated on two levels: his intelligence enables him to defeat his ugliness when he wins Anne, and his rhetorical tour de force allows him to be picked out as a fascinating object of sight by the same faculty that can kill him "with a living death" (I.ii.156). After twice circumventing the avoidance to which he was naturally doomed by sight (compare I.ii.151), Richard is willing to become an object for his own gaze. His villainy makes him worthy of a look, so he calls the sun—nature's condition of sight (and ultimately of ugliness) introduced in the ambiguity of the first sentence of the play—to "shine out." The vehicle that enables rejection is called upon to allow for a complicated belonging.

The split in Richard is fully revealed in his soliloquy at Bosworth Field, when he wakes up in horror after the ghosts of all his victims appear to him:

> Give me another horse! Bind up my wounds!
> Have mercy, Jesu!—Soft, I did but dream.
> O coward conscience, how dost thou afflict me!
> The lights burn blue; it is now dead midnight.
> Cold fearful drops stand on my trembling flesh.
> What do I fear? Myself? There's none else by;
> Richard loves Richard, that is, I and I.
> Is there a murderer here? No. Yes, I am!
> Then fly. What, from myself? Great reason why,
> Lest I revenge? What, myself upon myself?
> Alack, I love myself. Wherefore? For any good
> That I myself have done unto myself?
> O no, alas, I rather hate myself
> For hateful deeds committed by myself.
> I am a villain—yet I lie, I am not!

> Tell them that God bids us do good for evil:
> And thus I clothe my naked villainy
> With odd old ends stol'n forth of Holy Writ,
> And seem a saint, when most I play the devil.

(I.iii.324–38)

For Richard's performative nature, see Rossiter (ibid, pp. 16–19); Thomas F. Van Laan (1978); Hammond's introduction to the Arden edition of *King Richard III*, pp. 112–14; and Gareth Lloyd Evans (1982, pp. 36–37).

> Fool, of thyself speak well! Fool, do not flatter.
> My conscience hath a thousand several tongues,
> And every tongue brings in a several tale,
> And every tale condemns me for a villain:
> Perjury, perjury, in the highest degree;
> Murder, stern murder, in the direst degree;
> All several sins, all us'd in each degree,
> Throng to the bar, crying all, 'Guilty, guilty!'
> I shall despair. There is no creature loves me,
> And if I die, no soul will pity me—
> And wherefore should they, since that I myself
> Find in myself no pity to myself?
> Methought the souls of all that I had murder'd
> Came to my tent, and every one did threat
> Tomorrow's vengeance on the head of Richard.
> (V.iii.178–207)

After the first prophetic exclamations comes his uncharacteristic cry for divine mercy. The cold villain would never have exclaimed, "Have mercy, Jesu!" Only in sleep could such a thought be formulated and voiced. While awake, Richard successfully pacifies his conscience: "I am in so far in blood," he says while contemplating the murder of Elizabeth's brothers, "that sin will pluck on sin. Tear-falling pity dwells not in this eye" (IV.ii.62–65). Elsewhere he produces a Nietzschean analysis of conscience as a means "to keep the strong in awe" (V.iii.310–11).

The disorientation involved in moving from sleep to wakefulness allows his submerged conscience to resurface and enables Richard to reflect upon his villainy. This time he does so not through cynicism or the shallow, unreflective kind of cleverness he usually employs but through the normative categories he had long abandoned. We witness "insight"— which I take to be a moment in which he gets to read himself through a frame of reference to which he was previously blind. He reacts by immediately personifying (and thereby externalizing) his conscience, and blames it for being a coward. The split is now fully revealed, making possible the schizophrenic dialogue Richard conducts with himself. He sets forth a chain of self-references: he fears himself, wants to fly from himself, wants to have revenge on himself, and hates himself. In all these descriptions, the villain is feared and hated by what can only be a Richard who conforms to the strictures of conventionality, the same one who delighted in descanting on his own deformity in the opening soliloquy.

Richard seems to divide himself between a bundle of conventional judging voices—which he calls his "conscience"—and the character he was determined to become—which he terms "villain." He moves in and out of these constructions—between the "I and I"—that make up his psychic ontology. The quickly "won" self-argument concerns what he is and what he feels toward it. The detached third person of "Richard loves Richard" gives way to the emotional first person: "O, no! Alas, I rather hate myself." Recognition, the process by which a particular description is accepted as true by this plurality of voices, then takes place. We shall later return to this crucial moment of recognition, especially to what Richard does *not* include in it.

Spitting

Why is it that just one scene after the opening soliloquy, with its elaborate discourse of the alienated and unloved, Richard not only is accepted as a lover but also refrains from following up this possibility? In what is undoubtedly the strangest scene in the play, he succeeds in wooing Anne after he has killed her father-in-law and her husband. The clever rhetoric Anne uses in the scene (esp. lines 74–89) makes it interpretatively implausible to regard her simply as silly or shallow. The peculiarity of the scene lies not only in Anne being insufficiently motivated to turn so quickly from the extreme hatred she manifests throughout most of the scene, to partial acceptance of Richard's wooing (one wonders if any motivation could count as sufficient for that), nor in the further implausibility involved in the public setting of the process (during her father-in-law's funeral), but also in the fact that—contrary to his opening soliloquy—Richard *is* acknowledged as a lover (at least potentially) and simply ignores the options such acceptance opens up.

For interpreters who refuse to take Richard's opening soliloquy at face value, this merely supports the dismissal of Richard's explicit motivations for his villainy. That would mean, however, that if one also dismisses ambition as a motivational factor as previously mentioned critics did, Richard's villainy simply turns out to be unmotivated. Such a view has been defended by regarding Richard as conforming to the mid-sixteenth-century dramaturgic convention of the Vice, a personification of diabolical evil that only seems to be motivated by human or rational reasons. But since Richard's villainy can be explained without dehumanizing him, there is no reason to fall back on a reading that simply demonizes Richard, thereby making him psychologically uninteresting.[20]

The insights contained in the opening soliloquy concerning Richard's psychological constitution make his "avoidance of love"—to employ Cavell's phrasing—only superficially illogical.[21] As we have seen, Richard's method of belonging is not to be accepted as what and who he is (a mechanism that ideally culminates in love), but to participate in his own rejection. This, and not his ugliness or his implied impotency, is the deeper reason why he "cannot prove a lover." This point is revealed by the close proximity of the argument in the opening soliloquy to its too obvious "refutation" in this scene. For an audience that does not limit itself to noting Richard's demonic rhetorical skill, thus duped to accept the way Richard explicitly asks his audience to relate to the scene, the proximity yields a further, sad characterization of Richard by revealing the extent of his alienation—that it has already become irremediable by any worldly fact. He does not even consider the possibility of actually loving Anne.

If Richard can be explained through his previous characterization, Anne cannot. Her positive response to Richard's wooing is outrageously unmotivated, and the very blatancy of this fact makes it implausible to

---

[20] Shakespeare was aware of dehumanization as a simplification of reading character. Henry V says: "There is some soul of goodness in things evil, would men observingly distill it out." The pattern itself, villainy as a form of love deprivation, is obvious in *King Lear*'s Edmond's awakened morality before he dies because he senses that he was loved ("Yet Edmond was beloved"). When Bradley contemplates this line, he notes in passing that the pattern appears several times in Shakespeare and "it strikes us that he [Shakespeare] is recording some fact about human nature with which he had actually met, and which had seemed to him peculiarly strange" (1904, p. 303). The tradition of critics (Croce, Hazlitt, Raleigh, Dowden) who perceive Shakespeare as a poet of tolerance is surveyed in Harbage (1947, p. 45), though I shall distance myself from that tradition by delineating a more ambivalent stance than compassion that the play's rhetoric weaves. Another difficulty I have with the Vice reading—used by Hammond (1981) who follows Spivack's major study on this point (1958)—is that inadequate motivation does not necessarily entail that the choice of villainy is irrational. Rather, it could itself be an insight concerning the nature of evil: that, as the cases of Edmond and Iago may be read as exemplifying, evil involves a *disproportionate response* to a cause.

[21] I recognize the force of reading this rejection of love through a Cavell-like interpretation: Richard avoids love because love requires allowing oneself to be seen by another, which Richard avoids—Richard's copious rhetoric of self-exposure is thus an elaborate mode of evasion, as are his calls to be seen. In contrast, the interpretive route I am pursuing requires relating to Richard's self-talk as genuine description of his state of mind rather than an evasion.

dismiss it simply as an aesthetic fault in the play. Nor could one see the scene as merely exemplifying Richard's rhetorical abilities or exhibiting what R. G. Moulton calls Richard's "fascinating power" over his victims.[22] No degree of rhetorical force or fascination could plausibly explain Anne's acceptance of Richard under the circumstances. Could there be some sexual pull that attracts Anne to Richard? Anne's description of her husband as "gentle, mild, and virtuous" (I.ii.106) (a line that could be acted as referring to her late husband rather than to her father-in-law) may disclose that he was worthy but sexually boring. Her latter reference in the play to Richard's bad dreams, and that she did not get a night's sleep, suggests that they slept together each night—which is not always the case with married royal couples, who go to each other's bedrooms only for sex (cf. Hamlet's demand of Gertrude to "refrain tonight" from going to Claudius's bedroom). This may imply intimacy and a strong sexual bond between them, which can be played up in performance.[23] Yet such a generous view of their long-term relationship is difficult to maintain. Anne's complaints about her sleep tell us something about Richard's conscience (which, we know, awakes at night). If Shakespeare was interested in hinting at physical intimacy, he would have added less oblique hints that this was so (compare Cleopatra's wish to be Antony's horse, Juliet's desire to be enjoyed, or Desdemona's heart, "subdued to the utmost pleasure" of her lord). As for Richard, his dismissive "I'll have her, but I will not keep her long" (I.ii.234) hardly intimates aroused erotic interest, and his casual dispatching of her, after she has served her purpose when he moves to wooing Elizabeth's daughter without any misgivings (IV.ii.50–51; IV.iv.283), suggests that Anne has never worked herself out of being merely a pawn in Richard's instrumental calculations.

So what turns Anne from dissmisal to acceptence? Insight into this question is gained when one drops the attempt to remotivate Anne. Respecting her irrationality is achieved by outlining the point the play makes by portraying her consent as the culmination of an irrational process. That the scene involves wooing that succeeds contrary to reason is, in fact, consistent with Richard's seemingly irrational persistence in his villainy, given the possibility of love. For both of them, logic breaks down. Richard holds to a conclusion of a refuted argument, and Anne

---

[22] Moulton (ibid, pp. 97–98).

[23] I am grateful to this book's reviewer for calling my attention to the possibility of such a reading of the scene.

accepts a wooer contrary to her better judgment. Both of them are explainable if we regard their actions as conveying a deep sense of this scene: that belonging overrides rationality. The need to belong is brought up in the context of ultimate separation of Anne from her familial context: a funeral—a process with which Richard interferes and that he eventually spares Anne the need to complete. But while this explanation might clarify why accepting Richard must in fact be insufficiently motivated, it does not yet tell us precisely how Richard succeeds in promising Anne belonging.

In the middle of the scene, she spits at him. With her spit "hanging" from his face (line 151), he woos and wins her. The spitting is, in fact, the turning point of their dialogue, since it is followed by her gradual acceptance of him (it is also their first physical contact). Their discourse turns from legalistic argumentation and verbal fencing to actions. This process begins with her spitting, followed by her inability to stab him, her inability to ask him to kill himself, her acceptance of his ring, and, finally, her granting him a favor by leaving. What allows Richard to move confidently from words to self-endangering praxis is the discovery of her weak spot in the lines that lead up to the spitting:

RICH. It is a quarrel most unnatural,
To be reveng'd on him that loveth thee.
ANNE. It is a quarrel just and reasonable,
To be reveng'd on him that kill'd my husband.
RICH. He that bereft thee, lady, of thy husband,
Did it to help thee to a better husband.
ANNE. His better doth not breathe upon the earth.
RICH. He lives that loves thee better than he could.
ANNE. Name him.
RICH. Plantagenet.
ANNE. Why that was he.
RICH. The self same name, but one of better nature.
ANNE. Where is he?
RICH. Here.

She spits at him
(I.ii.138–48)

Richard discovers in these lines that Anne is accepting his identification of a "better husband" (line 143) with someone who loves her *more*. It is the discovery of her self-centered conception of love—revealed by her aroused curiosity when she wants her new lover to be named—that enables him to win her. Asking for the name, she in practice accepts his justification of Edward's murder. All that is left for Richard is to convince her—through what she will retrospectively refer to as "his honey words" (IV.i.79)—that such a lover exists.[24]

Spitting, like the barking of dogs, is communication that is a withdrawal from the realm of language. It is aversion not supported anymore by argumentation or reasoning (note that in line 140 above, Anne still wants her quarrel to be "just and *reasonable*"). From the moment Anne reaches that stage, Richard can quickly manipulate her to accept him. Anne moves from cursing and dehumanizing Richard—comparing him to animals or to supernatural entities—to rehumanizing him through arguing with him, and from that to an insupportable aversion, which collapses into acceptance. This is an elaboration on the same pattern of response to Richard we have already noted in the opening soliloquy, when Richard moved from curse-like self-descriptors, to extrahuman aversion, and from that to his own method of belonging. Though with Anne, Richard in fact turns the internal conversation of the opening soliloquy into an actual dialogue, duplicating its stages one after the other. In one way, this reemphasizes a movement. In another, it exhibits the familiar way in which internal structures get imposed and limit external relations thereby revealing the sad nature of Richard's unloving narcissism: he will only see his own reflection wherever he goes, not only in terms of the image perceived but in terms of the manner of perceiving it as well.

Success

The man determined to prove himself a villain has succeeded. His soliloquy after his nightmare at Bosworth Field makes that clear. The thousand tongues of his conscience all condemn him for a villain, and now he is in a position to assess his success. It is not clear what his verdict is. He hates himself and has no pity for himself. He knows that no one loves him or will pity his death. He acknowledges his crimes in all their gravity and does not attempt to justify them. But do such words manifest regret?

---

[24] He will later (IV.iv.294–324) appeal to such a notion of love in Elizabeth too—asking her to replace her love to her murdered children with love to future grandchildren—but this time he will fail (one wonders whether this is merely a difference in the characterization of Anne and Elizabeth, or a suggestion concerning a difference between the love of a spouse and the love of a child).

Was this not precisely what he set out to do? Was he looking for love or self-love when he made villainy a vocation? Was not this exclusion from the sphere of love already an established assumption on which he built his argument for choosing villainy—an assumption he not only considered true but also *made* true in his rejection of Anne?

The reentrance of conventional belonging—the need to be loved—so violently silenced in the opening soliloquy, overlaps the climax of belonging through self-hatred. At this point, Richard fears and wants to flee from himself. He wants to have revenge on himself. He says that no "creature" loves him (note the return to an alienation that includes more than humans). We already know that through this "descant" on his moral deformity he belongs, so we may conclude that achieving self-hatred is a culmination of his successful attempt to prove himself a villain. But embedded in the same moment of the realization of his sad success is its cost and what he had to give up. Gone is the delight he used to experience through self-hatred. Plain, conventional, banal love is what he craves now.

Here we should expect regret. Hastings acknowledges his mistake in such a moment of recognition. So do Clarence and Buckingham, each explicitly regretting his previous actions (cf. Marlowe's *Dr. Faustus*, V.i.69, or Tourneur's *The Atheist's Tragedy*, IV.iii.212–45; V.ii.255–66). In Richard's speech, however, there is no remorse or regret, only pain and fear. What may be concluded from the textual evidence is that, for him at this moment, his life is a miserable one. This by no means implies that he regards his choices as mistakes. The text's subtlety here is easy to overlook because Richard mentions many close notions, such as guilt and sin, and he makes a case of his unhappiness. Nevertheless, there is no regret. Moreover, regret is missing not only from the words of his soliloquy but also from his actions following it. He does not change at the last moment like Edmond, and does not even contemplate such a change.[25]

Frustrating the audience's natural expectations for regret is even more disturbing because another structural expectation of dramaturgy—that Richard and his accomplices be punished—is fully met by Shakespeare. Nemesis works in calculated and subtle ways in this play: each crime

---

[25] Heilman (1964), too, sees no regret in Richard's soliloquy, but regards this as indicative of the immaturity of the play. He seems to base this conclusion on the assumption that moral feeling and perspective are required for deep self-knowledge. He does not argue the point, so it appears that, at base, he simply cannot envision an evil that remains untouched by moral scruples.

meets with its appropriate punishment.[26] But retribution is not enough, and, in Richard's case, it is not accompanied by regret. This absence of regret uniquely allows the work to position the reader between two reactions. On the one hand, there is the ethical condemnation elicited by the unfolding of a certain chain of fictional events, a condemnation that Shakespeare surely emphasizes and reinforces when Richard moves to infanticide and we are left to note the discrepancy between his own reaction to this horrid event and those of Buckingham or his supposedly heartless assassin. On the other hand, when we resist the poverty of the Vice reading and take up the details of the language through which Richard casts his motivations, we note that the play's psychologically rich characterization of Richard does not refuse us something like understanding—through the deployment of an amoralist who chooses villainy not out of some general, philosophical, consideration but out of the painfully personal.

Indeed, one of the ways through which choosing morality has been traditionally defended is by attempting to ground moral action through the desire to avoid pain. Afterlife punishment in its theological or Platonic variation is an example of such justification. If the avoidance of suffering supports a choice of conduct, however, then what do we say to someone for whom such avoidance requires immoral performance? In real life, one would lecture to Richard, urge him to take up therapy, or send him to jail, depending on when in the story one finds him. But responding to literary characters does not require us *to do* anything. Nor do I perceive a danger of empathy to Shakespeare's Richard turning into compassion extended to actual child murderers—a threat that appears to be a serious source of concern for some critics of the idea of empathy through literature. For it is not only in its closeness to life but also in its distance from it, in setting in motion responses that we need to fight away in non-fictional reality, that literature creates unique understanding. Richard turns villainy into a way through which a basic human need can be met and satisfied. It is certainly not the only way open to him but—as his rejection of Anne makes clear—his constitution blinds him to any alternatives (to re-emphasize this blindness: after she yields to him, he never contemplates the possibility of actually loving her). Paradoxically, the need to belong, which is at least in part responsible for normative conformity for most people, causes Richard to choose immorality.

But an understanding of his actions "from within" is certainly not the

[26] See Moulton (ibid, pp. 107–24); and Rossiter (ibid, pp. 2–3).

only constituent of our response to the play, even when we choose to relate to Richard's language as a genuine indicator as to his experience. A different dimension of this response includes an experiential understanding of amoralism. The kind of moral skepticism that Richard embodies is not merely a stage in intellectual discussion but also an experience in which a strong need to maintain and reassert one's moral beliefs and sentiments clashes with a conceptual impasse. This text can position us precisely at this emotive and intellectual point. The literary tools of character and plot bring forward many of the same sentiments and principles that are used in interpreting, judging, and relating to nonfictional events in a compassionate way. At the same time, we are challenged by the skepticism that underlies this work. Richard's choice of villainy means he would, on one level, agree with any *particular* ethical condemnation of him that an audience might entertain—indeed, he readily employs them himself—but, on another, challenge the entire framework from which that judgment was initially produced.

As for an audience's ability to meet Richard's challenge, here it is important not to underestimate the actual degree of helplessness of moral philosophy in the face of amoralism. Bernard Williams (1985, ch. 2) has convincingly argued that a philosophical justification of morality of whatever kind cannot constitute a definite answer to the ethical skeptic, since the latter can always dismiss any rational, compelling reason to choose morality through preferring immorality over rationality. This route is *precisely* the one Shakespeare builds into Richard's (and Anne's) characterization. The constitutional presuppositions of Richard are such that, for him, psychological needs override philosophical claims. This disposition is itself unassailable by philosophical argumentation precisely because such a preference limits the power and scope of a tool that presupposes reasoned argument. Richard is unphilosophical through and through. He never attempts to formulate a philosophical defense of his actions (though we noted implied routes he could have followed). He does not relate to himself through generalizations concerning conduct or human nature. He holds to a conclusion of a refuted argument. If he was, indeed, a living interlocutor, why should a philosophical defense of morality matter to him? In fact, Richard never doubts that his actions are wrong, and it is absurd to suppose that what he requires for the mending of his ways is some general explanation why he should be ethical. Philosophers can, perhaps, deal with skeptics who commit themselves to rational debate, but they have nothing to say to skeptics who are indifferent to rationality, or who challenge the need to be rational all

PHILOSOPHICAL CRITICISM IN PRACTICE

the time, being willing to alternate between rationality and irrationality. Shakespeare's *Richard III* presents just such a position.

Philosophy in Literature

Where does this leave us?[27] I began with the danger of extending empathy to evil characters. People worry, for example, that judges trained by empathic readings of literary professors will too readily understand the villains they encounter and will create an unjust legal system. Yet reading literature is unconstrained in a way that need not carry over to other contexts. Being disposed to understanding literary characters rather than evaluating them does not typically involve paying practical prices. There can be such prices—one thinks of literary works that make one understand the joy of Nazism, and such could achieve canonical status, say, understanding pedophilia in *Lolita*—and this counts against indiscriminately advocating whatever literary experiences happen to support—a position no one holds anyway—not against being disposed to understand rather than judge. Banning literary arguments simply because literature can be evil or create morally dubious states of mind is as plausible as banning standard, nonliterary arguments since Nazis and pedophiles use them as well.

Empathic zealots are not a genuine threat, but the detailed empathic experience I outlined enables a more specific response to the said dangers of empathy. Even when the literary portrayal of evil is enticing and powerful, as it is in this play, and even when one allows the work to make its case for an immoral character in the strongest way, empathy is not the only constituent of aesthetic response. If a reading as generous as this one is to an evil character includes dimensions of response that counter empathy and conflict with it, then, a fortiori, more balanced readings of evil characters are even less likely to be "taken in" by the immoral potential of literature. The overall response good literature of this sort creates is never simple, one-sided identification. Literature's moral dangers lie elsewhere (one kind of danger I have in mind is the way by which texts can naturalize and make unproblematic morally dubious

---

[27] Reading Daniel Statman's work and several conversations with him on the relations between empathy and justification have caused me to modify the view I expressed at this point in the two previous published versions of this reading.

connections—for example, a reader feeling that it is not right for Othello to kill Desdemona *because* she was faithful).

What, then, is this complex experience this work creates in "us"? (To repeat, first-person plural terms in this book are to be taken as invitations to what we can fruitfully become as readers, not as descriptions.) To begin with: empathy. *Because* this is a reading of a play (rather than a courtroom in which Richard is on trial), it permits a more complex, aporetic response than one-sided condemnation. For an audience that refuses to dismiss the details of Richard's characterization, the possibility of maintaining simple condemnation fails as it failed for Anne when she allowed Richard to explain his actions. A consistency thus appears between fictional elements and actual response patterns. Affective relationships within the fictional domain predict and reflect the positioning of the reader, which the textual rhetoric achieves.[28]

The metaphor of positioning makes it possible to explain the special way in which this play enables relating to conceptual content, and this concerns a second dimension of our response to the play: the one involving challenging Richard's amoralism. Explanation, understanding, or compassion to Richard never turns into hearty justification, and involves an opposite wish to find *the* reason that shows why he is wrong rather than simply evil. I have just endorsed Williams's view that there is no such knockdown reason, and that the encounter with this limitation is a second constituent of the response to this play. Facing amoralism is here an experience of skepticism, rather than some grasp of its conceptual message (that message being that choosing morality cannot be justified). Skepticism presents an impasse that—one could recall one's first encounters with it—is not experienced merely as an intellectual puzzle. For readers who share Anne's response—a mixture of condemnation, fascination, and understanding—this work of literature reenacts something of the richer, complex frustration involved in encountering skepticism for the first time. This includes a repeated use of synonymous adjectives to describe what is feared and hated, a feeling of impotence that finally resolves itself into condemnation. *Richard III* forms an experiential structure in which the

---

[28] This analogy between fictional occurrences and actual response patterns is not unique to *Richard III*. I shall argue for a similar parallelism with relation to *Hamlet* and *Romeo and Juliet*. For other ways in which other plays anticipate actual response patterns to them, see Jane Adamson (1980, pp. 4–5, 19–20, 85–86), Janet Adelman (1973, p. 189), and Stanley Cavell (1987, 54, 84–85).

limits of philosophy are not only comprehended but also acknowledged in a way that responds more fully to the different kinds of claims that skepticism makes, as well as to what skepticism sets in motion.[29]

But the play challenges philosophy—at least one dominant version of it—in another way that does not depend on the possible existence of a knockdown antiskeptical argument that I may have been missing all along, and this makes for a third constituent of response this work elicits. The play casts amoralism in terms of a secondary, derivative formulation that emerges from basic needs (rather than an abstract position). It thus pushes us into a metaphilosophical stance that is continuous with Nietzsche's subordination of the philosophical to the psychological, or the metaphilosophical assumption built into the early and middle Platonic dialogues that insist on examining positions only after they have been embedded into actual and articulated lives. I prefer Plato's picture of interpenetration between needs, dispositions, and adopted philosophy manifested in many of Socrates' interlocutors to Nietzsche's cruder one-directional subordination of reason to needs. Both, however, urge us to avoid any conceptual analysis of positions that ignores the lives who will plausibly endorse them. From this perspective, Shakespeare's play not only supplies literary flesh and blood to amoralism, creating a believable exemplification of it, but also facilitates its evaluation.

I have been arguing that Richard's life is sad, even when we recognize its power, liveliness, and moments of extravagance. We see a man setting out to be something he dislikes, and achieving this. There is something profoundly tragic in this movement, and taking *The Tragical History of*

---

[29] In his influential discussion of acknowledgment in relation to skepticism and Shakespeare, Stanley Cavell argues that the lesson skepticism asks us to digest is that the world is not out there to be known (it is not a knowable fact) but to be accepted, much as other minds are not to be known but to be acknowledged (1987, 94–95). For Cavell, modern epistemology is an attempt to transform or evade the ethical stance that acceptance of the world requires. Richard III provides an intriguing challenge to Cavell's suggestion that skepticism should invoke a moral response. The challenge for Cavell emerges when moving from epistemological skepticism (which is what Cavell is focusing on) to the moral skepticism that underlies amoralism. Both kinds of skepticism (moral and epistemological) utilize the same arguments, differing only in subject matter, and both were known to early-modern thinkers. And it is precisely the acknowledgment of others, the acceptance of them, that the moral variant of skepticism challenges. Cavell's wise discussion of acknowledgement and skepticism appears to presuppose that the ethical stance itself is in some sense insulated from the skeptic's challenge. Cavell's thinking begins from Descartes, which is why the notions of acknowledgment and acceptance sound reassuring. But what shape would it have had if it took its starting point from Callicles?

Richard III to be a tragedy, rather than a history in which we are merely horrified at Richard's climb and satisfied at his fall, permits his many "tragic mistakes" to emerge. These all relate to his blindness to invitations for meaningful contact and acceptance—his brother, Anne, even Buckingham offer him many kinds of love (familial, marital, friendship) throughout—and he is not merely refusing them but is also unable to register these offerings. That is to say, when we give his mother's hatred of him its due importance in relation to Richard, and yet do not allow it to mask other reactions to him, Richard's story turns out to be one of a *misperceived* alienation rather than simple exclusion.[30] We confront a hardening, a closing off from insight, with which skepticism is connected when it is plausibly endorsed in a life.

Noting these missed opportunities does not amount to a conceptual confrontation, a solution of ethical skepticism in its skeletal argumentative shape. While this may disappoint some, I gave my reason why we shall never have such a solution and how the play creates an experience of this limitation rather than simple comprehension of it. *Richard III*, I argued, is a constructed, particularized experience of philosophy's limitation in confronting radical ethical skepticism. But the play does more than this. In creating the "if only" effect of a tragic mistake ("If only Macbeth had not killed Duncan"; "If only Lear would have kept his kingdom undivided"; "If only Othello would have listened to Emilia") a lived option comes across as deficient. Richard's life revolves on a lack, not of features or of fair proportions as he fancies it to be, but of perception. The experience the work creates is thus not only, finally, one of defeat in the face of skepticism, but one in which this particular skeptic elicits from his reader: "If only he could see." This "if only" response is experiential, rather than merely conceptual, in two ways ("conceptual" being the state of comprehending the claim that alienated individuals sometimes exhibit systematic misperception). First, this response will probably not arise in anyone who refuses the dimensions of the text that aim at knowing what it is like to feel alienated. Anyone who relates to

---

[30] Misperceiving what others communicate to him rather than responding to genuine dislike is what differentiates Richard from other familiar alienated villains. Here are some lines from Frankenstein's creation, when he explains to his creator why he turned evil: "Cursed creator! Why did you form a monster so hideous that even you turned from me in disgust? God in pity made man beautiful and alluring, after his own image; but my form is a filthy type of your's, more horrid from its very resemblance. Satan had his companions, fellow-devils, to admire and encourage him; but I am solitary and detested." Shelley, *Frankenstein*, p. 126.

Richard simply as a dramatic convention or a fascinating bad guy will most likely not experience anything like this regarding his misperceptions. Second, this "if only" response involves something like personal care, rather than noting a psychological idiosyncrasy (the difference between this and the first experiential pattern is that it is possible to know what a person's situation is like without caring for him).[31]

This experience connects with therapeutic and educational aspects of moral choice in important ways. But it also has a more narrowly philosophical import, pertaining to understanding, since amoralism is presented as deficient perception and thus a form of misunderstanding. Of course, moral characters can also be misperceiving important details and some literature achieves its effect precisely through creating a discrepancy between the reader's knowledge and the moral character's outlook (one thinks of *Candide* or Sade's *Justine*) thus ridiculing a crude endorsement of morality. But the particular power of Shakespeare's depiction of Richard is that, although he walks under the banner of disenchantment, cynicism, and nonconformity, Richard remains sadly ignorant of the complexity through which people actually relate to him. In an important way, Shakespeare thus turns him and his flashy amoralism into an oversimplification, a deficiency in knowing.

Such a presentation of amoralism is rhetorical, as the connections between amoralism and blindness are contingent. Shakespeare could have been harder on himself, presenting a skeptic who perceives these offerings of love and yet refuses them. In stressing these particular and contingent links, Shakespeare's play moves us from the conceptual to the worldly—that is to say, while there is no conceptual necessity binding amoralism with blindness, such connections are there, or tend to be there, in life. Refusing a stance of Bardolatry, we can now ask to examine such a claim about the world against surveys or criminological statistics that strive to be empirical in a more direct way. Yet, even if a meaningful survey can be thought of, an attempt of this sort presupposes that

---

[31] Brudney (1998) and Nussbaum (1990) both speak of perception and misperception in characters they analyze as part of moral readings. My emphasis on the interconnectedness of such perception with a broader experience of the work enables answering the critic who would press to know why one requires literature, rather than, say, psychological case studies, if it is manners of perception or misperception that one is looking for. For Cavell, perception and misperception relate to one's own capacity to disclose oneself to others and so, reading Richard through Cavell's terms would mean that his blindness relates to him shunning others and perhaps himself. In contrast, my reading examines the possibility that Richard knows himself well, and still misperceives others.

we should give higher or equal weight to self-reports of actual skeptics than to the penetrating insight of an author. One wonders what statistic can possibly validate this last particular bias.

When we avoid the false assumption of an epistemological equality that could decide contingent matters, we are left with claims that compete for our assent and are based on nothing stronger than the way they cohere and make sense of our experience. Is this type of knowing weaker than what rigorous philosophy should allow? It is only so for a philosophy regulated by a notion of understanding that demands more than mere, plausible, knowing.

Upon One Bank and Shoal of Time

THEY CONSIDERED HIM HONEST and "loved him well," a valiant, worthy gentleman. A brave man, the bridegroom of Bellona, the Roman war goddess. He won "golden opinion from all sorts of people," but all that changed. Instead, he became despised for his treachery and feared for actions that knew no moral bounds. From murdering his king to killing his past friends, from that to infanticide, Macbeth's story, at least from the perspective of others, is one of a change in reputation.[1] Yet, from his own point of view—an outlook that never experiences a good name or, for that matter, anything else as an accomplishment—things are somewhat more complicated than a simple story of loss.

There is something hollow in Macbeth. What is missing is not motivation for his actions—his "vaulting ambition" is supposed to cover that—but a sense of motivational depth. What worries us as we read the play is the emptiness of Macbeth's ambition.[2] He wants to be king—that much is certain—yet this desire was not always in him. It overtook him only when a chance for advancement appeared. Ambition can overwhelm, and so our difficulty in relating to Macbeth stems not from him being overtaken by a new desire. The alien quality of Macbeth lies, rather, in the way in which he never enjoys his accomplishments. There is never happiness or satisfaction in the man. Not when he returns triumphant from fighting Macdonald. Not when he becomes a king. Not when he secures his reign. He never hints how he wishes to put to use the power he so desperately wants to have. Like Richard III, Macbeth never dwells on the object of his ambitions. However, whereas in the former one detects an unmistakable delight that accompanies his villainies, a sense of the proud performer calling attention to the atrocities he commits, Macbeth remains an unhappy, frightened man. One wonders why it was that he wanted to become a king in the first place.[3]

---

[1] See, in the following order, IV.iii.13; I.ii.24; I.ii.16; I.ii.54; I.vii.33. All references to *Macbeth* are to Nicholas Brooke, *The Tragedy of Macbeth* (Oxford: Oxford UP, 1990).

[2] For similar impressions and suggestions as to why ambition cannot sufficiently explain Macbeth, see R. A. Foakes (1982) and A. P. Rossiter (1961, pp. 218–19).

[3] For a suggestion according to which Macbeth's unhappiness results from his murdering the pleasure principle, see William Kerrigan (1996). Macbeth's pervasive unhappiness is one factor that should count against some suggestions regarding his underlying motivations.

Nihilism—which I shall soon argue is the philosophical concern that underlies *Macbeth*—could be presented as a philosophical position. A nihilist rejects any endowment of value to states of affairs, feelings, lives, actions, or dispositions. We tend to associate the term with authors of the last two centuries, but the idea is at least as ancient as *Ecclesiastes* (2:11) and probably surfaces in less explicit forms at one time or another in any life. When it is explicitly formulated, the position could take the form of dismissing any criteria according to which values may be ascribed. Another formulation is showing that value is always relative to some perspective that one has no reason to privilege. At its extreme, nihilism is irrefutable. The argument will be that since philosophical discussion is limited to rational debate, the best philosophy can do in answering a nihilist is to show that ascribing value is a rational—justified, beneficial, end-serving—act. However, philosophy is reduced to silence if the value of rationality—or the value of always being rational—is questioned. The catch is that a nihilist will have to acknowledge the value of rational debate in order to listen to philosophy in the first place.[4]

The impasse philosophy leads to when foundational questions of value arise should make us look hard for alternatives. I suggested that turning to literary works is one such route. In my discussion of *Richard III*, I argued that the play enables a deeper grasp of the amoralism that it depicts. "Deep" there meant that through portraying a plausible existential framework in which immorality becomes an explicit choice, literature forces us to go beyond the hypothetical smiling skeptic that haunts philosophy and that one never meets. We grasp the intellectual and emotional underpinnings of moral skepticism as it arises in a lifelike situation. We get to know how skepticism is experienced, as well as sense (again) the impotence that consists in an inability to ultimately ground a condemnation of intentionally chosen villainy. In terms of confronting amoralism, I claimed that there is something sad in Richard, since his jubilant villainy springs from his systematic misperception of complex reactions to him that may have made his life better or happier for him in

---

Kristian Smidt (1969) claims that his ambition stems from a desire for external praise, for "pomp and ceremony." Donald W. Foster (1986) suggests that Macbeth wishes to create himself and not resign to gains got through chance and time. Apart from being poorly supported by the text, the last two suggestions as to Macbeth's motivations cannot explain why Macbeth remains unsatisfied after he achieves what they suppose he is after.

[4] For an elaboration of this argument, see Frankfurt (2004, pp. 24–26).

his own terms. In moving from philosophical terms to quasi-therapeutic ones, I am not advocating a critical stance in which one tries to make literature's great villains go away by turning them into well-adjusted citizens. Shakespeare's characters are not there to be healed by the critic. Yet, the shortcomings of characters sometimes indicate the flaws of philosophical positions when these positions are endorsed in a life. More precisely, some positions attract those who are partially blind.

Richard challenged morality. Macbeth is a nihilist. Both mostly avoid philosophizing. I begin by working out the details of a full vision of nihilism. My emphasis will not be on the "position" as it is argued for but rather on the psychological and existential aspects with which nihilism is connected when it surfaces in a life. Unlike the previous reading, here, noting such details would not elicit empathy from us but would make for a different kind of reading experience. Through contrasting nihilism with its opposite, Shakespeare achieves one of the strongest moments of the play. In the closing sections, I inquire into this contrast not only aesthetically but in terms of the way it stages a philosophically formative experience that challenges nihilism.

Postponing

Let me begin with some of Macbeth's more revealing lines near the end of the play, when he hears of his wife's death and his nihilism emerges as an explicit position:

> SEYTON. The queen, my lord, is dead.
> MACBETH. She should have died hereafter;
> There would have been a time for such a word—
> Tomorrow, and tomorrow, and tomorrow,
> Creeps in this petty pace from day to day,
> To the last syllable of recorded time;
> And all our yesterdays have lighted fools
> The way to dusty death. Out, out, brief candle,
> Life's but a walking shadow, a poor player
> That struts and frets his hour upon the stage,
> And then is heard no more. It is a tale
> Told by an idiot, full of sound and fury
> Signifying nothing.
>
> (V.v.17–28)

The surface sense is of a general belittling of life, but the details of this speech also expose some of the finer aspects of Macbeth's nihilism. The traditional signifier-referent hierarchy underlies life's shadowy insignificance for Macbeth. More than a chain of sounds that signify nothing, life's empty value results from such sounds forming part of "a tale" conducted on a "stage." The histrionic, fictional context turns life from a chain of meaningless sounds into a process that is also charged with being ontologically inferior ("a walking shadow"). Even this is not enough as the tale is told by an idiot. The living are all "fools." So life ends up being not only a valueless copy but also one that is foolishly tailored. Explaining these lines from the perspective of an actor, Ian McKellen has (ingeniously) noted that, since the reference to the "poor actor" is actually mouthed by an actor, Shakespeare here enables the theatrical to merge into the real. A real actor has to give voice to lines that reflect on the temporal limitations of his actual worldly effects before reaching the nihilistic conclusion that, supposedly, he says merely as part of a role.

Let us avoid the temptation to reduce all this into a philosophical position and instead move closer to the existential subtleties that make up this nihilism. If Macbeth ever cared for anything outside him, it is for his wife. However, hearing of her death, he scolds her for dying at a time in which an approaching battle precludes mourning for her. More than indicating lack of feeling (one suspects that too), Macbeth says that dying at the right time would have enabled emotion to take place.[5] It is not so much the possible belief in deferral of feelings that should interest us here, but the very idea of postponing as well as the connections the speech draws between postponement and nihilism. Examining the temporal structure of the lines can yield insight into these links. We note that life's petty pace does not merely creep in day after day but tomorrow, and tomorrow, and tomorrow. Macbeth first seems to be referring to life's petty stuff. However, the "this" in "this petty pace" also refers to the triple "tomorrow" of the previous line. The meaningless pace is thought oriented toward a future, a tomorrow. The speech thereby connects its semiotic theme with its temporal one in that in both, the given (present, word, sound) points beyond itself. In both, the end is either a

---

[5] The centrality of time and Macbeth's relation to it has been repeatedly investigated. Luisa Guj (1986) counts forty-five uses of the word in the play. Foster (1986) sums up much previous discussion of the idea that time serves as redeemer and contrasts it with his own view that Macbeth's conflict is with time and its limitations as such. Guj, too, explores this theme in stressing Macbeth's attempt to obliterate the past and stop the future. I shall concentrate on a different aspect of the relationship.

dusty death, to which all yesterdays point ("light"), or a nonexistent referent. Times and signs point beyond themselves to nothing and expose the nihilist's lived experience. Nihilism is not merely an experience in which things are hollow and valueless but a mode of nonattachment that relies on a manner of looking that goes beyond what there is.[6]

Postponement is introduced in Macbeth's first (interrupted) aside in his "nothing is but what is not." The oxymoron is supposed to capture thought smothered by "horrible imaginings" and "surmise" (I.iii.140–44). The real and substantial in thought ("present fears") gives way to the possible and hypothetical. To those who look at him in his rapt state, he makes the excuse that he was thinking of "things forgotten." Lost in a future or a past, Macbeth's brand of nihilism involves circumventing times and things, a process that enables maintaining the belief in their worthlessness (the scene ends, incidentally, several lines later, when Macbeth defers his talk with Banquo to a more appropriate time). A somewhat different sort of dismissal of the present resurfaces in Macbeth's aside when he decides to kill Banquo (III.i.58–69). The witches' prediction that it is Banquo's children and not Macbeth's who will be future kings not only empties Macbeth's present accomplishment in his own eyes but induces a fascinating shift in his own self-understanding. Macbeth suddenly talks as if he murdered Duncan just for the sake of his own future offspring. Such remotivation and recasting of personal history reveals the mechanics of postponement and the strategies through which nihilism works. Deferring the experience of an achieved accomplishment is mediated not only through endlessly relegating value to the future but also by positing the accomplishment in a broader context than the one that would have conferred value upon it. The accomplishment becomes a means rather than the end it was initially conceived to be, and nihilism is enabled through this instrumentalization and diminishing of value.[7]

The reunion scene between Macbeth and his wife also exemplifies postponement. She asks him to place himself beside the time and only look like it—"to beguile the time, / Look like the time". This parallels through

---

[6] Cavell claims that *King Lear* creates a lack of presentness in its readers, who do not allow themselves to be present to what is here and now, leading to a form of blindness that duplicates the blindness of the characters (1987, p. 119). Readers who are persuaded by Cavell can then relate to Macbeth's nihilism as an embodiment of a general tendency to avoid presentness. Macbeth then allows us to examine our disposition to avoid what we have (in contrast to Macduff, who I will soon discuss).

[7] Regarding a different Shakespearean variation on the idea of losing value, see L. C. Knight's (1959, pp. 137–38) comparison of Macbeth's nihilism with *The Rape of Lucrece*.

rhetoric the relations between Macbeth and time—more specifically, his own evasion of his time. All three lines Macbeth speaks through this entire scene are set in future tense. We also note what should by now seem unremarkable: after she asks him to set himself by time and resemble it, Macbeth replies by asking her to postpone talk ("We will speak further").[8]

Finally, on postponement, note Macbeth's deliberation before the murder:

> If it were done when t'is done, then 'twere well
> It were done quickly; if th'assassination
> Could trammel up the consequence and catch
> With his surcease, success, that but this blow
> Might be the be-all and the end-all—here,
> But here, upon this bank and shoal of time,
> We'd jump the life to come. But in these cases
> We still have judgment here, that we but teach
> Bloody instructions, which being taught, return
> To plague th'inventor. This even-handed justice
> Commends th'ingredience of our poisoned chalice
> To our own lips. He's here in double trust:
> First, as I am his kinsman, and his subject,
> Strong both against the deed; then, as his host

---

[8] I need to say something about Lady Macbeth's role in all this. Lady Macbeth believes that Macbeth is a highly ambitious man who is yet "too full o'th' milk of human kindness." Yet the more one reads the play, the more one suspects that she deeply misreads her husband and that these lines are, rather, a projection of her own submerged morality (note, for example, the striking way in which she misreads him in III.ii.5–28: she believes that he is worried about his immorality, when he is in fact concerned with his fears of Banquo). Apart from the moments directly after he murders Duncan, and his attempt to avoid fighting Macduff at the very end of the play, Macbeth is not that worried about the immorality of his actions, while she certainly is. The tradition of regarding Macbeth as a noble, weak man tempted into evil by his wife, exemplified by readers such as Hazlitt and Johnson, or seeing him as deeply conscience-ridden, as does Bradley, disregards the way in which the two characters differ in relating to their crime. Such a reading also confuses—regarding Macbeth's supposed temptation by his wife—between being persuaded and *allowing* oneself to be persuaded. Against such readings, Richard Moulton (1966, pp. 144–67) makes a persuasive case for Macbeth's moral shallowness, but in the strict division that he sets between Macbeth as externality and his wife as associated with the internal, Moulton's reading is in danger of simplifying both. What has not been stressed enough about the so-called temptation scene are Macbeth's short but semantically pregnant lines before his wife "tempts" him. To her question regarding Duncan's planned departure time from their home, he replies, "Tomorrow, *as he purposes*" (I.v.59).

>   Who should against his murderer shut the door,
>   Not bear the knife myself.
>
> (I.vii.1–16)

Beyond simple avoidance of one's time, these lines further complicate Macbeth's relation to temporality by situating him outside time's flow. Upon a bank and shoal of time, stands this man, contemplating whether to jump into the life to come through Duncan's death ("his surcease"). More than alienating Macbeth further from his time by a figurative self-placing outside time, the figure articulates the disconnected manner through which nihilism relates to life. It also captures the attitude of relating to life as if plunging into it is some kind of a decision that awaits the proper justification. Shakespeare also exposes the fear of losing control and connects it with processing everything as valueless. Nihilism is not merely an intellectual position. When Macbeth does eventually mouth it in the lines about his wife's death, nihilism comes across more as a sad outcome than as a philosophy (think, in contrast, of the sharp intellectualized and icy nihilism of the type endorsed by Turgenev's Bazarov, or the more philosophically formulated antilife speeches of Hamlet, *Measure for Measure*'s Duke, or Spenser's Despair). Nihilism is less of a brilliant cynicism and more of a disability connected with anxieties of losing control that jointly underlie patterns of circumvention.

Happiness and Reality

Postponement and extemporal self-placing do not exhaust Macbeth's nihilism. Shakespeare connects these patterns of deferring to a pervasive hidden longing: the hope—perhaps always a silenced part of nihilism—that somewhere out there value may still be found (note Macbeth's vague allusion to "success" in the lines above). He says that if success is assured, he should act. But the clever expository scenes, in portraying Macbeth not simply as a successful warrior and captain but as outstandingly successful, complicate what success means for him. While Macbeth does mention losing the "golden opinions" others have of him, we get no sense of accomplishment, of an occupation with present success. Moreover, Shakespeare later gives Lady Macbeth lines—"our desire is got without content" (III.i.6)—that register precisely the emptiness (both in terms of lack of content and lack of contentment) of what she and her husband had actually achieved by attaining royalty.[9] The fact that we miss any reference on his part to his present success makes his pursuing a new success problematic. Success is processed by him solely in terms of external praise, which, in turn, is experienced as something that may be discarded.

All this links success to a sense of emptiness, a frightening void that opens up when one is suddenly aware of the limitations of accomplishment. The psychological pattern itself—which Freud, in a discussion that includes *Macbeth* as one of its examples, termed being "wrecked by success"—is reiterated both in Lady Macbeth and in Malcolm.[10] However, regarding Macbeth's problems with success, it is less the psychic mechanism and more the particularities of confronting it that are stressed in the play. Macbeth never contemplates his hollow response to his outstanding military achievement. He does what he knows only too well how to do: move on.

So we have a nihilism that does not collapse into fatalism. Macbeth incorporates a view in which all is meaningless with an estranged, unhappy vitality. At the same time, Macbeth's preoccupation with the body and particularly with blood, turns the body into a significant presence and realness. Hamlet or Richard III are also concerned with embodiment (Hamlet with the possibility of escaping it, and Richard with the desire to be seen). However, in Macbeth these tensions remain raw, hesitant, indecisive, perhaps because he lacks Hamlet's depths of reflectivity or Richard's unfailing convictions.

Unlike Hamlet—or, for that matter, Duncan and Malcolm, who both explicitly formulate an appearance-reality tension and, at least in Hamlet's case, attempt to transcend embodiment—Macbeth's relation to the corporeal is one of *encountering* it. In his world, everyone and everything is merely a means to an end that, when reached, turns itself into just another means. In these, Macbeth's circumstances, seeing another,

---

[9] Shirley Sharon-Zisser has called my attention to the duel meaning of "content" in this line.

[10] The former in her collapse after gaining the power she was long after and the latter in the mode of self-abuse he practices when he senses that his wish to become king might well be fulfilled (IV.iii.46–102). Interestingly enough, Freud's discussion (1957) of this mentions only Lady Macbeth as exemplifying the pattern and does not seem to notice the way in which Malcolm and Macbeth are variants of the same psychic type. Rossiter (1961) also perceives the links between success and emptiness in Macbeth, but unlike the suggestion I am pursuing, connects them to his own exemplification of the tradition of depersonalizing the characters and seeing them as part of one psychic entity.

an actual encounter, takes place when the body is suddenly perceived. For a man who persistently shuns reality, this appearance of reality superficially manifests itself through various relations of sight. His inability to go back and look at Duncan's body ("I am afraid to think what I have done; / Look on't again, I dare not") is the simpler of these (II.ii.50–51). More moving is his attempt to stare back at Banquo's ghost, trying to meet his victim's gaze. He initially structures his ability to look back at the ghost in terms of bravery. To his wife's angry "Are you a man?" he replies with "Ay, and a bold one, that dare look on that / Which might appall the Devil" (III.iv.57–59). Looking back at that which he irrevocably did, at that which stares back at him as a dead result and not as the instrumental moment that he initially conceived this murder to be, means that looking would involve a struggle. Daring to look—perhaps because in this man bravery can be manifested only through its links with the militant—immediately turns to threatening the ghost. But after he tries to intimidate the ghost, he returns to the ocular ("Avaunt, and quit my sight"), verbalizing his wish for bodies to be hidden.

For Macbeth, the stronger of these encounters occur when the body lets its inside liquid be seen. Everything seems to wear off except the blood of victims.[11] Blood is central in Macbeth's very first description by the captain:

> . . . . but all's too weak,
> For brave Macbeth—well he deserves that name—
> Disdaining Fortune, with his brandished steel
> Which smoked with bloody execution,
> Like Valour's minion carved out his passage
> Till he faced the slave—
> Which ne'er shook hands nor bade farewell to him,
> Till he unseamed him from the nave to th' chops,
> And fixed his head upon our battlements.
>
> (I.ii.15–23)

The bloody sword carving, ripping Macdonald the rebel apart from his navel to his jaws, decapitating him—this gruesome image is the first description of Macbeth in the play. Shakespeare supplies the details of Macdonald's killing. This may appear unproblematic in the context of a military report that has to realistically capture the language of a captain

---

[11] For one analysis of the centrality of blood imagery in the play, see G. Wilson Knight's two essays on the play (1964).

and the expectation for a violent retribution to a rebel. However, when we hear of another incident in which Macbeth kills:

> How it did grieve Macbeth! Did he not straight
> In pious rage the two delinquents *tear*,
> That were the slaves of drink, and thralls of sleep?
> (III.vi.11–13)

we suspect that the details of these offstage killings also impart an additional subtle characterization of Macbeth. This suspicion is strengthened when the commending report Duncan passes on to Macbeth regarding the latter's bravery in the battle, talks of Macbeth as making "strange images of death" (I.iii.96). Duncan's praise for Macbeth thereby retains an allusion to the specific *ways* by which Macbeth kills. The violence to the body—tearing it apart, opening up its borders (note the alarming metaphor of unseaming)—is a violation that, in light of the depth-structure of the work to follow, is more than proportionate punishment to a rebel. Rather, beyond the violence there is something altogether extramilitary that the contexts of battle and retribution permit, which would be impossible in other domains. The play connects disrespect for limits with a form of nihilism that never succeeds in finding value or realness. Searching for *some* kind of resistance is expressed by stressing the way through which Macbeth repeatedly annihilates the borders of bodies.

The centrality of blood is also why the two scenes in which Macbeth and his wife fail to wash the blood from their hands (II.ii.59–62; V.i.41, 48–49) create such a moving impression. It is not so much the crime that cannot be erased—that too—but more specifically the connection the body maintains between the crime and its perpetrator through the synecdoche of transporting of the guilt to one's part, to one's hand. More than articulating guilt, or the sense of one's crime as being an unconfinable contamination (blood turning the ocean red before it will be cleaned), the unwashable blood means that unlike all that can be removed, cast away, devalued, or postponed, blood is where Macbeth meets reality. In his angry world, in which success has little or no impact, in which power is pointlessly pursued, blood is palpable. Through the estrangement to their hands via these uses of synecdoche, the Macbeths manifest guilt's capacity to induce alienation from one's body. Embodiment exhibits that which performed the crime but also that which follows the perpetrator around. Guilt, like shame—emotions that inherently have to do with others and being perceived by them—involves resetting the relations between body and self. The body becomes something that one looks at anew and attempts relating to again ("What hands are here?"). The body, or more accurately, what "the body" has done, transforms one's identity from a brave general into an executioner ("these hangman's hands").

Shakespeare thus presents nihilism as more than practical skepticism. The nihilist's preoccupation with borders and limits is also a search for reality, for realness that the nihilist hopes will constitute resistance. Unlike his wife's talk of the dead as no more than pictures (II.ii.52–53), Macbeth, who relates to everything around him as signs, cannot accept his wife's semiotic relation to corpses. Evading one's moment has its limits. It is bounded by death, or more specifically, the deaths that he causes. These deaths connect Macbeth to his moment, even when the gains of not relating to what is now are at their most enticing. His inability to look at Duncan's body or his struggle to look back at Banquo's ghost is where his fears—the most pervasive state of mind he manifests throughout—suddenly connect him with what is present here and now.

In Macbeth's response to his wife's death, Shakespeare brings the psychophilosophical pattern I have been tracking to the tragic outcome such dynamics lead to. A man who persistently avoids, who endlessly defers emotion and a sense of accomplishment, someone for whom moments are only instrumental and thereby devoid of value, finally makes his nihilism explicit through identifying life with a tale signifying nothing. Both his love for his wife and his fears, the two emotions he does consistently feel, finally disappear, and merge into the embracing nothingness of everything else. "I have almost forgot the taste of fears," he says (V.v.9–15).

Moments later, when he gets word of his wife's death, he retorts with: "She should have died hereafter; / There would have been time for such a word" (V.v.18–19). Like everything else in his life, her death too is something he wishes to postpone. More significant is the reference to her death as a "word." The import of this specific verbal choice can now be gathered by attending to the context. The line is embedded in an enveloping expression in which all are but signs that signify nothing. Given the hierarchy between being and representing that governs these lines, her death too becomes but a sign. Her death itself is postponed to the "hereafter" in which she should have died. But even "there," in a future that shall never come, it is referred to as a "word" and thereby abstracted from the ontological event that it is to the semiotic device through which it is only supposed to be signaled. All dies. What now remains, as *Macbeth*'s movement reaches its end, is absolute hollowness. In his own eyes, he is naught but a faded old man who has lived "long enough," a sapless "yellow leaf" (V.iii.22–23).

Encountering

In the midst of all this circumvention and hollow action, Shakespeare situates one of his most moving scenes: the talk between Ross, Malcolm, and Macduff. More than an actual contribution to plot, the length of the preliminary dialogue between Malcolm and Macduff, before Ross arrives to report to Macduff the death of his wife and children, makes possible a build-up of sympathy to Macduff's straightforwardness and simple decency. Shakespeare seems to have wanted nothing more complicated than this for Macbeth's victim.[12] But more than opposing Macbeth's nihilism to Macduff's unsophisticated commitment to his family, the strongest moments of the scene capture the *resistance* to the desire to shirk from emotion as well as convey an insight as to what emotion is.

Initially, Ross is unable to tell Macduff of the murder of his wife and children:

MACDUFF.	How does my wife?
ROSS.	Why well.
MACDUFF.	And all my children?
ROSS.	Well too.
MACDUFF.	The tyrant has not battered at their peace?
ROSS.	No, they were well at peace when I did leave 'em.
MACDUFF.	Be not a niggard of your speech: how goes't?

(IV.iii.176–80)

Some things are impossible to say (compare Macbeth's inability to say "Amen" after he kills Duncan). Macduff senses the evasiveness and—

---

[12] G. Wilson Knight greatly exaggerates in thinking that Macduff was evil, or at least cruel, because he left his wife and children behind (1930, p. 151). In fact, Macduff has no reason to think that his wife and children are in danger (even if he is) and, in that, shows that his fault is not moral but of a more cognitive nature: it is that he underestimates the lengths to which Macbeth's disproportionate cruelty has gone. For a similar conclusion, see Arthur Kirsch (1984) and Kristian Smidt (1969).

note the present tense—asks for literal unequivocal information, which he gets:

MACDUFF. If it be mine
Keep it not from me, quickly let me have it.
ROSS. Let not your ears despise my tongue forever,
Which shall possess them with the heaviest sound
That ever yet they heard.
MACDUFF. H'm—I guess at it.
ROSS. Your castle is surprised; your wife, and babes,
Savagely slaughtered—to relate the manner
Were on the quarry of these murdered deer
To add the death of you.
MALCOLM. Merciful Heaven—
What man, ne'er pull your hat upon your brows:
Give sorrow words; the grief that does not speak
Whispers the o'erfraught heart, and bids it break.
MACDUFF. My children too?
ROSS. Wife, children, servants, all
That could be found.
MACDUFF. And I must be from thence!
My wife killed too?
ROSS. I have said.
MALCOLM. Be comforted.
Let's make us med'cines of our great revenge,
To cure this deadly grief.
MACDUFF. He has no children.

(IV.iii.199–215)

Macduff's repetitious questions force Ross to mouth and mouth again the literal language he is compelled to use. Ross moves to avoiding directness through referring to what he has already said: ("My wife killed too?" / "I have said"). But it is Macduff's focus on grief and his rejection of too quickly endorsing future-oriented emotions such as anger and the "medicine" of some "great revenge" that impart the deeper contrast between what these moments stand for and Macbeth's postponements. We first notice how Macduff tacitly accepts Ross's suggestion *not* to relate the manner of the murders. Malcolm, in his haste to convert grief into revenge, would not, if put into Macduff's place, spare himself the details. Macduff, in contrast, concentrates on loss and attachment and rejects Malcolm's attempts to exchange present grief for future revenge. Malcolm has no children. He cannot understand.[13]

After the pauses and questions comes feeling, itself structured through rhetorical questions:

> MACDUFF. He has no children. All my pretty ones?
> Did you say all? O hell-kite! All?
> What, all my pretty chickens and their dam
> At one fell swoop?
> MALCOLM. Dispute it like a man.
> MACDUFF. I shall do so:
> But I must also feel it as a man;
> I cannot but remember such things were
> That were most precious to me; did Heaven look on,
> And would not take their part?
> (IV.iii.215–24)

On one level, we note the opposition between feeling and the resistance to it, expressed by Malcolm's militant remarks that in these lines border on scolding. However, these lines are also about something much less obvious, about what feeling might mean. It is here that the romantic opposition between emotion and circumventing it that I have so far employed gains deeper dimensions. For, one may well ask, what is the type of oneness with the present I am opposing to a pervasive escape from it? It is Macduff's collapse to effeminate language, his "all my pretty chickens," that provides us with one answer.

Indeed, the feminine ring of Macduff's metaphor does not escape Malcolm. This much is evident in his reproving "Dispute it like a man" and in Macduff's reaffirmed masculinity in the lines further on when he refrains from playing the woman with his eyes (along with Malcolm's approving "This time goes manly"). Identifying grief and feeling with femininity is conventional. However, the lines imply more. To begin

---

[13] I am here following Brooke's reading of "he" in line 216 as referring primarily to Malcolm and not to Macbeth (see the Oxford edition, p. 192). There is a subtle development in Malcolm's character in the closing lines of the play. Shakespeare embeds a small episode in which Seyward receives news of his son's death. His startling cold response, in approval of the brave way his son died, creates a mirror-scene to the one discussed here, but note Malcolm's change in relating to the value of emotions unconnected to actions: "He's worth more sorrow, / And that I'll spend for him" (V.vii.80–81).

with, Macduff, in his "I must also feel it as a man" reply to Malcolm, associates the feminine figure with feeling *as* a man. He is not a woman. Rather, he feels, and does so as a man. This attempt to encompass feminine contents within a stable masculinity—or, more radically, to redefine manliness through potentially subversive contents—terminates when the options of crying and talk—much more directly affiliated with effeminacy—surface and are precluded as such:

> I could play the woman with mine eyes,
> And braggart with my tongue. But gentle heavens,
> Cut short all intermission: front to front
> Bring thou this fiend of Scotland and myself.[14]
>
> (IV.iii.230–33)

Emotion—and this is what I take to be the second, deeper meaning of these lines—is identified with a *destabilizing* of a determining formative category. Manhood shakes, is in danger of breaking down, and needs to be constituted anew. It is not a matter of changing gender-associated *expressions* of emotion. Rather, Macduff's "feel it as a man" points to the ontological level: a weakening of identity categories is identified with the feeling itself. An unsettling of formative categories is what intensive feeling involves, is part of what such feeling *is*. And the Macduff scene allows us to be even more specific: the destabilizing of identity works through permitting an antagonistic voice to sound through one's own mouth. In some moments of intense feeling, something altogether *oppositional* to one's sense of self becomes momentarily encompassed within, and projected as, what one is.[15]

---

[14] The uses of gender in this play have attracted much attention. For one discussion and many references, see Janet Adelman (1992, pp. 130–46). However, the reader may easily see that while what follows refers to sexual identity, the point I am making has little to do with gender.

[15] This is a pattern the play repeats. Lady Macbeth's reference to "unsexing" and her alarming antimaternal rhetoric regarding what she will do to a baby that she loves, iterates the same identification of emotion—this time a mix of ambition, coveting, determination—as a disruption of layers of identity expressed through voicing an alien rhetoric. Or, more obviously, note the way she picks out instances of unmanliness in Macbeth when he is afraid (I.vii.41–51; III.iv.57; III.iv.74), thereby setting the conventional identification of fear with a retreat from the masculine. These moments have, I believe, less to do with gender and more to do with connecting emotion (ambition, fear, grief) with a momentary *reshuffling* of identity. They are, moreover, moments that are not instances of avoidance but of intensive confrontation with what is real in one's time.

Philosophy and Literature

In *Macbeth*, Shakespeare depicts a complete movement of nihilism. He does not restrict nihilism to a "position" or a "thesis," but pictures it as existential hollowness, as a reaction to life that persistently bypasses the possibilities for meaning. Nihilism comes across as unhappy, but this does not of course count as a "refutation" of it. The response to nihilism is more complicated than confirming or refuting.[16]

Nihilism challenges a first-truth, a starting point that cannot be proven. Accordingly, there are no demonstrative arguments that can be set against it. What is needed is to establish some acknowledgment that things are valuable. Reasoned argument cannot ground recognition of this sort without first presupposing the value of rational thought, an assumption that a nihilist will not grant. For anyone who thinks that some first-truths are better than others, what is required, and rationally so, is a theory of rational, nonvalid argumentation, a rhetoric, which should be able to support a first-truth without pretending to constitute a proof. I am now in a position to specify the various layers that make up such rhetoric.

Shakespeare draws a powerful contrast between circumventing one's time and meeting it. Through Macbeth, Shakespeare captures an intellectual nihilism that emerges from a psychological and existential context. Through Macduff, he embodies an opposite capacity for allowing the present to speak. The length of the Macduff scene—longer than any other scene in the play and twice as long as almost all of them—suggests that whatever peak this scene includes requires a substantial build-up. Focusing on the peculiarities of Macbeth's nihilism should explain why such build-up is necessary. Duration is required in order to develop something altogether alien to the cold, dark, and bloody atmosphere the work transmits. This contrast is activated both between the heart of this

---

[16] Jesse Kalin (1976) has offered a more sophisticated version of a literary text "refuting" nihilism and thereby establish a first-truth. Kalin proposes that not fiction but the reader experience, when it is conceived as a recreation of the experience of characters, may function as a counterexample. If a philosophical thesis such as nihilism claims that nothing has value, then experiences in which one feels that certain things are meaningful contradict the thesis. For all its elegance, Kalin's paper deals only with a "descriptive" nihilism and is oblivious to the much more plausible "normative" nihilism. That is, if a nihilist says that experiences of value do not exist, Kalin is right. However, the nihilist's thesis is usually that such experiences exist but are irrational. No experience readers undergo would contradict a normative nihilism of this sort.

scene and the rest of the play in setting the differences between Macbeth and Macduff, and internal to the scene in opposing between Macduff and Malcolm.

Macbeth meets philosophy through this contrast. Embedded within an overall nihilistic context—a setting in which all is instrumentalized and deferred, within a gory, selfish, indeed hellish universe—is a moment that makes reading stop. Nothing less than feminizing a general is needed in order for us to catch the different voice. Only then do we perceive the alternative metaphysics of time and commitment to value that makes this confrontation a moment in which, long before they fight, Macbeth and Macduff oppose each other through the philosophies they embody. The battle is not between some sentimental romantic and a calculated technocrat but rather—and this is what creates the force—between two hardened generals only one of whom allows attachment to have its space. The very disproportion between the unending textual time allowed for nihilism and the short but sharp moment in which it is contrasted creates the absorbing way through which a life that acknowledges value comes across.

As far as philosophical interests are concerned, the text does not prove that one should ascribe value to things. It allows this first-truth to momentarily appear in an opposing context. It is now up to us to decide between the options Macbeth and Macduff exemplify. Yet the suggestive forces of the play do not aim at an impartial choosing on our part. In stressing the vacuous nature of Macbeth's world, his unhappiness, his essential dissatisfaction and the darkness of his universe, in opposing all this to the carefully structured Macduff scene in which emotion is not only established but is also highlighted as a moving moment of oneness with what is real in one's time, the rhetoric of *Macbeth* creates a reader position that responds to value when it appears and closes itself more and more to Macbeth's nihilism as the play progresses. Literary contrast of this sort is "rhetorical" in the Aristotelian sense of rational, nondeductive argumentation since, while contrast can turn some alternatives into plausible choices (in our case, choosing to invest one's world with value), such reaction by no means necessarily follows from it. Employing means of this sort in the context of philosophy is rational—though I am not yet saying that the specific response itself is rational—because when first-truths are concerned, no stronger means are available.

Against this, some may rephrase Ramsey, saying that what cannot be proved cannot be whistled either. In response, I claim that when proof is not understood as being restricted to achieving compelling assent but includes an establishing of plausible preferences, a rhetorically presented contrast of the kind Shakespeare stages constitutes a means for forming choices. We now need to move from the rationality of employing nonvalid moves in the context of first truths in general, to the rationality of the specific move I am describing. In what sense was this antinihilist preference *rationally* established rather than *merely* established as part of the reading experience that I have suggested? We also need to know why not simply ask readers whether they wished to live as Macbeth does, rather than belabor them with a detailed reading of his nihilism?

The answer to both questions is interconnected and relates to the makeup of basic preferences, to what philosophers would call "the metaphysics" or "ontology" of value. It is by dwelling on subtleties of circumvention, on the one hand, and noting the powerful particularities of relating to value, on the other, that a general preference is created out of experiences that are the formative constituents of this preference itself. These experiences are, at base, moments of recognition of particular patterns of circumvention (Macbeth), coupled with attention to a holding on to value (Macduff). A preference for the latter is thus formed. The rationality of such preferences (as opposed to them being merely established) consists of their relation with a broader wish for happiness (assuming that the preference for happiness is itself basic). The difference between this and a nonliterary employment of contrast (say, in the context of moral education where such contrasts are also often used) is that, unlike nonliterary rhetorical argument, we can perceive how encapsulating the move within an aesthetic context invites readers to *allow* themselves to be influenced and infiltrated when rigorous proofs cannot be given. On a deeper level, the creating of such experiences is itself a formation of preferences and values, and so one must undergo such experiences rather than hear about them through description or paraphrase.

An additional argument on behalf of literature's philosophical relevance that should be made here relates to belief-formation. Investigating patterns of belief formation is a necessary part of an inquiry into the concept of knowledge itself (rather than the concepts of value or nihilism). What we take to know, what we think we are justified in believing, is not limited to beliefs gained through argument but also includes beliefs that emerge from experience. Such experiential knowing should accordingly be investigated as part of any comprehensive theory of knowledge. Moreover, since some of these beliefs are philosophical ones—pertaining, in our case, to basic values—by studying their formation, philosophers do not simply sharpen their ideas about belief-formation but about belief-formation *in philosophy*. When attempting to understand belief-formation through aesthetic experience, this involves breaking up the experiential patterns that have been repeatedly mentioned in the philosophy-literature discussion (showing, conveying, witnessing, identifying, projecting, and responding) in specific and detailed cases. As for philosophy's need for literature, this last thesis is demonstrative (rather than rhetorical) in two ways. First, since belief-formation through aesthetic response is distinct from other types of belief formation, *studying* it is necessary for philosophy when the discipline is envisioned as including an inquiry into knowledge. Second, showing that such experiences exist enables the *specific beliefs* that emerge regarding processes of belief-formation and, ultimately, regarding the concept of knowledge itself, to be justified via appeal to such evidence. What matters, in this further respect, is not the truth of the beliefs I formed in my reading regarding nihilism but the simple fact that I formed them. The claim that philosophical beliefs do, at least sometimes, get formed that way is justified through simply pointing out a case—a reading—in which such formation took place.

But is the specific response pattern created through the experience I described the only possible one in the context of Shakespeare's play? While other commentators have responded to *Macbeth* in a similar way,[17] the obvious answer is negative. The importance of this interpretive freedom should not, however, be overstressed. A literary work is a collection of possibilities for structuring one's experience. A fruitful interpretation should be both a discovery of one such possibility and an invitation to accept it as a rewarding possibility. Such a view enables circumventing the question of subjective response. According to my interpretation, itself only an invitation, *Macbeth* offers us a certain experience. The reader need not worry that I am generalizing from my own subjective experience (though that is no disaster when response patterns are discussed). The impressions of Arthur Kirsch and Emrys Jones admit of the same experience. Such "data"—to employ a rhetoric some may prefer—is all that the last demonstrative thesis requires since it serves as "empirical evidence" that a certain process of belief-formation repeatedly results from attentively reading this play.

---

[17] See the closing paragraphs of Kirsch (1984), or Emrys Jones, who says of the Macduff scene that "this is the first time in the play that what we see on stage has the effect of simply moving us" (1971, p. 221).

As for the threat of instrumentalizing literature, focusing attention on epistemological processes rather than on ethical ones enables explaining the force that philosophical criticism has without endorsing the instrumental view of literature that has worried critics. If my claims above are correct, we need not choose between a didactic employment of literature, on the one hand, and an "Art for art's sake" approach that makes ethical features irrelevant, on the other. Instead, we can identify reading literature with an aesthetic experience and regard that experience itself both as a proper subject matter for epistemological inquiry and as what contributes to unique, "deep," moral belief-formation. Thus, investigating salient features of aesthetic response becomes an inquiry into the epistemic conditions that can accommodate greater responsiveness to moral insight. When the moral claim itself is a first-truth, such a shift in our responsive capacities can become a process we will rationally choose to undergo as a result of the impotence of conventional, argumentative philosophy.

Nihilism questions the very root of moral belief, the idea that some things have value. Philosophy can only respond to this challenge through presupposing the value that rational inquiry is supposed to have. This means that nihilism makes us confront a philosophical limitation. Meeting nihilism cannot, therefore, be confined to argument. Through contrast, aesthetic experience allows a preference for value to be formed. Formation is not conclusive justification. Nevertheless, it is something that can be done. Nihilism can be met, as this play meets it, through creating an experience in which value is perceived. Moving from this point to preferring value is a matter of succumbing to the text's rhetoric, of letting it resonate for a while.

Deciding to listen is, of course, never necessary. It is a decision, a choice. Nothing stronger but nothing weaker.

Love Stories

P<small>HILOSOPHERS OFTEN TALK</small> of the inappropriateness of philosophy, the sense of its simplicity in discussing love. Expressing such dissatisfaction is common, and is routinely made in many philosophical writings on the topic.[1] This chapter aims to explain the epistemological basis of this dissatisfaction, as well as to say how we may avoid it. I begin with the process of falling in love in *Romeo and Juliet*.

THE PROBLEM

Let us begin by sensing something of the evasive quality of *Romeo and Juliet*. The play does not seem complex. Indeed, it looks rather simple in the range of meanings to which it is tuned. If the Romantics are to be believed, the tragedy is primarily an exquisite eulogy for youth and first love—a love that is conceived as a totality of emotional involvement, commitment, and erotic expression. Yet reading the play in the way Haz-

---

[1]
> We suggested that theories about love, especially philosophical theories, fall short of what we discover in the story because they are too simple. They want to find just one thing that love is in the soul, just one thing that its knowledge is, instead of looking to see what is there.
> Martha Nussbaum,
>
> 1990, p. 283

> There is an air of paradox surrounding an attempt by philosophy to deal with the passions . . . It is the bloodless abstractions of philosophy that would seem farthest from the stormy vehemence of the passions. A philosopher trying to understand a passion would seem like a cynic trying to understand the feelings of two people in love.
>
> Robert Solomon,
> 1976, p. 1

> I took the opportunity to demonstrate how incorrigibly stiff philosophy is when it undertakes to lay its icy fingers on the frilled and beating wings of the butterfly of love.
>
> Arthur Danto,
> 1991, p. xii

litt, Coleridge, and Schlegel have done is invalidated by elements of plot that seem to be there precisely in order to block this reading. Mercutio makes sharp ironic remarks concerning Romeo's infatuations (". . . We'll draw thee from the mire / Of—save your reverence—love, Wherein thou stickest / Up to the ears" [I.iv.41–43]).[2] He also describes Romeo as trivially sex-crazed rather than heavenly possessed by love ("For this drivelling love is like a great natural that runs lolling up and down to hide his bauble in a hole" [II.iv.91–93]). Such remarks are one important way through which Shakespeare restricts a reading from being overtaken by passion alone. But the biggest obstacle for such a reading is the peculiar fact that Romeo is introduced *already* deeply in love with another woman.

Presenting a hero with shallow emotions in a tragedy of love seems blatantly wrong. Commentary has avoided this conclusion by dismissing Romeo's love to Rosaline as false or solely sexual.[3] Such an impression in fact endorses the views of Mercutio and Friar Laurence. Friar Laurence never did believe that Romeo loved Rosaline (II.iii.77–78), and Mercutio considers the entire affair as a rather comical case of unfulfilled desire. This, though, is hardly how Romeo sees things. There is, no doubt, emotional and linguistic development in Romeo. His love for Juliet is much deeper than his pining for Rosaline. But doubting his love for Rosaline is plainly contradicted by the reports of the depths of his despair: "Many a morning hath he there been seen, / With tears augmenting the fresh morning's dew, / Adding to clouds more clouds with his deep sighs; / But all so soon as the all-cheering sun / Should in the farthest east begin to draw / The shady curtains from Aurora's bed, / Away from light steals home my heavy son / And private in his chamber pens himself, / Shuts up his windows, locks fair daylight out / And makes himself an artificial night" (I.i.129–38). Claiming that such a depressive state results solely from an unsatisfied sexual appetite is unpersuasive.

So we hear that nothing can replace Rosaline in Romeo's heart ("The all-seeing sun / Ne'er saw her match since first the world begun" [I.ii.94–95]), but then we are to simply accept the fact that all this is gone as soon as he accidentally sees Juliet. Such an achievement has been

---

[2] Brian Gibbons informs us as to the play here on "save your reverence" and *sirreverence*—"a euphemism for human dung" (1980, p. 108). All references to *Romeo and Juliet* are to the Arden edition.

[3] See, for example, Ifor Evans (1959, p. 80–82) and M. M. Mahood (1968, p. 61). Such impression recurs in many other commentaries.

difficult even for very sympathetic readers.[4] Can one really believe that the love of someone confessing to having been "stricken blind" by Rosaline, someone to whom all other beauties are but "a note" indicating the one who surpasses them all (I.i.230–34), can disappear, change its object, merely because of a moment of sight? Does not such characterization block the attempt to sympathize with what Romeo later says to Juliet regarding the depths of his feelings for *her*? Does not the whole tragic effect of the work suffer because of this diminishing of Romeo?

The second chorus excuses the change from Rosaline to Juliet through the mutuality that was missing from Romeo's one-sided love to Rosaline.[5] Yet this justification—altogether missing from the first Quarto—is not dramatically satisfying. To begin with, Romeo confesses to loving Juliet moments after seeing her (I.v.51), *before* he could have possibly known or guessed about mutuality. However, things are not only chronologically awkward but also substantively dubious. If Romeo was indeed willing to die for Rosaline in that day's afternoon, it is hardly a persuasive justification to appeal to the fact that his falling in love with another women in that day's evening is the result of having some sense of being loved back.

Moreover, two additions of Shakespeare to his source—Brooke's *The Tragicall Historye of Romeus and Juliet*—further intensify the problem. To begin with, Shakespeare compresses the time frame from several months in Brooke to five days including the turn from Rosaline to Juliet. It is not so much that this makes the change from Rosaline to Juliet quicker in Shakespeare. In both plays, the switch itself is fast. But the grave costs Romeo immediately has to pay for his love, when only days or hours ago he loved another, along with his never questioning commitment, make him a potentially unpersuasive and mechanical hero. Secondly, Friar Laurence mocks him at length for his changed disposition (II.iii.61–80). Such mockery is nowhere to be found in Brooke's description of the same scene. The fact that it is mockery and ridicule and not merely a questioning of his

---

[4] Hazlitt (1817) thought that the episode "is perhaps an artifice (not absolutely necessary) to give us a higher opinion of the lady [Juliet]" (pp. 114–15). Notice the "perhaps" and the parenthesized remark, which stand out as the only points of humble critique in Hazlitt's praise for the play.

[5] Notice the subtle contrast here between Shakespeare and his source. In Brooke the description is almost identical, but the explanation does not appeal to mutuality but to a mechanical picture in which a new love replaces an old one, just like a new nail can drive an old one out of a piece of wood (see Brooke's *The Tragicall Historye of Romeus and Juliet*, lines 203–8, in the edited version supplied by the Arden edition).

transformed state of mind is also significant. Shakespeare thereby appears to invite a reading according to which there is something altogether ludicrous in Romeo's love. Opening up such a possibility through showing a dreamy hero that is merely "in love with love" seems inexplicable if we assume that a tragic effect is ultimately intended.

Some Replies

To begin with, this entire problem may be dismissed through contending that love, in the period's conceptualization, is a somewhat laughable malady, fit subject for jokes—not of serious reflection. Substituting a love object will thus not shock anyone, and in fact occurs at times on the Elizabethan stage (I already mentioned Anne's implausible turn to Richard in the outrageous wooing scene, but think too of Kyd's *Spanish Tragedy* [I.iv.60–63] in which Bel-Imperia casually turns her love object from Andrea to Horatio with small attempts at self justification). In the next chapter, I shall devote more space to the love-as-fatuous-malady claim (usually attributed to Dickey and Babb), both to its historical inadequacy and to the error of supposing that conventions exhaustively determine dramaturgic choices. Here I limit myself to claiming that the idea that there was such a "convention" is unlikely. Hammon's turn from wooing Rose to courting Jane (moralistically opposed to the erotic constancy of Ralph and Jane) in Dekker's *The Shoemaker's Holiday* is certainly connected with and strengthens his shallowness. The same value scheme figures in Shakespeare's own *The Two Gentlemen of Verona*: Proteus's move from fervent devotion for Julia into an ardent infatuation for Silvia is also a turn from being an amiable youth into becoming that play's villain (II.vi), and he is strongly reproved for his turn of heart by Silvia (V.iv.45–49). On the other hand, Castabella of Tourneur's *The Atheist's Tragedy* wins moral sympathy by insisting on maintaining attachment to Charlemont in the face of strong pressure to change her love object. An even clearer statement regarding the moral import of erotic constancy is expressed by Spenser's Guyon, who responds to Mammon's attempts to have him change his love object by saying, "To Change love causeless is reproach to warlike knight" (*The Faerie Queene*, II.vii.50). So it is far from obvious that early-modern audiences would have simply dismissed the erotic substitute as unimportant. The source-play alterations I have mentioned already suggest that, whatever his audience may or may not have expected, Shakespeare seeks to emphasize the problematic nature of the erotic switch. The idea that we should mark off this problem through some dramaturgic norm becomes even less appealing when we note the way in which so many characters—Mercutio, the Friar, the Nurse, Juliet—enforce on Romeo the issue of erotic constancy and reliability. The play, it seems, will not allow us to belittle the significance of the migration from Rosaline to Juliet.

Some of those who have not simply dismissed Romeo's love for Rosaline as unimportant, or as manifesting some convention, have suggested why appropriating the Rosaline affair from Brooke's novella is justified. One may follow Hazlitt (1817, p. 115) and claim that Shakespeare is showing how overwhelming loves are sometimes not those where one turns from absence of feeling to passion but from a weaker to a stronger love. A second possibility, and one that satisfied Coleridge (1960, p. 6), is that through stressing Romeo's nonproblematic shift from Rosaline to Juliet, the love object becomes a contingent catch of a psychic state that already hunts. But we may elect to avoid adding missing justifications when Shakespeare employs an unlikely one (or, according to the First Quarto, does not supply one at all). The unsaid and inexplicable in a literary work is not necessarily there to be "solved" through adding speculation—filling out, as it were, the missing parts. Sometimes it needs to be explained as such. Interpretations that allow for the possibility that Shakespeare embeds gaps in plot, motivation, and characterization in his plays should explain how such points cohere with more general meanings that these works establish. In what follows, I claim that respecting this muteness reveals the overarching philosophical considerations that underlie this play.

Suspending Doubt

In sharpening Romeo's instability and in making him face the unreasonable manner in which he so casually replaces the object of his infatuations, Shakespeare presents a context in which doubts, skepticism toward one's own certainties, *should* have been invoked. Shakespeare makes it increasingly difficult for Romeo to blind himself to the threat that his past emotional instability poses for the veracity of his present feelings. Loving Juliet carries costs as grave as dismembering himself from his family, foregoing his name, and even losing his life. These should have made him more responsive to the demand Friar Laurence makes of him to examine his inner state. The Nurse also asks him about the seriousness of his feelings for Juliet (II.iv.158–68). Even Juliet's words should have made him question the stability of his emotions: "O swear not by the moon, th'inconstant moon, / That monthly changes in her circled orb, / Lest that thy love prove likewise variable" (II.ii.109–11). In the morning of this same day, he was willing to die for Rosaline. Yet, in the face of all that these people tell him, Romeo never engages in self-examination.

A striking example of this refusal is how Romeo answers the Friar's mockeries: "I pray thee chide me not, her I love now / Doth grace for grace and love for love allow, / The other did not so." (II.iii.81–83). Romeo is basically duplicating the argument of the chorus, appealing to the mutual nature of his and Juliet's love unlike his feelings for Rosaline. His reply is particularly interesting in the context of self-examination since it is a glaring evasion. It says nothing about the stability of his own emotions, which is what the Friar was questioning. After all, Romeo could prove fickle hearted in a mutual love story. This possibility should alarm Romeo in the face of all he has to give up, but he does not hear this. What he attempts instead is for the Friar to believe that this love has some better prospect of working out. The Friar is questioning him about his self and his knowledge of himself, but all Romeo wants is the Friar's blessings.

Shunning introspection is connected with Romeo's unreflective nature throughout the play. Indeed, it is difficult to miss the plain, trigger-response way in which he moves to action. He fights, falls in love, and decides to kill himself, all without hesitation or meditation. In this he manifests not only the conventional shirking from reason in the face of eros (Friar Laurence calls him both mad and drunk [III.iii.61, 83]) but also what appears to be a shallowness of emotion. And yet Romeo's characterization, the intensity and originality of his language, his cleverness—manifested most clearly when he outwits sharp Mercutio—as well as the simple fact that both expert as well as lay readers for centuries now have related deeply to him and his love for Juliet instead of condemning his superficiality and remaining unmoved by this supposed mechanical nature—all make it impossible to dismiss him as shallow. Stressing only Romeo's unreflective aspects therefore makes for a flawed account regarding what we perceive.

What hidden elements prevent the audience's disconnection from Romeo? What stops us from endorsing Mercutio's cynicism or Friar Laurence's fatherly bemusement? A clue to an answer may be indicated by Romeo being not merely unreflective in his practice but also explicitly attacking philosophy and its value:

FRIAR L. Thou fond mad man, hear me a little speak.
ROMEO. O, thou wilt speak again of banishment.
FRIAR L. I'll give thee armour to keep off that word,
Adversity's sweet milk, philosophy,
To comfort thee though thou art banished.
ROMEO. Yet 'banished'? Hang up Philosophy.
Unless Philosophy can make a Juliet,
Displant a town, reverse a Prince's doom,
It helps not, it prevails not. Talk no more.
FRIAR L. O, then I see that mad men have no ears.
ROMEO. How should they when that wise men have no eyes?
FRIAR L. Let me dispute with thee of thy estate.
ROMEO. Thou canst not speak of that thou dost not feel.
Wert thou as young as I, Juliet thy love,
An hour but married, Tybalt murdered,
Doting like me, and like me banished,
Then mightst thou speak, then mightst thou tear thy hair
And fall upon the ground as I do now,
Taking the measure of an unmade grave.

(III.iii.52–70)

Philosophy is useless and blind. Romeo does not require some abstract advice, a "dispute" as to his "estate," but someone who feels what he does. Dismissing philosophy coheres with the portrayal of reflective wisdom (Friar Laurence) as cold, nonpenetrating, and, ultimately, the origin of all disaster. Rejecting philosophy is also in line with the transformed status of the supposed wisdom of the elderly: Brooke's introductory note to his readers applauds such wisdom, presenting it as what the young couple rebelled against, damning themselves through that very rebellion, whereas in Shakespeare such "wisdom" leads to catastrophe through its insensitivity. Romeo is not merely unphilosophical. After Romeo's display of wit, Mercutio praises him for his *regained* "art," which is also a regaining of his old self ("Now art thou sociable, now art thou Romeo; now art thou what thou art, by art as well as by nature" [II.iv.89–91]). Mercutio's line discloses that Romeo is out of character when we see him, at least from the perspective of his best friends.

The play does not present a superficial protagonist, nor does it simply exemplify the love-as-folly convention that Shakespeare repeatedly invokes elsewhere.[6] Shakespeare is, rather, exploring the love-reason opposition as such, instead of exploiting its comic potential or relating to it as a given piece of common wisdom that is there to be endorsed. Love is presented as a motion of *withdrawal* from wisdom. In Romeo, this movement takes the shape of playing down certain possibilities of thought, a silencing of both internal and external skeptical voices.[7] Such selective awareness is not merely a condition for falling in love but an aspect of how love operates, of what it is. Love is a state in which some questions are never really perceived. In meeting such refusal in a lover, we do not perceive stubbornness *caused* by love but rather note an aspect of love itself. In some domains, allowing certain questions to be raised is a letting go of something that one has.[8]

This brings up a subtle difference between Romeo and Juliet. Unlike Romeo, Juliet does allow skeptical voices to emerge. She doubts Romeo's affections, employing conditional language: "Dost thou love me? I know thou wilt say 'ay', / And I will take thy word. Yet, *if* thou swear'st, / Thou mayst prove false" (II.ii.90–92); "*If* that thy bent of love be honourable" (II.ii.143). These conditionals could obviously be acted by emphasizing an attempt to extract more love-talk from Romeo, rather than imparting genuine disbelief. Such manipulative games will surely be in line with the way she is maneuvering him, his talk, and his actions in their first conversation (the three kisses she commissions from him). Yet even this would still mean that for Juliet, suspending skepticism is not Romeo's partial awareness but a choice. In opposition to Romeo, Juliet is always aware of the possibility of doubt, but opts for a willing blindness. She *decides* to believe him (II.ii.115). Possibilities are noted and ignored, rather than never perceived. This aspect of her erotic experience is further characterized through Shakespeare's differentiation of her loving gaze from Romeo's. While he is totally absorbed by her when he first sees her, the context supplying a faded background that makes her shine through and be even lovelier ("She doth teach the torches to burn bright"; "So shows a snowy dove trooping amongst crows"), her own loving gaze

---

[6] *A Midsummer Night's Dream* (III.i.132); *Troilus and Cressida* (III.ii.151–52); *As You Like It* (II.iv).

[7] Compare Hazlitt's claim that "Romeo is Hamlet in love."

[8] This last theme is not explored only in *Romeo and Juliet* but is also an underlying theme of *Othello*. In the latter, however, Iago does manage to establish a question thereby destroying Othello's love.

encompasses the context without subordinating it to what she desires. She manages to look lovingly at him while noting disharmonious elements ("Art thou not Romeo, *and* a Montague?").⁹

In Juliet, Shakespeare is interested in a gaze emphasizing care ("How cam'st thou hither, tell me, and wherefore? The orchard walls are high and hard to climb, And the place death, considering who thou art?"), rather than religiosity ("If I profane with my unworthiest hand This holy shrine . . ."); attention to context ("O Romeo, Romeo, wherefore art thou Romeo?"), rather than insulation from worldly matters ("With love's light wings did I o'erperch these walls"); awareness of the future ("If that thy bent of love be honourable, They purpose marriage") rather than a present that makes everything else vanish ("And I'll still stay to have thee still forget, Forgetting any other home but this"). All this indicates that Romeo's erotic experience is predicated on a narrowing of perspective, whereas Juliet's is a selective attunement to what she perceives. As for the inversion of these outlooks after sex (III.v.1–55), here I hesitate to read Romeo and Juliet through the same explanation. While an awakened realism after sex is a conventional piece of characterization regarding him, Juliet's ignoring of endangering reality ("It was the nightingale and not the lark") is less of a clinging for postcoital connection. Juliet engulfs Rome's erotic outlook, the way his love involves a disregard for reality. Sexual bonding for her means more than a unification of bodies. She allows his viewpoint to speak through her experience—communicating a merging of erotic perspectives and adopting the loved object's own favored erotic rhetoric.

Suspending Reality

Romeo's love involves not only ignoring the possibility of doubt but a suspension of reality. We note Romeo's disorientation: the way in which he

---

⁹ One could perceive this aspect of Juliet's erotic gaze as manifesting the courtly fascination with obstacles as constituting and interlinking with love. But I am less inclined to such a reading here. A de Rougemontean love of obstacles strikes me as a plausible reading of Romeo's killing Tybalt after he marries and before he has sex with Juliet, which I cannot dismiss as a simple outcome of Romeo's outrage or grief. Yet Romeo and Juliet fall in love with each other before they have a sense of the inappropriateness of their love story and so the search for impediments cannot be central to their erotic experience, and, while such striving may have awoken in Romeo, looking for obstructions when the possibility for a happy consummation of love arises, such needs are never there in Juliet.

does not know that it is morning in the first line he utters in the play (I.i.157), or his vague attention to significant things that others say: "What said my man when my betossed soul / Did not attend him as we rode? *I think* / He told me Paris should have married Juliet" (V.iii.76–78). But Romeo is not merely confused. He is, rather, presented as being in a dream-like state. Wakefulness and dream flow one into the other: ". . . I am afeard, / Being in night, all this is but a dream" (II.ii.139–40); "Said he not so? Or did I dream it so?" (V.iii.79). The love affair between Romeo and Juliet is itself structured somewhat like a dream: it takes place only at night; it does not respect social and familial affiliations, wishing it could be altogether conducted without names; it disregards reality (Juliet's refusal to accept the coming of dawn); it generates its own sense of time.[10]

Intriguing explanatory connections exist between the fuzzy ontology the lovers experience and a choice of rhetoric that would otherwise remain within the bounds of the familiar usage of erotic hyperboles. Suspending a well-defined reality involves deploying a language of approximations ranging over several domains: an inability to express one's impressions with exactness—"Is love a tender thing? It is too rough, Too rude, too boisterous" (I.iv.25–26); or to be precise regarding the loved one's attributes—"She is too fair, too wise" (I.i.219); "Beauty too rich for use, for earth too dear" (I.v.46). In these, the description operates not through a positive term but through a relational predicate that will not do because of some disproportion: there is a roughness that one can bear, but not the roughness of love. There is a beauty that can be "used" (sexualized) though not Juliet's.

Bracketing off reality in the hazy domain of love also takes the rhetorical form of an inability to count, which Juliet repeats: "But my true love is grown to such excess / I cannot sum up sum of half my wealth" (II.vi.33–34); "My bounty is as boundless as the sea, / My love as deep: the more I give to thee / The more I have, for both are infinite" (II.ii.132–35); "Romeo is banished, / There is no end, no limit, measure, bound, / In that word's death" (III.ii.124–26). At its extreme, the opposition between love and actuality is manifested in Romeo's love rhetoric as challenging reality: he defies the stars and would swim to the shore of

---

[10] For similar impressions as to Romeo's dreamlike state, see Hazlitt's (1817, p. 114) or Norman Holland's (1970) discussions of the play. On how the lovers create their own sense of time, see Brian Gibbons's introduction to the Arden edition, pp. 55–60. On the contrast between the busy objective time and the quality of "stillness" that the affair has, see James Calderwood (1971).

the farthest sea. He repeatedly relies on hyperbole thus disclosing his hostility to facts. The use of hyperbole adds to the dissociation of the discursive universe that the lovers develop from the banal restrictions of the world. Such disconnection is aided by the extensive use of another figure: oxymoron, a device that many have noted to be the dominant rhetorical tool of this play.[11] Oxymoron, the figure that underlies Romeo's opening lines, creates a sense of dream-logic that eschews "correct" reasoning patterns. Hyperbole also contributes to the dreamy quality of the affair since, in the way in which it corresponds to the exaggeration of wishes, hyperbole is itself a structural feature of dreams.[12] Both hyperbole and oxymoron embody a stepping out of reasonable proportions and reasonable thinking, a forsaking of actuality.[13]

However, love in the play is not only an abandonment of the world, a dim or foggy experience, but also a penetration of it through heightened perception. The ordinary is seen anew, as in the balcony scene where Romeo whispers enchanted, "She speaks," or "See how she leans her cheek upon her hand" (II.ii.25, 23). The loving gaze is a new perceptivity of the hitherto unnoticed—unnoticed not because it has been hidden but because it was always there. You always saw it until you really did. Abandoning the conventional categories that structure perception involves substituting them for new, hitherto unseen and unimagined connections. The imaginative discourse of love establishes such links: seeing Romeo at night as a flake of fresh snow carried on a raven's back; envisaging Juliet as a teacher of a class of torches; explaining to them by her own example how they can shine brighter; wanting to be a woman's glove; wishing to be her sleep.

Sleep

Love and dreaming both involve a sense of disproportion, a dismissal of what is normatively and physically correct, a sense of fuzziness, a modified perception that involves both a new seeing and a new blindness. The most ordinary occurrences form the background to this shift to a new dimension. Shakespeare presents it through embedding love at first sight

---

[11] See David Lucking (1997) and James Calderwood (1971). Robert Evans goes as far as claiming not only that oxymoron is used in *Romeo and Juliet* more than in any other Shakespearean work but "more than in any other work in literature" (1966, p. 1, 29).

[12] Cf. Bert States (1989), p. 93.

[13] For the way Shakespeare endorses the traditional association between dream and madness, see Garber (1974, p. 5).

between moments of utter banality: servants tucking away some food for themselves, two old men recycling empty recollections, the kind of talk one never recalls having (Baz Luhrmann's production beautifully captures this relation of love's intertwining with the banal by staging Romeo's moment of love at first sight with a man urinating in the background; the movement to a novel dimension Luhrmann gets through plunging his lovers into water).[14] Suspending reality in this way is not a condition for love. This play makes no distinction between love as some clearly defined passion and its enabling condition: Romeo is afraid that being in night, "all this" is but a dream. His is not the story of a passion being enabled by something else, but *this* experience, this inability to leave her, has a dreamlike quality.

So self-doubt in Romeo never reaches the surface and this is part of the total transformation of his experience. But what about the reader? We could not have been affected by this tragedy so much had we kept questioning the constancy of Romeo's feelings. Through Rosaline, the play weaves a context in which such reservations should have been unavoidable not only for Romeo but also for us. Yet the play's greater achievement is that we seem to be blind or dismissive toward them.[15] Hazlitt, who loved this play so much, told us how to dismiss misgivings regarding the kind of love the play presents, contending that such qualms issue from "gray hair" conceptions of love. Willie van Peer, a recent critic, says much the same: those who dismiss the play act from "repressed emotionality, or a cynical disbelief in any utopian vision of the relationship between men and women" (1996, pp. 98–99). However, these are merely examples in a long tradition that misses the entire dimension of deferred

---

[14] For an examination of water imagery in the movie and an extended analysis of this adaptation in general, see Lehmann (2001).

[15] The following remarks concerning the relations between the blindness of characters and the parallel blindness of readers in *Romeo and Juliet*, should (ideally) be read alongside Stanley Cavell's claims about such a parallelism in *King Lear*. For Cavell, the blindness of readers implicates them in the tragedy (1987, 84–85), we become "implicated in the failures we are witnessing" and therefore share "the responsibility for tragedy" (p. 54). The blindness created by *Romeo and Juliet* and its relations to the characters is, however, of a different order. It is not the negative blindness that Cavell's reading of *Lear* would warn us against. Rather, it is a part of the experiential structure that constitutes love. The ocular figures that shape so many of our epistemological notions predispose us against blindness, taking blindness as opposed to understanding. I will argue for an opposite conclusion: sometimes it is precisely blindness that opens up modes of understanding, not only because it tells us something about blindness itself but also because it is itself an enabling condition, as well as a part of, the experience one wants to connect with.

doubts set in motion by the Rosaline affair. My own impression is that lay as well as experienced readers who have not examined the work in detail need to be reminded of the existence of Rosaline in the first place. This disregard is as telling as significant forgetting ever gets.

So how do we come to be as forgetful and dismissive of Rosaline as Romeo is? Do we dream through the play, like Romeo? Readers like Norman Holland and Brian Gibbons have indeed spoken of a dreamlike quality of the affair, and connections can also be drawn to more ambitious associations of literary response and dreaming.[16] I am not persuaded by these impressions (for me, Kafka's works are more persuasive contenders for such reading experience). A second alternative underscores the psychological pull of the play. Holland (1970, p. 53) suggested that the whole play is nothing "but the most exquisite expression of the child's inverted wish for love": "wait till I'm gone, *then* they'll be sorry." Such explanation fits in nicely with the possibility that some of us undergo a dreamlike response to this play. If dreams are sometimes or—according to Mercutio's Queen Mab speech—always wish-fulfillments (1.4.71–88), Holland supplies us with a substantial guess as to the subliminal wish that audience project on this play. But the problem with Holland's idea when it is supposed to account for the play's grip on the reader (which, incidentally, it is not meant to) is that assuming that a work plays on a certain wish or drive in the reader is never enough. A different work—for example, Brooke's *The Tragicall Historye of Romeus and Juliet*—could be an expression of an identical wish or need, yet can fail in capturing its reader. This is, incidentally, why any explanation that seeks to account for "pull" solely through projected psycholog-

---

[16] Speaking of the love affair, Gibbons talks of the lovers as being "spiritually remote from other characters and the concerns of this world" as well as encapsulated in a "dream consciousness" (1980, p. 70). His impression therefore attests to the dreamlike quality of some aspects of the play. Holland is more general and claims that "the entire relationship of Romeo and Juliet is treated as a dream" (1970, p. 52). One may go further with this approach, and turn to writers like Garret Stewart (1981) or Derek Traversi (1965) for whom all Shakespearean plays have a dreamlike quality. The most ambitious formulation of this option would be to follow those who claim that literature and theater in general are experienced somewhat like dreams. Indeed, Shakespeare himself has Puck ask us at the very end of A *Midsummer Night's Dream* to treat the play as a dream. The analogy itself is older (see Cope, 1973). For a recent inquiry into its theoretical plausibility, see States (1993), but also relevant is his (1989). Some of the authors in Rupprecht's anthology (1993) discuss the idea as well. The fact that we are discussing a play and not simply literature moves the work still closer to dreams since dream phenomenology is closer to the iconic representations of theater than to the more discursively oriented language of texts (see Eli Rozik, 1991).

ical mechanisms will not suffice. Even if we agree that such a projection is one response pattern this work invites, it remains to be asked how Shakespeare's *Romeo and Juliet* in particular succeeds in eliciting such projection from us.

If we avoid Holland's suggestion, it seems to me that we are left with no real alternative to that which some find to be an anachronistic, suspicious, or ideologically laden concept, but which I find unavoidable in discussing some works of literature—that is, the idea of artistic beauty. Not seeing that skepticism should have arisen in Romeo intimates to us a pattern of response that duplicates his own blindness regarding the stability of his emotions. For him, such blindness is achieved through divorce from reality and stems from Juliet's beauty. The blindness of enthusiastic reading is an effect of the strong formulation of love that the play articulates. In the fictional domain, a dreamlike experience involves perceiving the beauty of a person. On the level of response, forgetfulness results from moments in which one is overtaken by the beauty of fictions.

Philosophy and Literature

The self-proclaimed inadequacies of philosophical love-talk from which I began, need not designate the cognitive status of philosophical claims—that philosophical claims are inherently simplistic or obvious—but, rather, a sense of their qualitative deadness. That is, the shortcomings of philosophical discourse when it addresses love need not issue from restricted insight but from the low degree of responsiveness induced by philosophical argumentation. Yet, on its own, a declaration regarding philosophy's frosty critical distance does not substantially advance our understanding of the philosophy-literature links, since we may well feel uneasy about opposing a trusting, yielding, literary reading experience to a supposedly very rigid, unloving, critical, sense of self that a philosophical work asks its reader to maintain. Experienced readers of literature usually remain critical throughout the reading: sorting out elements, evaluating, comparing, stepping back and reflecting, asking for justification for this or that characterization or element of plot. Moreover, literary works can create anger or distance from the love relations they portray (Lawrence's *Sons and Lovers*, for example), yet still cast these in powerful and convincing ways. So it cannot be an accepting or yielding attitude we have for literature that promotes its greater capacity to capture or convey love. If we wish to substantiate the idea of a greater responsiveness that literature facilitates we have to be more specific about what such "openness" means.

Unlike other forms of intellectual activity, reflecting on love does not arise only from a desire to know what love is but rather from a need to perceive it. A theorist of love is less of a cartographer of an emotion, and more like the heroine of Delene Matthee's *The Day the Swallows Spoke*: someone who seems to be solely instrumental about diamonds, asking various questions concerning them—how they are classified, what the criterion is for authenticating them, how to comparatively evaluate them, and so on—but for her all along it is touching and playing with the diamonds that captures her eyes. The intellectual curiosity her questions imply only partially reveal what is going on, as alongside this inquisitiveness are other needs that have less to do with intellectual classification and more with recognition, touch, and play.

I wish to exploit this image regarding what may be involved in having an intellectual need and to suggest that in some fields of intellectualization—love being one—we want the object to be perceived through the theory. Some objects compel us *to rephrase* them. To lose sight of the hold these objects have, and the way in which this fascination asks to be translated into theory, will lead to insensitive theory. The obvious objection to this claim is to say that a reflection of the kind I am describing is not genuinely aimed at understanding (and is thus not philosophical) but is rather directed at consuming or articulating love through an intellectual prism. This criticism has some force only when it leaves out the fuller image of Delene Matthee's heroine, who is touching *and* talking of the diamonds she is playing with. This duel activity—reformulation and reflection—is what I tried to respect in my reading of the play.

We now have one answer to the question of philosophy's difficulty in discussing love. Philosophical discourse may be able to explain how love operates or what it is. However, it fails to enact the epistemic conditions that enable perceiving love. Such perception is required in a theoretical activity on love since what some of us need from such intellectualization is not only explanation but also reformulation. *Romeo and Juliet*'s reformulation of falling in love boiled down to experiences of blindness that paradoxically open up an aspect of the world, rather than block it from view. Once again, what distinguishes literary discourse from the standpoint of philosophy is not primarily that it is particular, evocative, figurative, or simply denser in such elements than other discourse. Rather, literature reshapes our listening capacities in certain ways. Through a rhetorical strategy that is enacted by this play both internally and in its audience, a certain selectivity of inputs makes perception possible. This reconfigured receptivity also explains why philosophers should contemplate the previous claims into the love-as-blindness theme or the epistemic advantages of silencing skepticism *as part* of a reading of a play, rather than lifting such insights out of the context of the work and assessing them as part of a theory of beauty.

My epistemological argument is consequently this: works of literature are structures of experience. Interpreting a text is a suggested way through which to accomplish such structuring or—if the work was known before—restructuring. Appealing to literature invites contemplating claims not through arguing for them. Instead, we are presented with an experiential possibility, a state through which we experience how things are. Philosophical readings of literary texts supply us with beliefs and ground them in a carefully constructed experience. In my own reading, these beliefs concern the relations between love, beauty, reality, and skepticism. If both the literary work and its proposed interpretation are persuasive, such beliefs can turn into experiential knowing. This means that, on one level, what reading or seeing a play achieves for philosophy is not a difference in the belief that is supposed to be known but in its grounds, in the way through which the belief is justified. To reemphasize a point elaborated on in the first chapter, a "ground" need not be a "reason." Experiences are not reasons, but they can form a part of what turns a belief into knowing (both in the sense that lacking them can itself lead to or itself be a form of misunderstanding and that having them modifies the depth or level of acceptance of a belief). As long as knowing is an epistemic relation involving the ground for belief and not merely the claim, there is a distinct mode of understanding that literature opens up, which cannot be reduced to the kind of understanding gained through descriptive language.

Knowing through experience is not necessarily better than knowing through argument. It may well be that one should modify for various reasons and arguments the way one experiences certain states. But things can also be the other way round—a belief supported by good argument should be modified since it strongly opposes one's sense of life. Banishing experiential knowing from the domains of philosophy amounts to giving up a mode of knowing that is at the very least as important as knowledge by argument. It is to opt for a philosophy that is both limiting and limited. And when philosophy attempts to address itself to life, such limitation could well result in a false philosophy.

Saying that literature can make us entertain certain beliefs in a unique way explains why literature is relevant for philosophy. But this is not all. Literature also supplies beliefs relating to the concept of knowledge itself. Reading literature enables distinguishing between different ways in which we can be made to listen. Philosophers reading literature get to explore contexts of discovery. Mega-epistemic notions such as "reader-experience" or "conveying" are unpacked into specific patterns of relating to sense. My own reading sought to show that there exists an experience of personal and aesthetic beauty that involves blindness. Erotic blindness is not merely an epistemic limitation but also a form of opening to aspects of the world. I supported this claim by showing how it has been repeatedly actualized in specific, real reading experiences of *Romeo and Juliet* that involved an important dismissal. Examining *Romeo and Juliet* and how some of us react to it imparts not only a conception of romantic love but also indicates how we recognize beauty. It tells us something about our perception and about how we can be made to listen. We need not oppose a critical, suspicious, philosophical reading experience to a trusting, yielding, literary one. If we must talk of trust, we may say that in rare moments when captured by some literary line, we also suspend reality, doubt, and reflection. All of these return almost at once. But for a few moments, we are blinded to doubt, which is what beauty of person and beauty of fictions involve.

Making Love

THE OPPOSITIONS BETWEEN LOVE AND REASON, romance and reflection, passion and marriage, emotion and insight underlie many passages in Shakespeare.[1] Such distinctions constitute a theme that should be all too familiar for contemporary ears, versed in rhetoric espousing *carpe diem* as opposed to staleness, intensity to a blunt and indistinguishable experience. In contrast, *Antony and Cleopatra* captures the subtleties of a mature love, both in terms of perceiving, maintaining, expressing, and respecting it, and in the struggles these involve. The play attempts the difficult task of articulating something that is unmistakably a form of love and yet never overwhelms, is always only a part of a plurality of voices. Gaining a more specific understanding of the details of such love is the subject of the following reading.

On the more theoretical dimension, I will avoid repeating arguments of the previous chapter regarding connections between poetic discourse and philosophizing on love, though they are relevant here too (since here I will also practice a mode of intellectualization that couples analysis with reformulation of love). Instead, the closing section of this chapter argues for the advantages of casting the familiar idea of representing contingency and poetic exemplification as part of the epistemological framework presented at the beginning of this book. I then defend a different modality of knowledge that literature creates, one to which I shall return in the chapter on *King Lear*, and that constitutes an addition to Ryle's knowing how/knowing that distinction. This chapter also includes

---

[1] In *A Midsummer Night's Dream*, Bottom says that "reason and love keep little company together" (III.i.137), and in *Troilus and Cressida*, Cressida says that "to be wise and love / Exceeds man's might." In *The Two Gentlemen of Verona*, the lover (Proteus) is described as being "yoked by a fool" (love), which therefore cannot be "chronicled for wise" (I.i.39–41). "You cannot call it love," says Hamlet to Gertrude, "for at your age / The heyday in the blood is tame, it's humble, / And waits upon the judgment" (III.iv.66–69). *King Lear*'s Edmond talks of the bastards begot though extramarital lovemaking that "in the lusty stealth of nature take / More composition and fierce quality" than the fools "got 'tween a sleep and wake" "within a dull, stale, tired bed" (I.ii.11–15). Mercutio, we saw, praises Romeo for his regained wit, implying a movement of withdrawing from reason that overlaps Romeo's love for Rosaline (II.iv.88–93). For numerous other examples of the theme in Shakespeare's contemporaries, see Lawrence Babb (1951, pp. 150–54).

response to a different charge of anachronism that philosophical criticism invites.

Mature Love

Compare Antony and Cleopatra with the youthful love of Romeo and Juliet. Romeo's love rhetoric, we saw, works through hyperbole and the language of approximations that cannot quite capture his love. Such rhetoric of transcendence of the worldly coheres with him picturing Juliet through angelic terms: she is a pure and holy saint worthy of worship. He never hints at sexual desire (unless one rather strenuously reads such meanings into one or two lines). Juliet overrides all other considerations for Romeo, without hope of setting compromises between his love and his obligations. Turn now to Antony. Antony's feelings, while they are unmistakably love[2]—love that like that of Romeo, eventually destroys Antony, costing him his life and his name—are never overriding. Unlike the younger lover for whom love makes every other consideration petty, Antony

---

[2] I shall discuss hostile reactions to the affair below. Apart from denying that what Antony and Cleopatra share is love, one other tradition of interpreting this play (that may well object to my characterization above) is that the play is not primarily "about" love. According to such critics—who base themselves on a supposedly informed historical assumption—the play is actually about the costs of vice. Now it may be true that, as Lawrence Babb says, "Elizabethans" would "necessarily" relate to any conflict between reason and love as one between virtue and vice (1951, p. 150). But aside from the sweeping generalization, such observation tells us nothing about the sort of manipulation Shakespeare may have intended for this, his audience's supposedly default impression. Citing approvingly Babb's observation, Daniel Stempel (1956) makes this mistake of moving from the assumption regarding the existence of a convention to the conclusion that Shakespeare must have necessarily conformed to it. Stempel is much more one sided than the studies he draws from. While heavily anti-Romantic in its orientation, Franklin M. Dickey's work (1966) on which Stempel relies, is much more balanced regarding the "Elizabethan malady" and argues for the existence of two visions of love. Dickey's version of history is, though, still one-sided. For example, Burton's *Anatomy of Melancholy*, mentioned by Dickey, does define love as a disease: "They that are in love are likewise sick; to be lustful, lecherous, wanton, to be rating in desire, is certainly to be sick" (1991, p. 658). Yet he finds it necessary to argue against opposing positions. For a richer understanding of love for Renaissance audiences, see Mark Rose (1968, pp. 1–24). Even Babb, on whom Stempel relies, is more ambivalent than Stempel, highlighting an ennobling aspect of love (rather than a simple identification of it with folly) that remains in Elizabethan representations of it (see Babb, pp. 154–56). Regarding Shakespeare, Babb perceives him as a skeptic regarding the love-as-malady pattern (p. 171).

enables his passion for Cleopatra to remain in disharmony with other aspects that are important to him. Romeo is overtaken by passion, suspending judgment and self-critique. Antony allows passion to overtake him completely only once, in an extremely important moment in which he follows Cleopatra's ship and thereby loses the sea battle at Actium. In all other moments, passion lives in constant tension with his other obligations.

Sex, in *Romeo and Juliet*, is on the whole implied, and is never discussed by the lovers, whereas it is explicit and frequent in the older couple. Antony constantly talks of "pleasure" (I.i.46–47; II.iii.39),[3] never utilizing the idealizations Romeo adopts. Others constantly refer to the lustful nature of his and Cleopatra's love (I.i.9; I.iv.26, 29; II.i.22–24; III.vi.94–95). Antony and Cleopatra eat. Romeo and Juliet never eat. In the latter pair, such refraining is continuous with the noncorporeal passion that possesses them. In opposition to this, Antony and Cleopatra's affair makes room for the sort of activities mature lovers share. There are recurring indications of enormous feasts and feats of eating (II.i.12, 23–26; II.ii.179–83; II.vi.62; II.vii.94). As early as their first encounter, they invite each other to supper. Enobarbus calls Cleopatra Antony's "dish," and this is not the only time Cleopatra is imaged as food (I.v.31; III.xiii.116–18).

Antony and Cleopatra talk. Already in Shakespeare's primary source, North's translation of Plutarch's *The Lives of the Noble Grecians and Romans*, Cleopatra's greatest assets are not her looks but her sweet company and conversation. Shakespeare stresses this by having Enobarbus oppose Cleopatra to Octavia's "holy, cold, and still conversation." Antony and Cleopatra laugh together. An incident is recounted when he is fishing and she sends a diver to attach a salt-fish to Antony's fishing rod "which he / With fervency drew up." Romeo and Juliet never laugh, imparting an intense erotic experience that never transforms from serenity into the sort of fun and games that underlie the affection between Antony and Cleopatra. Cleopatra's references to laughter—"O times! / I laugh'd him out of patience; and that night / I laugh'd him into patience"—conveys a romance that, unlike the younger couple, does not work through transcending life, through perpetually setting its intensities at odds with what life is, but rather structures itself through life and the daily pleasures it affords. We note Antony's suggestion to Cleopatra in the opening scene that they should go out and "note the qualities of people." Such gossiping, playing jokes on each other, laughing, eating, having sex, drinking, talking: these are the communicative acts that

---

[3] Citations and references follow Ridley's Arden edition.

invest this affair with its meaning—a meaning that avoids the grander gestures of Romeo and Juliet.

Love as Performance

The distinction I am after is this: mature love is not predicated on the existence of a consistent, underlying, unmistakable affect of the *Romeo and Juliet* kind. Rather, Shakespeare presents an alternative in which love is mostly an enactment of a set of practices shared by the couple. According to this vision, love is not something that one primarily feels but something that one does.[4] Such a "performative" conception of love, in which the category is created in praxis, not manifested through it, is exhibited in the very first exchange we get between Antony and Cleopatra:

> CLEO. If it be love indeed, tell me how much.
> ANT. There's beggary in the love that can be reckon'd.
> CLEO. I'll set a bourn how far to be belov'd.
> ANT. Then must though needs find out new heaven, new earth.
> (I.i.14–17)

The very first impression we receive of Antony is his reluctance to answer Cleopatra and tell her "how much" he loves her. Contrast this to the love rhetoric of Romeo and Juliet, in which ample references are made to the inability to count or measure one's love (II.ii.132–35; II.vi.33–34). Antony's shirking from such expressions, them being immediately extracted from him by Cleopatra, could suggest that he is being untruthful in his love proclamations. But the expository lines, the way by which Antony is directly portrayed (and some other matter I shall shortly discuss), show that he is unmistakably in love. What is also apparent almost at once is Antony's predilection for a love disclosed through actions rather than through oratorical performance. His decision not to hear the messengers and his embracing of Cleopatra manifest an action-oriented love communication rather than the grand loving eloquence she had asked him to produce.

---

[4] As we shall see, the specific practices Shakespeare presents enable perceiving something altogether different from the sort of practices, policies, commitments, and tacit contracts that philosophers have attributed to the action-oriented aspects of love. For these, see Vincent Brümmer (1993, pp. 153–54). Brümmer follows Van De Vate's (1981) as well as others who connect love with commitments and the expectations that these involve. The practices that Shakespeare presents in this play have nothing to do with commitments.

In terms of mature love, the reluctance to engage in love-talk is perhaps natural when low-keyed love is experienced. If love is the manic state Plato's *Phaedrus* envisions it to be, its overwhelming nature turns hyperboles into the most fitting communicative vehicle. But language seems incapable of expressing nonoverwhelming love without being offensive. Imagine, for example, that Antony replies to Cleopatra's need to "have a bourn set" by saying that he loves her moderately—that, yes, she is a source of happiness and delight for him but, no, he would not swim, like Romeo, to the "farthest shore" for her. Antony does produce the required hyperbole by his "new heaven, new earth." Yet his initial disinclination is revealing. Antony's avoidance of love-talk and preference for embracing is a feature one senses in many mature loves, in which loving hyperboles are gradually replaced by personal, idiosyncratic practices (he calls me "my serpent of old Nile," says Cleopatra in I.v.25). In Cleopatra, such a performative model of love takes the form of theatrical displays of love (Cleopatra never conducts such exhibitions when Antony himself is there). It also involves creating confusion and conflict in Antony, thereby extracting performances from him.[5] Common to these games is that the feeling of being loved is made possible through compelling the lover to give up something of importance, in which aspects of the self are relinquished and a willingness to be remolded surfaces in him.

A love predicated on the other's willingness to decompose, to fall from wisdom, status, manhood,[6] kingdom, reputation, and all Antony loses further on in the play (ultimately life) is more than simply expressive of

---

[5] We note, for example, how she repeatedly implants conflicts between his devotion to her on the one hand, and some other contradictory element for which he cares. She then has the satisfaction of seeing him resolve such conflicts, always, of course, in her favor. In the opening love-game, she succeeds in forcing him to "set a bourn" as to how much he loves her, although he believes that estimating love is fit for beggars. She then plays with him, insisting that he should hear the arriving ambassadors, *herself* counting the various reasons why this is necessary. She then has the pleasure of seeing how his desire to be absorbed by her overrides his political obligations.

[6] For Antony's receding from the sort of exemplary manhood he embodied in his past, see for instance (I.ii.83; I.iv.4–7; III.vii.13–15, 69; III.x.23). In Antony, love involves a willingness to withdraw from his favorite sense of masculinity, and this to the amazement of those around him. Such readiness to jeopardize and damage the source of his self-respect and reputation, his manhood, connects emotion with *playing-up* possibilities that stand in opposition to one's sense of self. The *Macbeth* reading exemplifies a similar connection between emotion and a reshuffling of formative categories of the self. The difference between the two plays is that in *Antony and Cleopatra*, we perceive effeminization magnified from Macduff's intense moment into a prolonged process.

Cleopatra's domineering personality or possessiveness. Love is not merely exhibited by the desire to intervene and reshape the lover's attachments to parts of himself, his reputation, or to cherished moments of his past. The purpose of these games is to create and amplify her presence in the mind of the lover. Unlike North's translation of Plutarch (Shakespeare's source for the play), which mentions direct physical presence—". . . never leaving him night or day, nor once letting him go out of her sight . . ."— in Shakespeare, presence is created through more complicated mental manipulations. Obstructing the natural flow of Antony's thoughts, instilling conflict within him, changing his state of mind, whatever it is: "If you find him sad, / Say I am dancing; if in mirth, report / That I am sudden sick." Indeed, in their very first meeting, as reported by Enobarbus, Antony invites her to supper, but "she replied, / It should be better he became her guest." Such a reversal of Antony's plans should not be taken lightly since, as Enobarbus goes on to say, Antony never "the word of 'No' woman heard speak." Cleopatra also creates presence by sending messengers every day to him to the extent that she is willing to "unpeople Egypt" (I.v.77–78). Love, for her, means never disappearing from the lover's mind. Such is the conception of love underlying the operations of this seductress.

As for seduction and what being a seductress may mean, Shakespeare does not employ the conventional conception of love-teasing as a future-directed fantasy that the seductress maintains and never satisfies. Cleopatra's games with Antony involve intensifying passion through gratifying it (II.ii.236–38). At (I. Iii. 87–91) she wants to tell him "one word," though she says she forgets what it is. She thus keeps her lover suspecting that she always has one more untold secret. Alluding to significant undelivered information is a mode of frustrating continuous with other forms of teasing. We note an incident in which she asks to see him and then purposefully exits before he enters (I.ii.82–84). In Plutarch's *Lives*, Cleopatra is much less crafty and sophisticated. She starves herself, at one point, to get Antony's pity and attention through her "weeping and blubbering" (p. 257 in Ridley's Arden edition). Shakespeare refuses to use such whining as a game worthy of his heroine.

Unlike heavenly Juliet, who is there only to be gazed at, Cleopatra comes across through the sounds of flutes and numerous scents. She is a total experience, there not simply to be looked at in pure, holy, untouchable bliss but rather, desired, felt, smelled, lived with. In opposition to the perfect Juliet, Cleopatra has many blemishes. She is neither young nor chaste. Unlike the many allusions to her beauty in Plutarch's *Lives*

(p. 246–47) or in another potential source, the Garnier-Pembroke play, *The Tragedie of Antonie*, in Shakespeare no one directly refers to her as beautiful and there is an explicit disclosure of to her "wan'd lip" (II.i.21), "tawny front" (I.i.6), and her being "wrinkled deep in time" (I.v.29).[7] Cleopatra's beauty is a recollected experience pertaining to the first impression she made in the past. That first impression was complex: her marvelous appearance upon the river of Cydnus, forming a detailed picture of pleasure, eloquently described by Enobarbus through appealing to every sense, was not perceived by Antony. What he saw was the town square in which he was sitting being emptied of people who are going to gaze on the *local* queen, leaving him to sit alone and whistle to himself. In fact, if beauty "can settle the heart of Antony," says Maecenas, "Octavia, rather than Cleopatra, should be Antony's choice (II.ii.241–43). Yet, it is Cleopatra and not Octavia who is loved by a man who has a third of the world at his feet.

Maintaining Doubts

We may have misgivings about some of these games as constituents of a loving relation that we may desire for ourselves. And yet, many of us will sympathize with such a humanly livable vision of love. It is certainly an attractive picture. Unlike the intensities of *Romeo and Juliet*, such a conception does not jeopardize or make stale the milder romances most of us experience. We do not become liars who have given up on life, exchanging "cold comfort for change." Rather, it enables us to look for achievable minor moments and respect them as forms of genuine love. This comforting sense of becoming a legitimate liver and lover is created by the text's rhetoric through casting it as a love of such a grand pair. The godlike scale of Antony and Cleopatra can make any love that is worthy of them appropriate for us too.

But we must ask, is this love? As could be expected, Shakespeare does not simply present an unambiguous comforting vision. The more one

---

[7] Bullough argues the Garnier-Pembroke play to be a potential source (p. 231). For Cleopatra's beauty in that play, see lines 430–36 in the text as supplied by Bullough. If Shakespeare was following a source with regards to Cleopatra's beauty, it is probably Daniel's *Tragedy of Cleopatra* in which the Cleopatra is certainly not beautiful: "What, hath my face yet powre to win a Lover? / Can this torne remnant serve to grace me so . . ." (1070–71). All references to North's translation of Plutarch are to the text as given in the Arden edition.

contemplates the subtleties of their relations, the more the disturbing aspects of it surface. These relate to the inevitable anxieties that accompany nonoverwhelming loving as well as the fear that performing and acting run dangerously close to *play*-acting. For Antony, this means never knowing whether Cleopatra truly loves him, forever shifting between competing thoughts about her true feelings. Cleopatra fears losing Antony and is compelled to keep playing the shifty games she perpetually devises. Edward Dowden was right to note that for all their magnificence and fun Antony and Cleopatra torment one another in setting off these anxieties in each other.[8]

Let us avoid asking whether such love is happy or not (which will involve unpacking "happiness" in this context). All forms of love involve some apprehensions and are therefore not entirely happy. Instead, let us return to the insights into mature, nonoverwhelming love. Casting things this way—descriptively rather than normatively—enables relating to the evaluative anxiety, to the question whether or not this is truly love, as an *intrinsic* component of the relationship. If Antony and Cleopatra epitomize mature lovers, mature love is an erotic bond that is preoccupied with the question of its own existence. Such worry sets it apart from romantic love of the Romeo and Juliet kind, where skeptical voices within the couple are either dismissed (Juliet) or unseen (Romeo). Indeed, as I have argued in the previous chapter regarding *Romeo and Juliet*, the latter sort of love seems to be predicated precisely on ignoring or being blind to the possibility of doubt.

Doubt is an intrinsic component in mature love: it can always surface and constantly needs to be fought off. Doubting the existence of the love also means that, although in mature love affect is distilled into practices, the idea of some clear-cut separation between emotion and its expression never disappears entirely, and remains in the background. When the separation appears, it underlies a questioning as to the status of loving actions; whether they are hollow rote or practices invested with meaning. A loving experience in which skepticism perpetually needs to be fought off, also explains why both Antony and Cleopatra have something extreme and exhibitionistic in their love-talk.[9] The idea of love as other-oriented

---

[8] Edward Dowden (1875), cited in J. R. Brown (1991, p. 40).

[9] When Antony embraces Cleopatra in the opening scene, he says to their attendants: "the nobleness of life / Is to do thus; when such a mutual pair, / And such a twain can do't, / in which I bind, / On pain of punishment, the world to weet / We stand up peerless." The exhibitionistic ring is also there in the scene reported by Caesar, when Antony divides his

performance—this time in the histrionic sense of performing—can be further understood when connected to another practice which both Antony and Cleopatra engage in: moving into and out of names.[10] Cleopatra conceives of the return to names after they argue as a return to love and a retreat from the accusations Antony levels at her. Unnaming and renaming connects personal identity with love, suggesting that moving out of love—or, at the very least, allowing hostile feelings to surface and be directed at the lover—is experienced as a loss of identity. Names, for these two, function not simply as designators or descriptive words as they did for Romeo and Juliet (as arbitrary signs of the "What's in a name?" kind) but as honorific titles. Being an Antony or a Cleopatra is a grandness they have to live up to. The names are the couple's joint idealized identity, and include a regulative element indicating what they *should* be.

The regulative role of names and the desire to exhibit love suggests that in mature love there is a story that is maintained by a "we."[11] In *Antony and Cleopatra*, the story is one of fun, endless banquet and, again, of eating (the return to names leads to a feast Cleopatra will organize for her birthday). The story also involves ostentatious manifestations of their non-human magnitude. But, like other narratives of identity, this one too necessitates suppressing subversive voices coupled with a growing realization of their existence. In opposition, romantic love of the Romeo and Juliet kind can bear nothing more complicated than uniform experience. One is blind to doubt, and self-critique becomes impossible. This also explains why Antony and Cleopatra quarrel, whereas Romeo and Juliet never do.

An Unseen Body

Given Antony's suspicions regarding Cleopatra's true feelings, and in light of his belief that she betrayed him at Actium, we too have our

---

empire in the "market place" in "the public eye" (III.vi). It is perceptible in Cleopatra, when she tells her escorts: "O Charmian! / Where think'st thou he is now? Stands he, or sits he? / Or does he walk? Or is he on his horse? / O happy horse to bear the weight of Antony! . . ." (I.v.18–21). Such rhetoric, with its sexual overtones, seems to be more of a performance of love conducted for the sake of those around her, than an uncalculated imparting of emotion.

[10] "what's her name, / Since she was Cleopatra?" (III.xiii.98–99); "But since my lord / Is Antony again, I will be Cleopatra" (III.xiii.186–87).

[11] The idea of love as creating of a "we" is analyzed both in R. Solomon (1981) and in R. Nozick (1991).

doubts as to whether or not she loves him. These doubts cannot, however, persist because when he dies she says this:

> O, wither'd is the garland of the war,
> The soldier's pole is fall'n: young boys and girls
> Are level now with men; the odds is gone,
> And there is nothing left remarkable
> Beneath the visiting moon.
>
> (IV.xv.64–68)

And later she says this:

> His legs bestride the ocean, his rear'd arm
> Crested the world; his voice was propertied
> As all the tuned spheres, and that to friends:
> But when he meant to quail, and shake the orb,
> He was as rattling thunder. For his bounty,
> There was no winter in't: an autumn 'twas
> That grew the more by reaping: his delights
> Were dolphin-like, they show'd his back above
> The element they lived in: in his livery
> Walk'd crowns and crownets: realms and islands were
> As plates dropp'd from his pocket.
>
> (V.ii.82–92)

Such accuracy in capturing one's sense of loss, an expression that J. M. Murry (1936) thought nobody could ever forget, is nothing but love. But notice that even in the context of the clearest expression of her love, Shakespeare is careful to avoid presenting Cleopatra's feelings as what they are not: these lines could have been voiced by a close friend (say, Enobarbus) and not necessarily by a lover. The lines express admiration of the highest degree, the loved one's uniqueness presented in terms of his relative value in comparison to others. To be sure, this is admiration distilled into love. But missing here is the erotic element that is expected in a lover and not in a friend. Compare this to Romeo's: "Eyes, look your last. / Arms, take your last embrace! And lips, O you / The doors of breath, seal with a righteous kiss / A dateless bargain to engrossing Death" (V.iii.112–15). What we witness in Cleopatra is loneliness and a broken partnership, a sense of abandonedment in a colorless world left lacking anything remarkable. But, unlike the centrality and particularity of the body stressed so much in Romeo's lines, for Cleopatra the body becomes an abstract giant, peeping dolphin-like above the element in which he used to live. Whereas Romeo virtually makes love to what for him is Juliet's dead body ("For here lies Juliet, and her beauty makes / This vault a feasting presence, full of light . . . O my love, my wife, / Death that hath suck'd the honey of thy breath / Hath had no power yet upon thy beauty . . . Beauty ensign yet / Is crimson in thy lips and in thy cheeks . . ."), for Cleopatra, Antony's dead body becomes nothing more than a cold case that previously housed his huge spirit (IV.xv.89). Thus, Cleopatra either metaphorizes Antony's body or trivializes it, never relating to it as what it is. For Romeo, on the other hand, there is nothing beyond present perception and its articulation. This creates the nonerotic sense of Cleopatra's lament.

Beyond merely portraying Antony and Cleopatra as more attuned to companionship and admiration whereas Romeo and Juliet as more erotic and body-centered, Shakespeare enables a particularized understanding of the makeup of these conventional oppositions. For what are "companionship" or "admiration," and how do they differ in a lover as opposed to a close friend? The answer begins with Cleopatra's lament over Antony above. We note a momentary willingness to endorse the other's ideal self-narrative, to relate to him not through just any possible perspective but through the one that *he* would have chosen (IV.xv.51–54). This is a loving act conducted after the loved one's death.

When Antony is alive, Cleopatra shuns direct love rhetoric to the extent that he (and we) distrust her feelings. Shirking from directness partly has to do with Cleopatra's explicit reference to the strategies and manipulations she thinks necessary in order to keep Antony. On another level, avoiding expression is also related to the character of mature love itself, a state in which passion transforms from an engulfing affect into numerous modalities of relating to the other. I am thinking here of Antony's protectiveness (going after her in the sea battle) and Cleopatra's possessiveness and jealousy (her talk with the messenger). My confidence in referring to "transformation" of passion stems from how these moments so obviously indicate that these people are in love. Protectiveness leads Antony to perform an unreasonable action, needlessly costing him the battle and, later, his empire and life. His action is unnecessary. Cleopatra is in no immediate danger when he follows her. This too conveys one of the many insights the play affords into love. Protectiveness (or, for that matter, possessiveness and jealousy) as parts of love are sometimes experienced as (and sometimes actually are) unnecessary in the sense that on examination they prove to be *disproportionate* responses to an external cause. In highlighting Antony's protectiveness at a point in which at least one commentator has experienced as "one of the greatest proofs of love that he can offer" (Burton, 1973), the play suggests that this exaggerated response is precisely how love is manifested.

As for Cleopatra, we know that she is in love not only through her envy of Antony's horse or her laments but also through a scene Shakespeare added to what he found in his sources. Shakespeare there highlights Cleopatra's possessiveness through her violence to the unfortunate messenger bringing her news of Antony's marriage to Octavia:

> MESS. Madam, he's married to Octavia.
> CLEO. The most infectious pestilence upon thee!
> [*Strikes him down.*
> MESS. Good madam, patience.
> CLEO. What say you? Hence,
> [*Strikes him.*
> Horrible villain, or I'll spurn thine eyes
> Like balls before me; I'll unhair thy head,
> [*She hales him up and down.*
> Thou shalt be whipp'd with wire, and stew'd in brine,
> Smarting in lingering pickle.
> MESS. Gracious madam,
> I that do bring the news made not the match.
> (II.v.60–67)

This scene cannot be found in North's translation of *Plutarch*, in Daniel's play, or in the Garnier-Pembroke work. When we ask for Shakespeare's motive in adding this specific scene to a work in which he was generally following his source, the answer is that nowhere, in Shakespeare's play, is the erotic element in Cleopatra's love clearer to us than in these moments when she hales the poor man up and down. Issuing one horrible threat after another, promising the panic-stricken messenger that she will melt gold and pour it down his throat, telling him that he has lived too long and drawing a knife—these cannot but dispel the sense of a cynical manipulator, convincing even the most suspicious of audiences that this woman's love—while it cannot be intimated directly to Antony—is genuine.

RESPONSE AND AMBIVALENCE

With this picture in mind, it is intriguing to note the subtle, *indirect* routes through which Cleopatra does manifest her companionship and admiration for Antony when they directly communicate. This requires understanding something as to the play's operations on some actual readers, as I will now argue for the importance of discrepancies between fictional and actual responses, and suggest how such gaps relate to philosophical insight.

It is a commonplace of this play's criticism that readers radically diverge in what it is they believe Antony and Cleopatra share. For some, the play portrays a celebration of love; for others, it is about a fool falling from power due to the operations of a crafty teaser. Usually, the difference relater to the particular critic's response to Cleopatra. Some interpreters, while admiring her characterization, detest her and these judgments then become the basis for an overall reaction to the affair. Such interpretation has to be ruled out not only because it is one-sided, ignoring precisely the sort of qualities that make Cleopatra a fascinating "piece of work," but also because of Shakespeare's selective employment of his source. Shakespeare makes no mention of some of the cruelties she performs in Plutarch—most obviously, her trying poisons on convicted men and applying "snakes and adders" to men "in her sight" (p. 268). In Flavius Josephus's *The Antiquities of the Jews*, Cleopatra poisons her fifteen-year-old brother and has her sister slain in order to inherit the kingdom (Bullough, p. 331). If these unfavorable critics are right, it is puzzling why Shakespeare eliminates such qualities.[12] Other readers adore Cleopatra. A third group opts for a middle way of one sort or another.[13]

Although in my reading above I did take sides in this dispute, claiming that Antony and Cleopatra do love each other, I suggest that when discussing reactions to this work we should avoid deciding between these response patterns. Instead, we can begin by accepting the arguments put forth by Adelman, Charney, Traversi, and others who take the ambiva-

---

[12] Shakespeare also omits some of Antony's flaws. Though Antony's treatment of Octavia is surely cruel, Shakespeare does not mention the two children Octavia had from Antony, or that he made her take an unnecessary journey while pregnant. Nothing remains of Plutarch's favorable profile of Octavia, in which she stays a faithful wife, refusing to leave his house in Rome, even though she knew of his life with Cleopatra, a virtuous choice that according to Plutarch made all in Rome hate Antony.

[13] Many studies give a comprehensive account of the diverging reactions to this play and I shall therefore avoid producing such a survey myself. For two such accounts, see J. Adelman (1973) and the opening chapter of P. J. Tracy (1970). For some negative accounts and remarks regarding Cleopatra, see William Hazlitt (1817, p. 74); Richard Moulton (1903, p. 129, 138), R. Ornstein (1966, p. 45), and Daniel Stempel (1956). For positive accounts and remarks, see A. C. Bradley (1941, p. 300) and G. Wilson Knight (1951, p. 310). For accounts arguing that Cleopatra incorporates both virtue and vice, see Clemen (1951, p. 167) and M. Charney (1961).

lent, aporetic potential of the affair as part of the play's meaning.[14] I shall immediately suggest that we need to complicate this account at least in one important way. For the moment, though, we can begin by noting how such an interpretive stance makes actual response-patterns resemble the position of the lovers themselves. After all, like the lovers, we too cannot always tell whether what we are seeing is love. But it is precisely through having the actual experience of readers *diverge* from that of the characters that this play imparts some of its deeper meanings. I am thinking here first and foremost of ambivalence itself.

One thought that this reading suggests is that mature love is about the ability to come to terms with an ambivalent stance to love, both to its existence and to its value. The recurrence of doubt is at perpetual tension with the opposing need for certainty. "Tell me how much you love" is the demand that opens this play, as if an assertion could dispel the anxiety that leads to the request in the first place. The need to be sure that one is loved underlies the performance of particular rites: extorting oratorical performance from the lover, asking for promises, demanding prices. If such oscillations between ambivalence and craving certainty encapsulate a fundamental tension of mature love, we may now obtain insight as to the recurring ambivalent *critical stance* to the work I mentioned above. While indecisiveness can be a justified critical stance of a reader, when it comes to the lovers themselves, ambivalence is not really an option. Perhaps in some hypothetical moment of detached reflection, actual lovers can accept the validity of two competing perspectives regarding what they share. But Antony and Cleopatra cannot operate for long in such precarious polyphony. They work themselves out of ambivalence not through putting on some false certainty (this last is a privilege of *Romeo and Juliet* type love, in which skepticism can be put on hold). In mature lovers, suspending doubt cannot be maintained, but neither can ambiguity. The latter threatens the relationship with detached intellectualism in which competing perspectives are allowed to have too much say. For mature lovers (at least for these two), receding from ambivalence works through avoiding direct expression of love (itself predicated on the distinction between an emotion and its manifesta-

---

[14] For a most persuasive interpretation espousing suspending-judgment as the reaction this play demands, see Adelman (1973, especially the first part—e.g., p. 15). For similar views, see D. Traversi (1963, e.g., p. 79) and Charney (1961). L. J. Mills (1960) lists the many central questions regarding Cleopatra that are left unanswered by the play and refers to Gamaliel Bradford who has, as far back as 1898, suggested that it is sometimes useful to regard aporias in Shakespeare's plays as intentional choices.

tions) and moving into the performance and loving action traced above. When love is channeled into action, when it becomes something one primarily does rather than feels, questions of inner truths are avoidable.

We can now connect this to the indirect manifestation of love. The scene I am thinking of is the one where Cleopatra refrains from approaching Antony when he is in shame after losing Actium. Being defeated in Actium because of what he regards as his foolish mistakes is the specific point of Antony's own tragedy. Connecting shame, loss of orientation, and a sense of lateness—"the land bids me tread no more upon't, / It is asham'd to bear me. Friends, come hither: / I am so lated in the world that I / Have lost my way for ever"—is when maintaining a self-image breaks down. This crisis lets in the weakness that has been perpetually fenced out as far back as the initiating scene of this play.[15] And it is precisely at a dramatic stage so pregnant with tragic potentials that Shakespeare opts for an effect not wholly tragic. Several readers sensed an intended comic effect due to the numerous manifestations of Antony's weakness that begin to bombard the audience: losing the sea battle because of vain and foolish considerations; his unstable shifting between despair and resolution; his unsuccessful suicide attempt; his being hauled up to Cleopatra's monument while she complains of his weight; his trouble of getting a word in when he is dying because she needs to talk (IV.xv.41–48).[16] But the response to weakness that the text configures here seems to me more complicated especially in relation to Cleopatra's acceptance of him and her perceiving his difficulty in accepting love at that state. While some readers find cause for smiling, Cleopatra does not. It is *through this discrepancy*, between the possible perspectives an outsider can adopt and the one a lover actually endorses, that yet another crucial insight as to mature love is conveyed. Antony is in a moment of weakness that he is not really prepared to accept as a possible state for him. Comforting him, as Cleopatra realizes and her attendants do not, will offend him. Even approaching

---

[15] Fear of weakness can already be discerned in North's translation of Plutarch. Antony is there presented as believing that he is a descendant of Hercules and trying to live up to the image in terms of deed and appearance: "This opinion [that he is a descendant of Hercules] did Antonius seeke to confirme in all his doings: not onely resembling him in the likenes of his bodye, as we have sayd before, but also in the wearing of his garments" (p. 241). The preoccupation with adopting Hercules' appearance, Antony's own identity not being good enough, shows that the connections between the militant, the heroic, and the fear of one's own weakness are constitutive of Antony already in Shakespeare's source.

[16] J. L. Simmons (1973, pp. 149–52), D. Stempel (1956), A. P. Riemer (1968), and Adelman (1973, pp. 50–52).

him is to disrespect his reluctance to expose or accept his vulnerability. Indeed, when she does eventually approach him Antony tells her that he is conveying his shame out of her eyes (III.xi.51). Only after his death wish—that she should not recall what he is now but what he was—do we realize what Cleopatra knew already here: that somewhere along the line Antony relates to her as an admiring audience that should never see him in his shame.[17] In not approaching him after Actium, Cleopatra shows that she realizes this. Such subtle moves, intended to enable Antony to persevere in regarding her as admiring him, are the sort of loving gestures we need to look for when mature lovers directly communicate.[18]

Moreover, when she finally approaches him, she not only diminishes her presence but is also accepting responsibility for his mistake. This is a loving act, which is, incidentally, one of Shakespeare's delicate additions to his sources. Plutarch and Daniel do not mention such uncalled-for acceptance on her part. In the Garnier-Pembroke play, she truly believes she is the "sole cause" of the loss at Actium (line 448 in Bullough's edition). Only in Shakespeare is Cleopatra made to assume guilt that she knows she does not have to take on. In this loving gesture, she is responding to Antony's actions at Actium. She realizes that going after her ship was not only a military mistake (which is all Enobarbus sees) but also a profound act of love. Her loving sacrifice is repaid immediately by Antony:

    CLEO.   Pardon, pardon!
    ANT.   Fall not a tear, I say, one of them rates
                 All that is won and lost: give me a kiss,
                 Even this repays me.

---

[17] Cavell, I take it, sees both Antony and Cleopatra as becoming each other's world and then withdrawing from being that (1987, pp. 24–29). Those who would follow Cavell in believing that skepticism underlies this play too (hence something in marriage makes up for the disappearance of the world) can relate to my remarks above as symptomatic of philosophical anxieties over skepticism that the play (for them) unfolds.

[18] Cleopatra's disorientation when they lose the battle further strengthens our sense of the consideration she here shows Antony. For Cleopatra, losing Actium has all the political and personal consequences of a queen losing a battle. Her lost sense of security is indicated by her language moving from assertions to questions. She becomes dependent on the opinions of her escorts and the judgment of Enobarbus. Moreover, since Cleopatra's love for Antony is a distilled form of admiration, a crisis in her emotional world is also to be expected when the great man fails. In Cleopatra's world, this "soldier's pole" failing in the battle, threatens to disrupt the projected elements that are regulative in her love story. Yet, throughout this crisis, she manages to choose the action that is most considerate to him. For a similar claim regarding the way by which kindness to a person involves not saying some things, see Daniel Brudney's discussion of *The Golden Bowl* (1990).

I claimed that through instances such as this, Cleopatra indirectly manifests her love.

Finally, at the exact moment of Antony's dying, the play shows how mature love involves *rechoosing* a privileged perspective of the loved one:

> ANT. I am dying Egypt, dying.
> Give me some wine, and let me speak a little.
> CLEO. No, let me speak, and let me rail so high,
> That the false huswife Fortune break her wheel,
> Provok'd by my offence.
> ANT. One word, sweet queen:
> Of Caesar seek your honour, with your safety. O!
> CLEO. They do not go together.
> ANT. Gentle, hear me . . .
> [. . . .]
> ANT. Now my spirit is going,
> I can no more.
> CLEO. Noblest of men, woo't die?
> Hast thou no care of me, shall I abide
> In this dull world, which in thy absence is
> No better than a sty? O, see my women:
> The crown o'the earth doth melt.
>   [*Antony dies.*]
>   (IV.xv.41–63)

Something altogether different than a comic effect is intended when she prevents him from speaking in the first lines above. In another scene of separation, when Antony departs for Rome (I.iii), Cleopatra interrupts him six times giving him no chance to talk.[19] Drowning separation with talk seems to be her method in coping with such moments. The specific nature of her words in both scenes is similar. In the earlier scene, she charges Antony with being untruthful and insincere. Here too he goes to his death hearing her loving accusation: "Hast thou no care of me, Shall I abide in this dull world, which in thy absence is no better than a sty?" His final thought concerns her loneliness and his blame in deserting her in this sty. But then, note Shakespeare's touch in letting her say (and Antony hear) just one more line before he dies: "O, see, my women: the crown o'the earth doth melt." In moving from blaming him to imaging

---

[19] For discussion, see Mills, 1960.

his dying as a decomposing crown of the earth, she finally lets herself recede into the adoring audience he always wanted her, as well as everyone else, to be.

Philosophy and Literature

Turning to the relations between literature and knowledge that this reading invites, we can begin with the idea of contingency: the conceptual connections emphasized in this reading are not necessary. As I have been urging previously, this need not alarm philosophers. One cannot erect valid arguments proving that mature lovers tend to communicate through practices rather than by expressing an overwhelming affect. Yet, confining oneself to valid argument—'valid' in the traditional sense of the impossibility of affirming the premises with the negation of the conclusion—is not only to err by adopting a limited conception of rationality but also by erroneously identifying truth with necessary truth. Realizing this brings up the need for nonvalid argumentative routes that can yet facilitate the process of rationally grounding contingent claims. One such informal move that rhetoric includes and that was often appropriated regarding the literature-philosophy connections is Aristotle's idea of implication from example. Authors such as Sirridge, Pollard, Nussbaum, and Eldridge argued that learning from the literary work—in our case, the details of a relationship—can be regarded as a process by which knowledge claims are derived from complex examples or counterexamples. Learning from a literary work is thus as rational as other noninductive implications that can legitimately be derived from examples. Claiming that this play generates knowledge will accordingly begin with contending that since Antony and Cleopatra exemplify something that pertains to mature lovers in general, one may cautiously generalize from them to others, or at least see that what is true of them can sometimes be reapplied.

The realization that these lovers "exemplify" anything is not itself supported by the literary text but registers something that the reader has independently sensed. This is how one arrives at another popular suggestion through which literature and knowledge are often woven together: the idea that literature can articulate experiences similar to and sometimes identical with those that one has in life. Is it anachronistic to endorse such a position, when accounting for our experience of a Renaissance play? I think not. Even more historicist-inclined critics have never denied that Shakespeare manages to capture some of the deepest thoughts and sentiments that we too entertain. Historical evidence as to early-modern love conventions points to ambivalent and conflicting attitudes some of which are certainly continuous with our own. It therefore appears at the very least as plausible to suppose that Shakespeare's audience would have found the play to articulate some of their sentiments in much the same terms specified here, as to suppose that these reactions are peculiar to us. Admitting such points of contact need not entail a belief in ahistorical *Aeternae Veritates* (though beyond dogmatic dismissals, I know of no arguments that deny the possibility of these). Nothing here depends on assuming eternal truths but on a minimal assumption that has never been rejected: texts written at different times and cultures have a remarkable capacity to come into suggestive meaningful dialogue with contemporary minds.

The existence of nonliterary examples and nonliterary linguistic formulations means that relying on articulation and exemplification cannot suffice in the context of an argument aiming to establish philosophical gains through the experiences that literature fashions. When we attempt to account for what such 'experience' may mean, we reach a third conventional route through which literature and knowledge have been conjoined. Literature "conveys" rather than simply "describes" knowledge claims. "Conveying" is a mode of imparting knowledge in which not only the intimated claim is at stake. Conveying is a mode of telling that involves configuring in highly specific ways the state of mind of recipients. It reenacts an experiential structure that overlaps and resembles the experience that it describes (though is not identical to it).[20] In literary texts, this is achieved through the suggestive capacities of the work. Suggestiveness is itself legitimate when something needs to bridge the gap between available rational support and the need for some stronger confirmation that one can never have. The argument above as to the contingent logical status of the knowledge-claims that are conveyed and the rhetorical distinction between conveying and describing are thus interwoven in the following way: the construction of a cognitive experience allows for some contingent insights—which, as I claimed above, are

---

[20] I will not enter the question of differences and similarities between responses as part of literature and nonfictional responses. "Resembles" above obviously requires further unpacking, but I think that it is informative as it stands: emotions elicited by literary works resemble but are not identical to emotions one experiences in relation to lived experiences. Acknowledging the quantitative and qualitative differences does not disqualify talk of resemblance.

themselves supported by the rational, nonvalid reasoning that the work prompts—to be embedded within a structure that "conveys" rather than simply "describes" them.

The terminology of conveying invites a different variation of the charge of anachronism. Asserting that the play generates given responses in its audience, when this is unpacked into particularized reception patterns, appears to again depend heavily on the sort of cultural sensitivities and narratives that different interpretive communities cultivate. Arguing that either Shakespeare or, to avoid intentional categories, his play "conveys" certain claims through emplotting them within complex experiences seems to dubiously presuppose that widely differing response patterns can be simply lumped together by an organizing perspective that is unaware of its own situated biases. The response to this complaint is that the reference to "experiences" above should not be regarded merely as descriptive terminology that designates what actual (past or present) readers or "we" undergo. The category of experience as used above and in this book as a whole is not a given but an invitation. Interpretations are *suggestions* as to ways for fruitful communication with texts. Such a metainterpretive stance diminishes the threat of anachronism since nothing depends on whether or not the proposed experiences necessarily conform to what a contemporary of the author would have naturally felt. Having said this, I do think that something is gained by showing that proposed response patterns are or have been shared by other readers (which is one advantage of analyzing works that have been heavily commented on before). The uniquely philosophical element of the mode of commentary that is proposed here is not, however, to simply record repetitive patterns of response but to reflect on these in relation to the conceptual content that the work exposes.

To stress again, such a vision regarding meaningful philosophical dialogue with the past does not imply some ahistorical intellectual stance in which all cultures and times are viewed from an allegedly unsituated perspective. It does not involve the threat of drifting "back toward a conception of art as addressed to a timeless, cultureless, universal essence," which Stephen Greenblatt warns of in the opening pages of *Renaissance Self-Fashioning*. The past's otherness should be respected since it is itself a source through which the dialogue with it gains much of its interest and import for people who are enmeshed in different conceptual nets. Otherness should not, however, turn into means by which the past is being progressively insulated, which is one—surely unintended—result of turning literary criticism into anthropology.

Articulation, exemplification, and unique intellectual responses are familiar features through which the links between knowledge and literature have been theorized, and connecting them in the way I just did covers most of the points argued for in this reading. A nonvalid yet rational move is being embedded within an aesthetic context that facilitates forming beliefs regarding contingent claims—that is, claims that cannot be rigorously established through argumentative procedures alone.

Grasping the disharmony between one's own response and the one the text portrays is another route that creates understanding. The divergences between actual response and fictional action enable the play to treat the problem of coming to terms with ambivalence as part of mature love. The play thus creates a gap between "our" own ability to maintain ambivalence regarding what Antony and Cleopatra share as opposed to the inability of the lovers themselves to maintain it. This positioning of the reader enables experiencing—not merely intellectualizing—something that pertains to ambiguity: a state of mind readily accessible when analyzing other relationships, but threatening when it comes to one's own. This emphasis on undergoing experiences rather than having them described is also how one avoids paraphrasing either art or the aesthetic experience.

But there is a further argument that should be contemplated in the context of specifying philosophical gains, one that deepens our perspective regarding what our notion of erotic understanding should encompass. I have so far proceeded with the assumption that "understanding" involves a collection of propositions that, through various justifications, turn into beliefs. In Ryle's terms, I was working with a "knowing that" concept of understanding. Philosophy-literature theory has known one very important addition to Ryle's "knowing that"/"knowing how" distinction: D. Walsh's "knowing what it is like." Writers who have underscored literature's ability to create empathy have appropriated Walsh's addition, arguing that empathic involvement enables us to experience what it is like to be in situations an "external" perspective of which tends to distort. But thinking of the way by which *Antony and Cleopatra* enlarges our understanding of love invites us to think of a fourth kind of knowledge: knowing the shapes through which things may come.

Knowledge is not merely a specification of our true beliefs. Broadly conceived, knowledge is a way by which we connect with the world. To sort out reality is to create knowledge that boils down to sharpened recognition, to picking out an entity as one thing rather than another. Some such knowledge can be reduced to "knowing that": we know *that* love can take the shape it has in this play. Since recognition is also an ability, some such knowledge can be reduced to "knowing how": the play enables us to know *how* to recognize some complicated forms that love may take. Yet knowing the shape that things may take is more than an improvement in recognition skills. It is also not merely growth in a body of beliefs. While these additions occur, the knowledge I am tracing primarily pertains to the scope and sensitivity of one's outlook, to the sharpness of one's response to vague and ambivalent inputs. We assess perceived inputs relative to some *background* that has now grown rather than be equipped with more perceptions. (An analogous example that may clarify what I mean by "background," as distinguished from the specific capacities that it promotes, is learning a new mathematical function, which is never simply reducible to merely knowing the answers to a set of new exercises. Pace those who will reduce all knowing to actual or potential behavior, learning such a mathematical function *manifests* itself in solving new exercises; it is not identical with it.) The love of Antony and Cleopatra does not primarily boil down to more beliefs or enhances capacities but becomes an additional coordinate through which we can describe other relationships.

Could such growth in understanding occur without literature, say, by reading this interpretation instead and avoiding the play? I think not. While some gains in understanding may be had by this method, the need to *implant* an additional coordinate of thought means that it is insufficient to grasp some themes as possibilities. One has to actually make them internal "talking" parts of one's perspective. Such internalization requires undergoing the experience of reading created by the powerful rhetorical capacities of poetry—the sort of poetry that J. M. Murry thought no reader could ever forget.

On Being Too Deeply Loved

I READ *OTHELLO* as a detailed portrayal of an erotic refusal on Othello's part. This reading is continuous with the corpus of scholarship on the play that (mostly implicitly) avoids the assumption that Iago's insinuations suffice to explain Othello's actions. Arthur Kirsch followed F. R. Leavis in highlighting how Iago simply echoes Othello's own words in the "temptation scene," thereby emphasizing that "the process we are witnessing is fundamentally an internal one" (1978, p. 733). As for attributing the tragic outcome to Iago's demonic rhetorical capacities that Othello is supposedly helpless to resist, this option is no longer persuasive since, as Leo Kirschbaum notes, Iago tells four different people (including, apart from the unimpressive Cassio and Emilia, the play's fool, Roderigo) that Desdemona is unchaste, and the only one who seems to believe him is Othello (1944, p. 158). Cavell (1987, p. 133) also notes Othello's tacit cooperation with Iago's accusation pointing out Othello's obsession with calling Iago "honest," thereby conveying strong suspicions in each of their exchanges. Cavell also says that if Othello would not have met Iago, he would have invented a different one (1987, p. 112). Mason, in discussing the temptation scene, comments that it is not always obvious who is leading whom. We need to add to these the moments in which Othello's suspicions of Iago turn into practical demands, as when he asks for ocular proof (III.iii.194), or when he personally interrogates Emilia (IV.II.1–18), or when, finally, he confronts Desdemona (V.ii.48–76). Apart from preventing his being taken for a fool, the more subtle function of these moments is to suggest Othello's over casual dismissal of the possibility that Iago is misleading him.

These considerations preclude agreement with J. W. Draper (1966) who accepts Othello's jealousy at face value, attributing it to the built-in jealousy of an oriental, a soldier, or a person with an inborn choleric humor. Jealousy is here a complicated outcome, not a cause, and the other explanations either amount to a stereotypically reductive view of the military or involve alienating Othello from any reader/viewer who happens not to share the theory of humors. In the context of resisting the erotic, of—to use Cavell's terms—avoiding love, the question to ask is why, for *this* man in particular, should there be such a temptation to fall out of love? Commentators have offered several solutions to this puzzle.

Othello is said to be a limited lover (or not in love at all); or sexually repressed; or else he does not accept various parts of himself due to the various dimensions of his otherness, so that he cannot be loved in his own eyes; or he is unable to come to terms with Desdemona's sexuality.[1] I shall not arbitrate between these interpretations or attempt to argue them away[2] since they contribute to an understanding of the various strands of meaning that create the play's richness. Many of them, however, are insufficient in one important respect. While they may succeed in explaining why Othello works himself out of love, they do not account

---

[1] Heilman (1956, pp. 216–18) sees here an insurmountable opposition between Eros and Agape in which the "unredeemed egotism" of a "man of affairs" nourishes "a large image of himself" and thus withholds himself "from a transforming devotion" (174). Othello's exchange of his "unhoused free condition" for Desdemona's love, which exceeds the "sea's worth" in his first avowal of love for her, reveals that for him love is a mode of negotiation and bargaining. Similarly, Slights (1997) talks of Othello as destroying love due to anxieties of losing control and becoming vulnerable. Kott (1966), Hallstead (1968), Greenblatt (1980), Snow (1980), and Cavell (1987) think that Othello unleashes Desdemona's frightening sexuality and that what transpires in him later is a manifestation of phobia (Cavell), or some Stoically inspired religious resentment of sexual overindulgence (Greenblatt), or the "post-coital male disgust with the 'filthy deed' of sexuality itself" (Snow, 1980, p. 388). Kirschbaum claims that Othello is an idealist escaping reality, swinging from "overtrust to unjust suspicion in a twinkling" (160); Kirschbaum links his explanation to Maud Bodkin's earlier suggestion that Othello cannot bear Desdemona's move from idealized lover to wife of flesh and blood. Othello's otherness and hybrid identity constitute a fourth possible explanation, that interweaves falling out of love to problems of self-acceptance. If he, indeed, lives in two worlds (Bartels, 1997), and if the play does involve a "progressive racialization of the protagonist" in which Othello reverts from being a Venetian to being the anonymous other (Neil, 1998, p. 374), or, alternatively, turns from being a baptized Moor, a "walking paradox," back to being a circumcised Muslim (Vitkus, 1997, p. 161), or, alternatively, if he is developing and internalizing the image of his blackness as pollution and himself as a polluter of Desdemona (Adelman, 1997), or if he becomes jealous since he cannot accept his own aging (Stavropoulos, 1987), or if he is being pushed by Iago to hate himself since he is *both* old and black (Kirsch, 1978), or suffers from subconscious shame due to his complicated status as outsider (Fernie, 1999), his inability to accept love would relate to difficulties that have to do with coming to terms with his own split identity. Desdemona reciprocates only one part of his complicated identity: one that other parts of him violently despise. Related to this is the view that Othello has no problems of identity: he simply cannot believe his own improbable love story (Hollingdale, 1989). There is also the Leavis view (1952), according to which Othello never loved Desdemona in the first place, or the idea that he loves Cassio, rather than Desdemona, and so the jealousy is nothing but the voice of his suppressed homosexuality (Feldman, 1952).

[2] I do argue, however, by way of exception, against the Leavis position according to which Othello is not in love at all. This interpretation tends to collapse when one watches any dramatization of the Cyprus reunion scene.

for his murderous violence, for the fact that Othello does not merely reject Desdemona or their love story.[3]

THE MURDER

I begin with these sentences from the last act:

> Yet she must die, else she'll betray more men.
>
> I would not have thee linger in thy pain . . .
>
> Have you pray'd to-night, Desdemona?
>
> (V.ii.6, 89, 24)

How can we make sense of Othello's surprising state of mind during his murder of Desdemona? What can explain the way in which he adopts the role of a stately, consequentialist judge, worried that Desdemona will hurt others, as if his course of action now were nothing but a deed for the sake of the community? What can we make of the way in which he takes up the practical concerns of the professional and merciful executioner, worrying that the punished subject has prayed, and that she will not suffer unnecessarily? And how should we understand his regained gentleness just before the murder (IV.iii.11)?

Shakespeare does not present the murder as the outcome of an emotional upheaval of the sort we see when Othello strikes Desdemona. There can be psychological explanations for this: the barriers that one

---

[3] The readings that stress Othello's otherness become more persuasive as explanations of the *murder* (rather than explanations of Othello's withdrawal from love) when connected with Karen Newman's suggestion (1994) that Desdemona is not simply murdered but is punished for transgressing her cultural limitations—Othello being the paradoxical tool for the revenge. The problem with this explanation is that it makes the dramatic force of the murder scene entirely dependent on Othello's skin color. The case against underestimating the importance of Othello's blackness has been ably made by Jyotsna Singh (1994) and Ania Loomba (1994) as well as numerous other contributors to the collections edited by Barthelemy (1994) and Loomba and Orkin (1998). Loomba (1994) claims (and partly shows) that one must not disconnect the relations between Othello and Desdemona from aspects pertaining to gender or "race." The important issue of Othello's skin color is, however, unrelated to the aspect of the play with which I deal here. One set of remarks regarding Othello's blackness (that does not concern the links between skin color and alienation) that does not pertain to this chapter's claims regarding Othello's sense of selfhood has been offered by Kenneth Gross (2001, ch. 4). Gross underscores the progressive blackening of Othello's reputation in his own eyes as a process in which various allegations gnaw at his sense of self, not primarily due to the significance of skin color but because of diminished reputation.

runs up against when murder is merely personal can be somewhat eased off when the murder turns into a mission; the murder could also be construed—as it was by the Victorian actor Edwin Booth—as an act of sacrifice, connecting the killing with Othello's awakened religious sense; aloofness in killing may also be resorted to so as to transcend a submerged conflicted state of mind. These explanations—or the one appealing to the irony of turning Othello into a missionary of justice as he is committing the worst injustice—are dramatically satisfying, but *Othello* also suggests a further philosophical insight.

OTHELLO'S LOVE

It is Othello's merging with impersonal operating—both in the sense of detaching himself from his own feelings and of his identification with and subordination to impersonal forces—that points to the submerged pressures underlying his withdrawal from love. Turning into an instrument through which something else is channeled is not simply associated with the experience of murdering but is a culmination of a movement that involves the entire play. *Othello* explores the potential inherent in a character whose ascent on the social ladder is predicated not on love and respect but on the *good use* to which he can be put. Aside from his status—which may also have to do with his being a mercenary and what this means in terms of value as exhaustively determined by service[4]—there are numerous references, by others and by Othello to himself, that emphasize the instrumental way in which he relates to himself and his worth, solely by reference to "service."[5] The play as a whole presents a movement in which

---

[4] The significance of what may be involved in Othello's status as a leading soldier who is not a Venetian is discussed in Vaughan (1994, ch. 2). I shall avoid entering into the question of whether he is a mercenary or a citizen, or attempting to balance his reference to his royal lineage with his slavery, in terms of expected audience response. Othello's social status is certainly not inherited. And this last assumption is not affected by differing opinions on these questions.

[5] "Employed" (I.iii.47), *borne* to the duke on "present business of the state" (I.ii.91), such is the instrumental language applied to Othello from the very beginning. It is, moreover, the way in which he perceives his own value in his first lines in the play, when he regards "services" to the state as the source of his security against Brabantio's accusations (I.ii.18). He talks, further, of his arms as that which "us'd / Their dearest action in the tented field" (I.iii.85), already introducing his agency as subordinated to forces that he does not identify with himself. Instrumentalization is also supported by the many references to sex as use (III.iii.277) or ab-use (III.iii.204, 271, 342).

structuring of the self and self-value as use modifies an erotic experience that initially resists these categories.[6] While *loving* is not a problem for Othello—love, in the period's conceptualization, is itself sometimes a form of passivity and instrumentalization (James, 1997)—being *loved* is another matter. Othello's strange state of mind during the murder is thus a *retreat* from a sense of being that exists and is esteemed without reference to social use—back into a self that is governed by external missions and causes. Love is a condition in which he momentarily circumvents his favorite self-conceptualization as a tool. Othello's difficulty with this sudden resistance to instrumental categorization lies in its bringing out anxieties and an imbalance that relate to existential patterns he cannot understand.

We can note this ambiguous pattern—wanting and not wanting to be a tool—as early as when he unfolds the manner and evolution of his love story. The context in which Desdemona hears his adventures and the details of his hard life is one of use. Othello was invited "oft" to her father's house to relate "the story" of his life. "It was," he says, "my hint to speak," and so he did, his sad life providing colorful entertainment in Brabantio's house. In the midst of this, Othello privately intimates his story to Desdemona, in response to which she gives him "a world of sighs." He closes his narration of their premarital relationship by saying:

> She lov'd me for the dangers I had pass'd,
> And I lov'd her that she did pity them.
>
> (I.iii.151–68)

There is, in this love, no mention of Desdemona's beauty, to which everyone else recurrently alludes (Othello will harp on her beauty only when he begins to lose her). In contrast to *Romeo and Juliet*, here there

---

[6] The notions of selfhood and subjectivity (e.g., Greenblatt, 1990, pp. 131–45) are awkward impositions in the context of early-modern texts, but they cannot be ultimately avoided by any commentary that explores how characters relate to their own lives. Nor are they anachronistic since, if theorizing on the period's self is to be accepted (Burckhardt, Taylor, Belsey, Ferry, or Maus), our own notion of self is already emerging in these early-modern texts. Camille Wells Slights (1997) connected Othello's self-understanding with the birth of individual autonomy predicated on self-control rather than the older concept of self as part of some larger cosmos. She regards the play as acting out the anxieties involved in the threatening possibilities of isolation that the new self-fashioning involves. I shall argue for a somewhat different construal of Othello. The specific dualism that Stephen Greenblatt (1980, pp. 242–54) argues for, between a self predicated on a collection of heteronomic narratives and the other, Desdemona, as a devourer of these, is closer to my own view, especially with regard to a self's discomfort with his self-casting. However, I do not share Greenblatt's emphasis on Desdemona's sexuality or the centrality of stories for Othello.

is no captivating moment of love at first sight, no bewitchment by a heavenly figure for which everything else becomes a vague context. Nor do we have the complicated entrapment of Antony whose erotic interest in Cydnus is kindled by teasing his pride. Antony is sitting in a quickly emptying Egyptian town square which everyone is leaving. They all flock out to see the marvelous *local* queen, a move that suffices to get him "ten times barber'd over" before he goes to Cleopatra. Romeo relates to a figure, Antony is aroused by the *effects* of a figure. Othello loves because he is pitied.

Desdemona's Love

Pity, when sincere, need not be condescending. Othello does not feel patronized by Desdemona but is erotically drawn to her by noting her response. Pity is a noninstrumental relation to people in which actions and states are empathetically read in relation to the formative circumstances that caused them. It is thus a virtue that makes people at least as important as their deeds. Othello falls in love when he encounters pity directed at him, when, for a change, he is not being used but is understood, becoming the focal point of another's reality. If we only have our eyes on the text instead of imagining the lines being acted, we may miss the effect of moments such as:

> DES. 'Tis as I should entreat you wear your gloves;
> Or feed on nourishing dishes, or keep you warm,
> Or sue to you, to do a peculiar profit
> To your own person
>
> (III.iii.78–81)

Or:

> DES. Why is your speech so faint? Are you not well?
> OTH. I have a pain upon my forehead, here.
> DES. Faith, that's with watching, 'twill away again;
> Let me but bind your head, within this hour
> It will be well again.
>
> (III.iii.287–91)

Or:

> DES. Alas the heavy day, why do you weep?
> Am I the occasion of those tears, my lord?

> If haply you my father do suspect
> An instrument of this your calling back,
> Lay not your blame on me; if you have lost him,
> Why, I have lost him too.
>
> (IV.ii.44–49)

All these lines force the actress to relate to Othello in a manner that centers on his well-being, that make him the center of Desdemona's world. The erotic charm in finding maternal comfort in a young woman is, in Othello, working alongside Desdemona picking out and relating to some preformed structure within him, which his own self-conceptualization resists. The sexual component in Othello's attraction is not a dominant part of it, though the play gives us no reason to doubt that it is there.[7] He is fascinated with her whiteness ("whiter skin of hers than snow," V.ii.4), her angelic look ("like one of heaven," IV.ii.37), her "sweet body" (III.iii.352), and he refers to his craving for her as "the vices of my blood" (I.iii.123). All this discloses sexual attraction, mingled with his self-image hungrily latching onto her admiration for him (her wish "that heaven made her such a man," I.iii.163). This interpenetration of the sexual with the self-commending will make the possibility of betrayal even more disastrous than it would for other lovers because it will not merely ignite erotic possessiveness but threaten to preempt her previous admiration for him.

In fact, Othello misreads Desdemona. He says that she loved him for his dangers. However, when she discloses her manner of falling in love, Desdemona does not recall the "dangers" that he focuses on, but refers to having seen "Othello's visage in his mind," "his honours and his valiant parts" (I.iii.251–52). Othello thinks that she was responding to his story, whereas she perceived and pitied some deeper foundation of his being, seeing his source, his being "born in the sun." She will continue separating his actions from him to the very end of the tragedy, not making much of his abusive language or the fact that he hits her, until finally she even manages to devalue her own murder.

Jane Adamson thinks that in all this Desdemona is showing that she is "quite unable to recognize or acknowledge any of his less than honorable and valiant parts," that "it is precisely her naive loyal devotion to her adored ideal Othello that blinds her to his reality until it is too late"

---

[7] I am not persuaded by those for whom Othello is positively frightened by Desdemona's sexuality. I will argue that he is frightened by Desdemona, but it is not her sexuality that causes this.

(1980, 218–19). But downplaying the loved one's actions is not always blindness. In Desdemona it denotes a mode of connecting with the lover in ways that transcend what he does. Her portrayal includes much more than the self-delusions of an abused wife: the play weds the range and depth of Desdemona's love with Othello's anxieties and limitations. In his repeated accusations of her being a "strumpet" or a "whore," Othello is pushing Desdemona toward those who, by profession, use love. He thus attempts to move her into a mode of response to him that he can make sense of.[8] This attempt latently underlies his violence as well. Whatever else it may involve, on some level, verbal and physical violence is also a call for response to one's actions. Othello would rather have such a reaction than continue to experience an unbearable penetrating love that sees through to his source. By way of this separation between what he is and his biography, Desdemona reflects onto Othello something to which he responds but never fully grasps. We see this when he says that Desdemona pitied his "dangers." He is not saying that she pitied *him*. He is thus identifying himself with his story whereas Desdemona's vision of self maintains a separation between people and their actions. And in his growing abuse of her, Othello wants this kind of love to stop somehow.

This love story and its tragic end are the outcome of a discrepancy between the service through which Othello structures himself and some flowing essence to which Desdemona's loving gaze is attached. I refer to "flowing" because Othello repeatedly images himself, his worth, his life, and his inner experience through aquatic figures (I.ii.28; III.iii.462; IV.ii.48–63; V.ii.269). The images of life as a stream, or the lover as one's "source," are conventional, but in Othello's case, they carry the additional association not only of a person who can be channeled but also of one who preserves something of his presolidified identity. Note too Othello's curious reference to chaos ("But I do love thee, and when I love thee not, / Chaos is come again"; III.iii.92–93), which reflects an inability to make sense of one's life. Othello's allusion to the chaos of Genesis before he loved Desdemona attests to the complicated experience of a life that is based, understood, and valued solely in terms of service. In one way, such a life seems clear-cut, its steps and curves making utmost

---

[8] The associative connections between sex and service (e.g., *King Lear*, III.iv.82–94) suggest that by harping on Desdemona's sexuality and her "use," Othello is able to fashion her into an entity that is analogous to his own service-related personality, thus making both of them part of the same world. I am obliged to Rebecca Gillis (Hebrew University) for calling my attention to the sex-service connection and to the passage in *King Lear*.

sense. There is also, however, that deeper confusion that underlies a well-ordered functioning, when one is not living a life but living a career. Othello is thereby referring to *the chaotic in regularity of function*, to living a well-regulated chaos.

The erotic bond that Desdemona promises is not one of biographies, like the sort of companionship notable in Antony and Cleopatra. Desdemona's offer is of a deeper level of connection, in which she sees as far as his watery, as yet unshaped, source. This is an offering that ignores the self's roots of respect and pride, and whatever has contributed to Othello's stand against the world, the self as a project, meticulously built over many years. This also means that a less penetrating lover than Desdemona would, perhaps, have survived. Thus Cleopatra's attunement to the magnanimous Herculean image that Antony constantly strives to live up to is, I have argued in the previous chapter, a loving choice among alternative, less commending, visions. And yet, like Antony, she is limited to a version of the self that identifies people with their actions and reputations. Cleopatra and Antony *waver* between diverging evaluative descriptions concerning themselves and their value that they either wish to maintain or dismiss, but never contemplate relating to each other in ways that go beyond such idealized descriptions. After all, standing "peerless," they form an unparalleled match for the whole world to marvel at. Othello shares Antony's preoccupation with forming and retaining an admirable image. But while Antony's experience is one of merging with this image—his tragedy consisting of a rupture forming between it and him—Othello *maintains* the gap from the beginning.

The erotic mismatch in *Othello* consists of Desdemona's penetrating loving gaze as unbearable for Othello, since it brings out something that resists reduction to the instrumental, a reduction that is what he is about. Othello's tragedy is that he should never have been loved, at least not like that. That is "the pity of it." If one perceives the dualism that tears apart Othello, one is also able to avoid taking Othello as merely manipulated by Iago. To say that Iago's naturalism and reductive outlook impress Othello as wisdom is surely to diminish Othello and to ignore the subliminal logic that leads to his *cooperation* with Iago. Instead, this marriage of minds (culminating in Iago committing himself to Othello's service) exposes Othello's attraction to an outlook that he understands and prefers to coping with the disruptive force of "too much joy." Iago is, in fact, Othello's mode of resistance and something in him is using Iago so that it can bloom to full expression.

And yet, though all this accounts for the willing recession from love and the collaboration with Iago, it does not explain the killing.

Othello's Tragedy

More than the discrepancy between the mild degree of love that he sought and the extreme one that he received, at the height of his "happiness" Othello discovers the violence of loving acceptance. Somewhere, Othello perceives that in Desdemona's complete loving devotion—which persists in spite of whatever monstrosities he can commit: it is a love that thus *cannot be lost*—a war is being launched against what he has worked his entire life to create. Something in this loving saint makes his personality irrelevant. On the most fundamental level, the tragedy is thus about the limitations of erotic bliss. It is about the psychological murder implied by the very idea of an erotic bond that transcends action and contingent biography. Such a bond is at once attractive (erotic acceptance that is conditional on accomplishment is unappealing) and, as Othello shows, also repulsive. The play is about the happy, painless destruction of a person that is conducted within the clasp of a loving embrace. This tragedy is so overwhelming precisely because it amplifies the loss within the confines of the supposedly sacred peaks of life.[9]

---

[9] Is love a "life's peak" for Elizabethans? Critics such as Babb (1951) or Stempel (1956) would have replied in the negative, telling us that love is not idealized but ridiculed or likened to an illness. More sensitive accounts, such as those by Dickey (1966) or Rose (1968, pp. 1–24), provide a much more ambivalent picture. "O sacred love, / If there be any heaven in earth 'tis love" says the Nurse in Marlowe's *Dido, Queen of Carthage* (IV.v.26–27), showing that the idealization of love did not skip over early-modern England. Of course, the idealization of love goes back at the very least to the courtly tradition (if not to Plato's *Phaedrus* or the Orphic roots of Platonic thought). The connection between erotic and spiritual bliss, or love as a form of moral improvement that is continuous with religious requirements, was built into the formation of the romantic ideal in twelfth-century France (de Rougemont, 1974, pp. 78–96; Hunt, 1960, p. 130). Thus, rather than touching a comic theme, Shakespeare was concerned with a state that included (and still includes) many religious undertones. The age and color difference between Othello and Desdemona as well as the self-created jealousy also cohere with courtly love's perpetual need for creating obstacles. In short, in spite of Puritan criticism (which only attests to the power and hold of its object), love was very much a source of idealization for Shakespeare's contemporaries (recall Romeo's religiosity in relation to Juliet). I would, however, add that unless one is implausibly supposing that artistic creation is exhaustively determined by social conventions, an appeal to social norms has limited value.

Othello's problems with happiness point to this tragic dimension already at the Cyprus reunion. "It is too much of joy," he gleefully tells Desdemona as they kiss, disclosing a resistance to the happiness provided by the woman who is his "soul's joy." Each time he mentions happiness and love, he associates them with destruction (II.i.189, 197; III.iii.91–93). This stands in sharp contrast to Desdemona's imagery of happiness, in which she wants it to grow further (II.i.194–95). Resistance to happiness may involve the anxieties set off by touching life's peaks. We note Othello's fear that not another moment like this will ever come (II.i.189–93), and we could also mention other patterns that may well be at work.[10] But there are also less expected strands of meaning here. In his endearing reference to Desdemona as his "fair warrior" when she comes in, his love-talk betrays a desire to annex her to his world, and this coheres with his need for a love based on biography. But as he is talking to her, looking at her as he does so, something in him realizes that this wish will not be fulfilled. Twice the "calmness" that he says she offers arouses in him thoughts of "death" (II.i.185–86, 188), and this in the context of the first words uttered in a loving reunion! If we ignore the kind of love Desdemona is offering, these words could be passed off for conventional figures or as standard Renaissance references to orgasm or some such. But in emphasizing the erotic anxieties of a

---

Marc Shell (1982, p. 64 n. 30) claims that in lines 25–40 in *The Pheonix and the Turtle*, Shakespeare makes explicit the annihilation-through-erotic-union theme. Readers who share Shell's understanding of these lines may feel that—given Shakespeare's supposedly direct preoccupation with the theme—my reading of *Othello* can be cast through more intentionalist language.

[10] Happiness is a condition of being rather than doing and this may explain something of the inability to contain it in an operator like Othello. This explanation and the one appealing to erotic resistance are associated with familiar themes in contemporary thought regarding the action-based constitution of masculinity and a couple's symbiosis as a threat. Note, for example, that when they meet at Cyprus, Othello storms off with no less than six allusions to himself and his love, while Desdemona instinctively replies with reference to "our love." This gets him talking of *his* joy and content, and when he does finally refer to them as a joint entity, he speaks of "discord." Age difference is also a factor. The love of young people tends to accommodate merging, whereas symbiosis is a problem for older individuals, who have already established a developed sense of self. Unlike the different ways in which Romeo and Juliet and Antony and Cleopatra are, respectively, matched in terms of age, in *Othello* Shakespeare is trying to capture the operations of age difference and the problems it creates. For an exploration of this last issue, and the subliminal connections between Brabantio and Othello as older men who share a paternal position, see Snow (1980) and Stavropoulos (1987).

mature character as opposed to the ease with which a young woman unproblematically turns into a lover, *Othello* highlights the self-imposed barriers that hold back the more disconcerting forces that operate within the erotic haven.[11]

The connection between love and war, previously discussed by de Rougemont and Firestone, usually brings to mind male aggression along with the entire symbolism of courtship or sex as a battle in which women are besieged.[12] But *Othello* presents erotic aggression as operating through more subtle routes that do not involve instrumentalization or ownership but are inherent in loving acceptance. Something in Othello tells him that he is under an offensive, that Desdemona's love is an attack:

> OTH. Think on thy sins.
> DES. They are loves I bear to you.
> OTH. Ay, and for that thou diest.
>
> (V.ii.39–41)

Love is a form of attack, as is sweetness, which is capable of killing: "So sweet was ne'er so fatal" (V.ii.20). And this connects with his strange desire to love her *after* he has killed her (V.ii.118–19) as well as with his

---

[11] Throughout the play, and in these scenes in particular, Shakespeare associates happiness, love, and the resistance to these with two kinds of knowing. Othello's conflicting desires are not presented merely as an opposition between the need to be loved and the need to avoid it but are complicated by a conflict between what one sees and what one suspects. The moving way in which Othello's suspicions disappear when he sees Desdemona, his inability to maintain his accusations as he looks at her, his inability to argue at length with her, all reflect the impact of immediate connection as it dissolves his older self. Looking at this woman tells him something while visual disconnection makes his destructive doubts gnaw from within. Shakespeare is thus structuring Othello's conflict as an opposition between two kinds of knowing: one is fueled by proofs and evidence, the other is created within the space of a gaze. And yet, neither is "knowledge." Beneath the language of assertions, proof, refutation, and judgment are forces of disintegration and resistance that are covered up by the terminology of knowing. Knowing, in *Othello*, has been extensively and variously discussed (e.g., in Heilman, 1956; Curtis, 1973; McGuire, 1973; Adamson, 1980; Cavell, 1987; and, in its complex relations with sexuality, in Parker, 1994). My reading differs from these in suggesting that the dualism of knowing and seeming to know, rejecting and embracing knowledge-claims, relates to the tacit war that underlies erotic happiness.

[12] On the general pattern, see Cooper et al. (1989). In Shakespeare, such imagery is exploited most obviously and insistently in *The Rape of Lucrece*. The older poem shares iconic similarities with *Othello* in having male aggressors standing over sleeping women, but, unlike the poem, the play stages reciprocal aggression.

suicide (which, incidentally, is a deviation from the source in Cynthio). Possessing her in the afterlife conveys the need to live this life to its end and to connect with the beloved only after the lover's older identity has been eradicated. Somewhere in his being, Othello discovers the annihilating aspect of love, and so acceptance of an erotic invitation is a modality of self-destructiveness (cf. Aristophanes' fable in Plato's *Symposium*, where the lovers who are uniting cannot really explain to Hephaestus, who inquires about their wishes, *what it is that they want*).[13] In this light, Othello's suicide is not simply the outcome of blame or shame or some other variant of self-hatred, but rather constitutes a final acceptance of the offering that is what Desdemona is and always was. He kills her, he kills himself, and only after this literal acting out of the abstract notions through which a non-biography-centered erotic bond makes sense, can he love her as he promised to when he talked of loving *after* killing (which is also why, for him, " 'tis happiness to die"). His suicide comes after a speech in which he asks to be remembered according to the most honorable moments of his biography. He then destroys this identity, dying, appropriately, "upon a kiss."[14]

Philosophy and Literature

Responding to the play in this way is reading against the built-in mystical and religious constituents that underlie the contemporary idealization of love. And yet, relating to the play as a progressive configuration of a spectacle of *Liebestod*, one that outlines what love's ideology masks—love as murder to both parties, love as an invitation to die, love as a war in which the previous self struggles to maintain its ground, love

---

[13] The formulation of love through the two-that-become-one scheme would have carried biblical weight for Shakespeare's audience. Referring to Genesis, James I says this about marriage: ". . . for she [your wife] must be nearer unto you than any other company, being 'flesh of your flesh and bone of your bone,' as Adam said of Eve"; "[treat your wife in all things as] the half of yourself" (James I. *Basilikon Doron*, p. 137, 141).

[14] Readers who are less skeptical than myself about the importance of sex in this relationship can read these remarks alongside Cavell's interpretation of the play. For Cavell, the murder scene enacts something of the missing wedding night, and in this sense, Cavell is also reading the play in terms of love as murder (1987, p. 132, 134). But unlike the process sketched in this reading, for Cavell, dying boils down to Othello deflowering Desdemona and thereby destroying purity (virginity) in himself (p. 130). If the previous reading makes sense, there is a process of erotic murder that has little to do with deflowering, and thus enables reapplication in contexts that do not involve virginity.

as happy suicide—explains the hold this play has always exercised on the audience.[15] Jealousy, otherness, shame, etc., can go only so far in making sense of our response, but they cannot account for the chilling sensation that any re-reader feels on meeting again that stage direction of the fifth act: "A bed chamber in the castle; Desdemona in bed asleep; enter Othello with a light." For what we are about to witness is not merely a man throwing away his happiness but the enactment of a cultural nightmare: the emergence of the suppressed perspective concerning what is supposed to be the pinnacle of one's life's experience.

On one level, Othello's tragedy relates to a willingness to withdraw from love because of difficulties with happiness and a resistance to being too deeply loved. It involves a murder (rather than leaving Desdemona or taking a lover—consider again Antony's much more prudent course of action upon his marital dissatisfaction—banishing her, or even having her secretly killed by an assassin, etc.) for reasons that go beyond the surface meaning, which consists of Othello reaching a stage of blinding anger due to skillful manipulations of his possessiveness. *Othello*'s movement culminates in an explicit destruction of what promises (and threatens) to be the source of his happiness. In one way, the murder is thus *a compressed visual representation* of the whole tragic movement as a prolonged iconic depiction of a most extreme form of resisting happiness. Being extreme, the tragic representation thus personifies, captures, and amplifies what some readers/viewers experience in mitigated form in their own inner lives (the dramatic device itself, an allegorized externalization of a battle within the soul—psychomachia—was often deployed in morality plays). As in the Platonic analogy of learning, what is said in small letters by looking at the larger ones, self-knowledge and self-shaping are achieved through a hyperbolic personification of lived conflicts.

The play enacts the mechanisms of love as war, love as destruction of the loved one, and love as a mode of self-annihilation. It does not simply

---

[15] The *Liebestod* motif is usually understood in terms of love *leading* to death (Northcote, 1984) rather than love as a form of dying that we see here. Shakespeare's *Romeo and Juliet* exemplifies the former pattern, though the closing picture of love inside a tomb is richer than merely chronological or causal relations. De Rougemont associates love with death through romantic love's craving for obstacles, death being the ultimate obstacle and therefore an ultimate source of attraction. This thesis is a more useful explanatory tool in relation to *Tristan and Iseult* rather than Othello, who is talking of afterlife reunion. A more interesting source for comparison with *Othello* are the myths of lovers who go to Hades—undergo a symbolic stage of dying—so as to retrieve their loved ones.

show that love can turn into violence (given jealousy, lack of security relating to one's otherness, sexual anxieties, a Iago, etc.) but presents a vision in which love *is* violence. A personification of the inner forces by dramatic roles would have been a conventional theatrical norm for an audience accustomed to morality plays. But we need not suppose that Shakespeare's contemporaries related to the play in the way I am describing here, or that Shakespeare necessarily intended it to be seen in this way. Interpretation is not an art of deciphering but a mode of fruitful communication with the work's potential meanings. An interpretation is a discovery and acceptance of one of the suggestions that jointly constitute the text. Interpretive discourse itself offers its findings as a rewarding way to relate to the text—which explains the feeling of some interpreters that they become, in some sense, part of the authorial act rather than its detached observers.

To relate in this way to *Othello* is to use it against the entrenched ideology concerning the supposed best in life. *Othello* can, through this reading, turn into a *critique*, albeit one that differs from nonliterary ideological criticism in its manner of operation. It uses the language of personification of forces and creates a condensed icon embedded in a richly configured experience instead of taking recourse to discursive understanding. Deciding whether this last modality of thought is or is not an advantage depends on the relative sympathy or antipathy to epistemological assumptions and argumentation procedures that have been established by Enlightenment philosophers and the post-Ramist rhetorical ethos that they instilled. If logos is a necessary advance over mythos; if contexts of discovery are irrelevant to questions of justification; if justification needs to be always universal and public; if suggestiveness is always illegitimate manipulation; if the aesthetic/emotive/imaginative is opposed to the cognitive, then we are surely degrading cultural criticism as well as this play in opting to see it as a critique. And yet, if the argument of the opening chapters is correct, assent to the Enlightenment argumentative ethos involves losing contact with important sources of understanding.

In contrast to this method, philosophical criticism of literary works constitutes a method that ultimately enables new dimensions of moral life to be meaningfully addressed. The primary focus of such criticism is fashioning the epistemological conditions for thought that manages to avoid simplistic cleverness. One such condition is working oneself into a position in which aspects of one's own formation can be related to anew. The epistemological advantage of doing this specifically through literature is that employing the existentially superficial tool of argument in order to think against powerful and numerous symbolic, aesthetic, emotive, and metaphysical links that have been introduced throughout one's early (and not so early) socialization is doomed to have limited success. But greater effectiveness may be achieved when one begins to think through a richer language that itself not only involves direct nonliterary ideological criticism but activates these further structures as well.

Read as a critique, *Othello* is not an attack on love, and I have therefore avoided connecting it with contemporary rejections of the inherited erotic ideology. It is, rather, a condensed focus on the violence inherent in the very idea of deep erotic attachments. This, on its own, does not mean that such bonds should be avoided, and so here the play is not read as a dismissal of love but as a mode of *distancing* from its idealization. The power of such *literary* critique, and its special advantage when compared to nonliterary philosophical criticism, lies in its reliance on the very same thought structures that form the idealization in the first place. Such a destabilizing of a deep-seated ideal is the prime condition for its assessment, which is one way in which the philosophical analysis of literature can constitute a condition for moral thought.

The problem with this formulation of philosophy-literature connections in this play is its suggestion of a misleading picture according to which, after the conditions for meaningful critical thought have been established, we can somehow conduct a straightforward evaluative inquiry in which we weigh and decide between the pros and cons of the current erotic ideology. While such a procedure is possible, it does not capture a more interesting contribution that "literary critique" facilitates. For what does it mean to "morally assess" an engrained erotic ideology? We tend to conceive of thought that is directed to embracing or rejecting. But Nussbaum and Diamond have urged that there are acts of thought that take place while reading literature that are themselves morally worthy and so constitute moral activity. They have said this regarding empathy to characters, but there are other acts of this kind. When in *The Relevance of the Beautiful* Gadamer identified art with symbol, he explained the phenomenology of symbolic thought through a process of participation and self-completion that the symbol offers to the temporally limited self. Choosing to relate to something as symbolic is thus choosing a completion of one's identity (which also explains why attacks on symbols can hurt as they do; selves, rather than objects, are being offended). Literary works can thereby turn into more than aesthetic objects to be contemplated at one time or another: they become invitations for a completion of one's identity. Choosing to relate to *Othello* as a love-as-death spectacle, entering and reentering the closing scene where a direct act of violence reciprocates indirect violence, is thus not merely an operation of thought but an act of self-creating that is itself the taking of a moral stance in relation to erotic ideology, a stance in which the very idea of loving violence can meaningfully resonate. We thereby allow Othello to enter much more than a bedchamber with his light.

Doing Nothing

H<small>AMLET</small> plays many games with ears, hearing, and audibility. Norman Holland (1958) claims that the word *ear* figures twenty-five times in *Hamlet*, more than any other of Shakespeare's works. Mary Anderson (1991) counts at least 184 references to eyes, ears, seeing, and hearing in the first two acts. Ears differ from eyes—the other faculty heavily alluded to in the play—in their constitution as entrance. Unlike other sense organs, the ear promises almost limitless exploration of interiority. Such a metaphorical identification of the ear as the body's gate is made explicit not only in the allusion to Horatio's "fortified" ears but also in the story of the ghost for whom the poison poured through "the porches" of the ear is imaged as quicksilver, coursing "through the natural gates and alleys of the body" (I.v.66–67). The body is likened to a town, the entrance to which is through the ear. Shakespeare's employment of audal imagery is continuous with some Renaissance anatomical and physiological conceptions of hearing as a process involving penetration of the body. Such preoccupation is exemplified in anatomical and musicological treatises that repeatedly invoke architectural imagery that invites exploration through specific allusions to penetration.

My topic will be the significance and function of this imagery in relation to the self-action dynamic presented in the play. This requires first noting the associative clusters involving penetration and possession that the use of acoustic imagery would set in motion in Shakespeare's contemporaries. To begin with, ears are repeatedly described in early-modern texts through architectural imagery in which the ear's inner structures are portrayed as rooms, corridors, chambers, windows and doors.[1] Whatever enters the ears is conceived as a powerful, at times

---

[1] Mondino dei Lucci wrote of "the *cavity*" or "the *twisted cavity*" in which is "implanted the auditory spirit" that is to be found in "every ear." Volcher Coiter's description of the process of hearing describes "the *passage*" of sound as "carried through the *twisting and turning windings* of the ears." The allusion to winding paths appears earlier in Avicenna in his *Canon Medicinae*, and another early writer, Albertus Magnus, conceived of the "*cavity*" as a "resonating *chamber*." Helkiah Crooke's *Microcosmographia* refers to sound as carried "through the *windowes* of the stony bone [. . .] into the *winding*

violent, entity, capable of transforming the hearer. Renaissance anatomy and musicology connects this theme to a counterocularcentric philosophy, upholding the superiority of hearing to sight (Febvre, pp. 432–37; Tomlinson, pp. 134–44). Sound is superior to sight—a hierarchy repeatedly employed to distinguish the respectable "auditors" of drama from its unsophisticated "spectators" (Gurr, pp. 85–97)—and the terms of the hierarchy between sound and sight are frequently cast through violent terms in which sound "insinuates," "seizes," "reshapes," "strikes," and, in general, possesses the listener.[2] I mean to discuss some of the ways through which audal imagery underlies the play's presentation of personal

---

burroughs, and so into the *labyrinth*." Thomas Willis's *De Anima Brutorum* is even more explicitly eucological in his imagery. He adds to the *fenestre ovalis* an entire discourse embellished with architectural imagery. He talks of doors, caverns, passages, arched meanders, chambers, and dens. He even refers explicitly to architects who could copy the design. The sources for these quotations are as follows: Mondino, Coiter, and Willis are collected in Crombie (1990, pp. 385, 386, 392–93); Avicenna and Magnus are from Burnett et al. (1991, p. 60); Crooke is from Gouk in Burnett et al. (1991) as are the references to Scaliger and Crooke in the next footnote. All emphases in this and the next footnote are mine.

[2] J. C. Scaliger claimed that "we learn things through the hearing more easily than through the sight, because the voice affects us more by *inflection* and *insinuating* itself into the sense." Helkiah Crooke claimed that things that are heard make a deeper impression on the mind. Much earlier, Boethius remarked in his *Fundamentals of Music* (p. 181) that "indeed, no path to the mind is as open for instruction as the sense of hearing. Thus, when rhythms and modes reach an intellect through the ears, they doubtless affect and *reshape* that mind according to their particular character." This remark echoes Aristotle, who, while claiming that sight is the superior sense for the primary needs of life added that "hearing takes precedence" for "the developing intelligence and its indirect consequences" (*De Sensu* 1.437a). Invoking an old conceptualization, Francis Bacon's *Sylva Sylvarum* alluded to the "similar nature" and "affinity" that "tunes and aires" have to our "affections" in order to explain why it is "that the sense of hearing *striketh* the spirits more immediately than the other senses." More than any other sense, hearing has a "present and immediate *access*" to the spirits. Harmony "*entering easily*," has the power to "*alter* the spirits in themselves" (Experiment 114). In his antitheatrical treatise, *The Schoole of Abuse* (1579), Gosson claims that poets are worse than cooks or painters, because "one extendeth his art no farther than to the tongue, palate and nose, the other to the eye, and both are ended in outwarde sense, which is common to us with brute beastes. But these [the poets] by the privy entries of the eare sappe downe into the heart, and with gunshotte of affection gaule the mind where reason and vertue shoulde rule the roste" (p. 22). Marsilio Ficino's language is even more extreme: this influential authority refers to the audal effect through words and music as "*penetrating* the depths of the soul" more strongly than all other senses. Such sound "seizes, and claims as its own, man in his entirety" (Walker, p. 137; Tomlinson, pp. 137–44).

disclosure, insulation, penetration, and genuine communication, and will explore some of the wider implications of these moments in relation to the play's problematization of action.

Doing

"The play's problematization of action" obviously refers to Hamlet's delay, an issue many Shakespearean scholars would dismiss as a tedious, ill-formulated puzzle. I am focalizing response patterns to the play, so for my purposes it is sufficient that many readers sensed and continue to sense a problem of delay. Accordingly, nothing in what follows depends on there being a genuine puzzle. I do, however, think that there really is such a problem in the play, both in Hamlet's own inability to fathom his hesitation, and, more importantly, in the philosophical potential Shakespeare draws out of delay, which markedly differs from other treatments of delay in popular revenge plays of the time. Early-modern avengers are often criticized for delay, but the dramatic solutions to this have nothing to do with the relations between being and doing on which Shakespeare focuses. Kyd goes for plot devices that explain delay, Middleton is after an aesthetics of revenge, a search for the right vindictive spectacle, Chapman is interested in an all-embracing stoicism, and Tourneur's hero waits for divine justice to take its course.[3] Shakespeare brings out an entirely different range of philosophical meanings that relate to the very attempt to organize one's life through action. These cohere with (though do not necessitate) a dramatic focus on inaction. This option is more interpretatively satisfying than dis-

---

[3] Kyd's Hieronimo (*The Spanish Tragedy*) is blamed by Isabella for delaying his revenge, but the accusation is implausible since he moves toward revenge as soon as he authenticates Bel-Imperia's original letter. This only superficially resembles *Hamlet*, as in the latter play Hamlet accuses himself for delaying *after* he verifies what the ghost tells him. Vindice's delay in Middleton's *The Revenger's Tragedy* is justified through an aesthetics of revenge, as he is looking for the appropriate vindictive spectacle when he avoids killing Lussurioso (see 2.2.87–90). Charlotte charges Clermont with unmanly procrastinations in Chapman's *The Revenge of Bussy D'Ambois*, but in that play the justification appeals to the radical stoicism that Clermont endorses throughout, and his claims against the senselessness and immorality of the revenge ethics (3.2.97). Charlemont, of Tourneur's *The Atheist's Tragedy*, basically waits for divine intervention, thus upholding the biblical "vengeance is mine" and showing that delay is theologically justified in terms of allowing divine justice take place. In the end of that play, Charlemont thus "sees" that "patience is the honest man's revenge" (5.2.276).

missing Hamlet's second speech of self-reproach by contending that Hamlet simply does not notice that he never has an adequate opportunity to kill Claudius, and so it is strange why he must be so hard on himself, which is what dismissing the problem of delay ultimately amounts to saying.

But let us set aside the disagreement regarding the question of delay, and focus on relations between response patterns to the play and the themes that it directly explores. Commentary concerning the question of Hamlet's delay—that is, documented patterns of reader-response—forms a rich range of actual responses to inaction. Some explanations aim to bypass the psychological puzzle by appealing to dramatic considerations, suggesting, for example, that through highlighting inaction. Shakespeare resists "the structural syntax of revenge tragedy" (Calderwood, 1983, p. 28), or through denying that there is a problem of delay. Yet, when the psychological question is confronted *as a problem*, something is already said about the reader's own projections. Attempting to explain or supply excuses for the delay is itself already an endorsing of a tacit identification of subjectivity with agency. The same projection is revealed when interpreters do *not* feel a need to explain other aspects of the play—for example, Laertes' nondelayed resolution and action. In the two soliloquies of self-reproach, it is obvious that Hamlet himself does not know why he hesitates. He even says as much (IV.iv.43). If we respect this answer, and that the play does not supply us with a better one, we can regard this epistemic limitation not as a riddle to be "solved" but rather as the assigned position to which the play's rhetoric moves its audience. So, instead of illuminating Hamlet's delay, let us instead explain *what* is being achieved by making delay a problem.

Doing Nothing

A focus on delay highlights a certain tension between what one may, for lack of better word, problematically call a "self" (Ferry; Greenblatt, pp. 131–45) and performance. Hamlet shifts easily from one to the other in cases of role-playing when it is precisely performance that sets up the gap between what one is perceived to be and what one is. The magical pull of intentional role-playing stems from the capacity to keep an aspect of the self encapsulated and unperceived. Action through playacting offers safety and enables impenetrability, broadening what one experiences to include numerous entities that one dons merely as play.[4] For Hamlet, playacting facilitates the seductiveness of remaining undetermined. Hamlet is disoriented when the role must turn into a large-scale, self-determining action that is really him. When his performance is not a piece of play-acting, the action is either immediately reactive, or involves him being perceived by others and judged. Inaction in these moments will be no less determining of what others take him to be. The delayed vengeance is different. Only he knows of it. No one expects him to take revenge. (Horatio, who later in the play learns the truth, is close enough to him to be nonjudgmental.) Hamlet allows procrastination to take place only in the private sphere.

In his resistance to take on the role of avenging son, Hamlet discloses the wish to remain undefined, open-ended, unorganized. Stanley Cavell has read the play in terms of a resistance to enter the world, an attempt to "hold back from existence" (1987, pp. 13–14), as one possible response to skepticism (since the existence of the world cannot be assured, Hamlet's fantasy is not to be admitted into it, to remain unborn). I wish to dissociate Cavell's remark from the context of skepticism, and to integrate it into a reading of the relations between delay, the play on senses, and a non-agent-oriented sense of self. Avoiding disclosure is, in Hamlet, related to the desire to sustain the potential, as yet nonactualized aspects of being. This resistance occurs in a maturing man—one who, like Hamlet, is precisely at the stage of being pressed into moving from primarily potential agency (a prince, a student), to being *this or that*. We encounter again an awareness of the residual, preformed "that within" that Desdemona picked out (and loved) in Othello, and that Hamlet will not give up on. We note that his idealizations of and repulsion with humanity or women are all general. He harps on the nobility of man, not of a particular man. Gertrude's frailty becomes the frailty of all women. Ophelia does not "jig and amble"—it is women who do that. And being or not being rather than living or not living is how he articulates his suicidal thoughts (if they are such). The bewitching "to be or not to be," rather than "to live or not to live," sets the generalized pitch, designating existence as a

---

[4] William Empson (1986) supplies an interesting explanation how Shakespeare manages to underscore Hamlet's theatricality as a problem for his own audience. Hamlet repeatedly calls attention to his own acting (jokingly to begin with), and this partly in order to meet the possible fatigue of the audience with the overfamiliar norms of revenge plays and self-blaming would-be avengers. For Empson, after focalizing self-theatricality in this way, the audience will be left wondering about such a stance rather than vexed by its reintroduction.

nonactualized entity. Nothing is less determined than just "being." This is what marks the difference between this soliloquy and other despair literature of the time (the Duke's exchange with Claudio in *Measure for Measure*, or Spenser's Despair). Hamlet's father too is no father but a god, there to be worshiped rather than just loved ("an eye like Mars to threaten and command"). This manifests more than incapacity for personal love, but also indicates repulsion from actualized personalities.[5]

The relations between performance and self are first set by the ghost's demand of Hamlet, in which action (revenge) is so naturally supposed to spring from filial love. The Pyrrhus and Priam story that haunts Hamlet also invokes these relations. The language of that tale involves most of the deeper structural components contained in the model of an "overtaken" self that the play will later problematize: "control" and craving its "loss," being "overseized," allowing oneself to be "used" by another (or by a father), and waiting to be "possessed" by passion. It is unsurprising that the simplistic model of self and agency deployed by both the ghost and the actor reciting the Trojan tale (whom Hamlet praises for so easily responding to the "cue" for passion) cannot really work for Hamlet. Hamlet's preoccupation with the tension between appearance and reality undermines the possibility of his believing that performance can be nonproblematically indicative of self. After all, Hamlet believes in an internal and unactable truth, in having "that within which passes show" (I.ii.85), and in this he probably goes beyond other sixteenth-century conceptualizations of the seeming/being gap that center only on the possibilities of dissembling and not on the more radical ones of nondisclosure (Ferry, pp. 212–14). Something in Hamlet is *radically* divorced from the sphere of action. This self-conceptualization he sets in opposition to Claudius's conception of grief as being reducible to performance (I.ii.87–101). An inwardness that cannot be acted is an idea that also opposes the action-centered subjectivity that Hamlet continually encounters in Fortinbras and Laertes, the other two sons with whom he repeatedly compares himself.

I am suggesting then that Hamlet's internal logic rejects equating the totality of what he is with an agent and, at the same time, he is also

---

[5] Historicizing this sense of self is not simple. "The birth of individuality in the Renaissance" in the older writings on "the birth of the self" has now been refined in numerous ways. In forthcoming work of mine, I relate the preoccupation with money in early-modern drama and poetry to the emergence of an identification of the self with possibilities associated with the vertical and horizontal mobility that characterized early-modern England. But Hamlet's "that within" seems even more abstract than possibilities, going for a nonlinguistic, predefined core.

strongly drawn to such a reduction. Perhaps it is the promise of certainty, the illusion of knowing through performance what one really is and what one truly feels, that charms Hamlet into recurring blindness. Hamlet fluctuates between competing self-descriptions in an all-embracing vagueness. When no other way can stabilize a suspected self-description, performance becomes the route that promises verification. And yet, Hamlet's painful awareness of the gap between what is seen and what is prevents him from maintaining this illusion for long.

To avoid actions that exhaustively determine what one becomes is to resist converting the self into an agent. Acting or, more specifically, a *nonproblematic* move from resolution to action is how such a reduction is established. Turning selves into agents is what Hamlet encounters in those around him, and it is what he wishes for himself. However, inexplicable, mysterious nonaction permits the gap between the disclosable and the hidden to come into (or more accurately remain in) existence. Shunning disclosure issues from a vague awareness of the existence of "that within which passes show," of a part in one's being, a "mystery" that Rosencrantz and Guildenstern seek to "pluck out" (III.ii.356). Hamlet's dying wish to "report me and my cause aright / To the unsatisfied" (V.ii.344–45) registers his own sense of his separateness from others, since all other characters misinterpret him. No one knows the cause of his melancholy, if it is melancholy, and all the reasons they give for it—unsatisfied love for Ophelia (Polonius), his mother's hasty marriage (Gertrude), unfulfilled ambition (Rosencrantz and Guildenstern, and perhaps suspected by Claudius)—are partial at best.

Replacing wrong or incomplete descriptions of Hamlet with a correct one that Horatio is meant to posthumously produce can, it seems, remedy this estrangement. But Hamlet's encapsulation goes deeper than his death wish suggests. For Hamlet (and for *Hamlet*), disclosure is avoided not only by engaging in pretense or by deferring action but also more radically by altogether dismissing language. Hamlet's dying words include the request that his story be only *"more and less"* (V.II.362) related to Fortinbras. As for the rest, "the rest is silence" (V.ii.363). What is not included in the necessarily vague description of events that Hamlet's "more and less" prescribes must remain outside discourse. The sense of futility in exposing himself through language is evident in Hamlet throughout the play. It is precisely revealing himself through language, through words and more words, which he not only shuns but violently despises (II.ii.578–82). Turning from Hamlet to *Hamlet*, the very last moment in the play—the gunshot—is meaningful sound, which is supposed to "speak loudly" (V.ii.405) for Hamlet, according to Fortinbras, but is yet a "speaking," which is crude sound and not elaborate language. By ending through nondiscursive sound, the play, like Hamlet's last words, closes by moving outside linguistic expression.

Such self-understanding registers limited contact with others. Yet Hamlet's need to remain undisclosed is paradoxically—though perhaps typically of such drives—linked with an opposite desire to be internalized and met. Since eyes are limited to picking out one's external part, Hamlet's wish to be internalized proceeds through a different sense that, while bearing its own limitations, is able to (partially) convey interiority.

Ears Again

Bodily infiltration through the audal, invoked by Shakespeare's use of acoustic imagery, meets the self/performance and encapsulation/disclosure dualities in several ways. Of all the characters in the play, Hamlet is the only one who uses the questioning idiom of "Do you hear?" during conversation (II.ii.519; II.ii.531; III.ii.62; V.i.283). His concern about success at achieving specifically audal contact marks both a fear of seclusion and a desire to be internalized through sound. This could have been an anticipation of Hegel's phenomenology of sound—sound as unveiling one's "inner life." But merely this cannot satisfy Hamlet. Disrespecting language and shirking from linguistic expression turns acoustics into no more than an approximation. Contact remains a fantasy. The heart of his mystery must remain silenced. And yet, while an aspect of Hamlet's self cannot be touched, he still tries to reach and affect another's. This is conveyed by another feature of audal imagery: Hamlet's preoccupation with violence done to ears.

There are connections between Hamlet's numerous figurative appeals to acoustical injury,[6] and the violent ways in which the various Renais-

---

[6] Hamlet considers ill-spoken words concerning Horatio to be "violence" done to his ear and asks Horatio not to use such words (I.ii.170–71). He is jealous of the player who could "cleave the general ear" with horrid speech (II.ii.557), and it offends him to hear a player "split the ear" of the groundlings who are capable of nothing (III.ii.10–11). Criticizing Laertes' exaggerated bemoaning of Ophelia, Hamlet echoes the arresting of motion by sound in the Pyrrhus and Priam story, and asks: "whose phrase of sorrow / Conjures the wand'ring stars and makes them stand / Like wonder-wounded hearers?" (V.i.248–50). It is violence to his mother's ears that he sets out to perform by "speaking daggers to her ears," an achievement that is confirmed by Gertrude almost word for word (III.iv.95).

sance tracts surveyed earlier portray the modification of the mental through sound ("inflecting," "reshaping," "striking," "altering," "insinuating," "seizing," "claiming as its own"). Beside these links, Hamlet's obsession with the theme of verbal violence done to ears (cleaving, splitting, stabbing, wounding) opposes perverse and nonperverse modes of penetration. The entrance of language through the ear thereby gains sinister overtones. Tropical violence done to ears signifies disrupting change that centers not only on the personality in general but also on the specific constituents of it that accommodates receptivity.[7] Hamlet wants to alter others through the audal. His fear of separation is revealed in his concern about being heard in his repetitive "do you hear?" Ears are thus exposed as that through which a manifestation-transcending aspect of self paradoxically hopes to "appear." However, for Hamlet, mere entrance is not enough. Hamlet seeks not only to penetrate Gertrude (the only character in the play that he does reach through audal infiltration) but also to metaphorically violate with acoustical daggers that through which he enters. To the many psychoanalytic readings of Hamlet's relations to his mother from Jones to Adelman, we may add the footnote that this is an inversion of the desire to enter a virgin: a wish to be the last.

Contact

Hamlet's talk with his mother—the most passionate moments in the play—is where all the themes I treat here connect. The self-knowledge Hamlet intends Gertrude to reach is assimilated with self-penetration, and this is done specifically through the senses,[8] through exposing Gertrude to the outpouring of audal daggers that ultimately yield self-knowledge.[9] Unlike Claudius, for whom reflective art—*The Mousetrap*—was sufficient in propelling active self-judgment, Gertrude's language consistently casts self-knowledge in the passive: the outcome of her being

---

[7] These remarks could be usefully read alongside an analysis by Kenneth Gross (2001, ch. 1) regarding a different dimension of violence conducted through and at ears in the play. Gross is focusing on slander and defamation.

[8] For connections between inwardness, penetration, and the female body that may be perceived in the scene, see Maus, p. 193.

[9] The process I am now describing should (ideally) be read alongside Hillman's (1997) rich discussion of the interpenetration of sense-talk and knowledge in the play.

brought to that state by Hamlet. He is the one who turns her eyes inward. He is the one who "cleaves her heart in twain." However, Hamlet turns Gertrude's process of self-knowledge into a cooperative rather than a passive enterprise. She is brought to a state of participation in what culminates in the breaking of her heart.

The breaking of the heart via audal daggers is consistent with Aristotle's influential theory of perception. Sound, according to Aristotle's *On the Parts of Animals*, literally enters through the ear, is conveyed by the blood, and is heard in the heart, the organ responsible for all conscious sense perception (656a, 656b, 666), and several Renaissance authorities followed this conception.[10] The heart is posited as the target for audal penetration at the beginning of the scene (hoping that it would not be "proof and bulwark against sense" [III.iv.38]). The use of language that challenges again and again the adequacy of Gertrude's senses (III.iv.72–81), while at the same time itself piercing through the alleys and cavities of a sense, brings together the themes of acoustics and penetration with that of touch. Contact is foreshadowed by the grabbing of her arm (or by whatever action it is by which he forcefully prevents her from leaving at the beginning of the scene). It is also anticipated by his references to her moving from detached naming ("You are the queen, your husband's brother's wife / And would it were not so, you are my mother" [III.iv.14–15]) to the ironical ("good mother," "lady" [III.iv.27, 30]), to the intimately passionate ("Mother" [146], employed but twelve lines before the breaking of her heart).

The climactic cleaving of the heart—that is, contact—is the precise point where Hamlet moves to demand a specific performance from Gertrude and to explicitly readdress her with the relations between performing and self. He demands that Gertrude avoid sex with Claudius: "For use," he tells her, "almost can change the stamp of nature" (III.iv.170). That is to say, acting in the proposed way could come close (only close, "almost") to changing what she is. It is after the breaking up of the senses into their parts in Hamlet's speech that Gertrude is

---

[10] T. Wright acknowledges it as a possible account of hearing, though he did not accept it: "The third manner [...] is this, that the very sound it seelfe [...] which passeth thorow the eared and by them unto the heart, and there beateth and tickleth it in such sort, as it is moved with semblable passion." Scaliger located sense perception in the heart since the spirits around the heart are supposed to take in the trembling motion of music and are stirred up. Helkiah Crooke followed up this account (Gouk, 1991); see, too, the citation from Gosson above (note 2).

shown to be not only metaphorically blind but also literally blind to the reappearance of the ghost. Ironically, it is she—who thinks that "all that is I see" (III.iv.133), who continually mistakes appearances for reality—who turns out to be the one person who does not perceive what Hamlet, as well as the audience and previous characters, have all seen. This blindness is even more noteworthy since she is repeatedly alluded to in the play through references to her sight.[11] Hamlet demands a specific performance from Gertrude after discovering her blindness. No longer occupied with his own insulation, he still senses a part of her that defies his moralizing (III.iv.146–57). And so he will mold her into action that is bearable for him rather than cope with that which passes show *in her*.

It is thus that both of them resist maintaining the fleeting moment of contact. To Hamlet's distinction between "use" and "nature" (performance/self), Gertrude's response is "What shall I do?" (III.iv.183). Instead of looking upon the black spots in her soul, her own "that within," all she understands is action ("What wilt thou *do*?" [III.iv.20]; "O me, what hast thou *done*?" [III.iv.24]; "What have I *done*, that thou dar'st wag thy tongue / In noise so rude against me?" [III.iv.38–39]; "What *act* / That roars so loud and thunders in the index?" [III.iv.51–52]). But it is her final words in the scene, her exaggerated metaphorical reference to being killed by Hamlet's words ("if words be made of breath, and breath of life, I have no life to breathe what thou hast said to me" [III.iv.199–201]), that denote a change. What begins by this numb queen's complaining of Hamlet's accusation as being audal overexposure—of the "noise" he makes (III.iv.39) or by asking what act it is that he blames her for that "roars so loud in the index" (III.iv.52)—ends with metaphorical nonbeing, with a retreat from the desire to maintain a self-conceptualization after what Hamlet has said. She realizes that, now, nothing can be *done*. And placing her in a position in which she can *be* rather than *do*—at last to lament rather than to transform grief into action that makes up a life that supposedly must go on—is Hamlet's small victory.

---

[11] Claudius, who incidentally is compared in this scene to "a mildew'd ear," always refers to Gertrude through notions of sight and *never* through those of sound (III.i.32; V.i.291; V.i.293; V.ii.314). The significance of this should not be overlooked, since Claudius is meticulous in his distribution of words about the senses. To Laertes, he always uses metaphors of sound and never sight (IV.v.94; IV.v.202; IV.vii.3; IV.vii.33; IV.vii.40).

Philosophy and Literature

Grief, for Hamlet, cannot simply be reduced to action. Genuine mourning should put a stop to life; deautomate and destabilize the move to action. This is where he begins in this play, and it is at such a point that he places Gertrude, though only momentarily. Grief is a state that opens up and *justifies* lingering between being and acting, a state to which he is drawn. We cannot know whether a preexisting philosophical fascination with the loss involved in becoming an agent *causes* Hamlet to use grief, or whether it is the other way round: his bereavement bringing out the philosophical experience. Causality aside (if there is causality here), *Hamlet* presents a state that cannot be reduced to depression or shock since it includes an opening up to a non-agent-based sense of life that is not essentially related to grief. Taking revenge is to transform sorrow into actions. In a way it is like crying (Hamlet never cries). In a deeper way, it is to be a Gertrude. Modifying grief into action is thus to avoid a deeper form of mourning. In one way, the refusal to reorganize active life around a powerful new state is a recognition and respect of that state. But in Hamlet, lingering in this state also opens up the problematic nature of the very idea of an active organized life, the awkward relations between life and its regulating structures.

The more abstract concerns that underlie the play are that self-exposure and communication require an assent to be merely partially perceived. We become an object of reference for others through being reduced to some of the roles that we don as performing agents. Trying to remain undisclosed, *doing* nothing, is the attempt to resist this reduction. *Hamlet* is a play about such an attempt. The reasons underlying the resistance escape the person involved and, the play suggests, *must* escape him because of what he regards as the essential defects of language. Words reduce the self into a collection of descriptions that supposedly capture and stabilize what one is, thereby enabling reference, signification, and evaluation. Hamlet's fantasy is Othello's nightmare: the former wants to remain undefined and be contacted as such, while for the latter such contact is too much, annihilating his established personality. *Othello* and *Hamlet* are in this sense one play: one about the wish to be rather than to be an agent, while the other is about the desire to be identified with an agent rather than to just be. One protagonist embodies the loss experienced in moving from being to being an agent, while the other stands for the opposite loss: the pain of perception that penetrates beyond one's agency.

In terms of the philosophy-literature links, if Shakespeare was in fact a philosopher interested in communicating through systematic presentation the resistance to being disclosed, there is a point at which he would have necessarily failed. The descriptive language of systematic presentation—conceptual truth-claims and argumentation—can refer to "passing-show" aspects only through referring to them negatively (one thinks of the *via negativa* tradition in theological contexts). But when one tries to say what a nondisclosed aspect of self is, as opposed to asserting what it is not, one is reduced either to silence or to the language of approximations (both options, as we have seen, are employed in this play). It is at this point that we can easily fall into the usual philosophical violence of eliminating what we cannot reduce to our modes of description.

One could ask about the truth of such a model, whether there really are parts of the self that cannot be imparted. But with reference to the links between philosophy and literature, I wish to focus now not on the truth-value of this model but on what is involved in *communicating* such a claim. As far as such communicating goes, there is a point at which a certain model of self may only be sensed. "Sensing" is a slippery notion. Attempting to say what is sensed through a systematic discourse seems to require dropping the claim for its alleged ineffability in relation to that discourse. We can, however, become vividly aware of alternatives without being directly told what they are. The literary work's ability to construct a cognitive experience can induce such awareness. By compelling readers to project their predisposed conceptions of subjectivity and agency, literary works enable reading not only the play but also the conceptual structures and the emotional dispositions that determine our own thinking. The distance achieved by such repositioning in relation to ourselves allows for freedom in sensing alternative schemes, ones that can never be fully brought to the surface and that must remain opaque.

I have been arguing that what *Hamlet* reflects—and a play's purpose, Hamlet says, is always to reflect (III.ii.20–25)—to those who recognize in it a problem of delay is an embodiment of a part of the self that has nothing to do with agency. This is how delay is not explained away but, rather, explained as such. By creating an experience that complicates the move from resolution to action, the play sets in motion a fascinating parallelism between the fictional occurrences and real response. Hamlet explicitly commits himself to the idea of an ineffable passing-show constituent of subjectivity in the first lines he utters. The existence of such an aspect is a possibility that the audience is invited to contemplate through their own experience of the play.

The experience *Hamlet* creates involves a particular projection that is being manipulated in a subtle way. A repeated response to this play is the attempt to remotivate Hamlet's procrastination instead of seeing unjustified inaction as the aspect to be explained. The play-audience relationship thus frustrates certain explanatory dispositions. The existence of an inexpressible drive that blunts Hamlet's purpose, the fact that nothing in Hamlet or in *Hamlet* sufficiently clarifies it, means that this play cannot be penetrated through identifying the self with an agent. Positioning the audience or the reader in such an aporetic stance lets them experience the breakdown of a self-conception. Disorienting the audience in this has led Thomas Hanmer and T. S. Eliot to find an aesthetic fault in the play. More fruitfully than these, one could see here the reduction to impotence of a basic conceptualization that, like Gertrude, we readily (if not automatically) employ.

Looking back to the chain of explanations for delay and their consecutive refutations, one can imagine Shakespeare purposely planting textual time bombs to explode as soon as the need arose to disprove an explanation. Whether the vindication for delay was that Hamlet is overly intellectual, lacks opportunities to kill Claudius, does not know what he wants, or disbelieves the ghost (and when he does believe it, it is too late), the textual evidence that refute it are all there. He is not a coward. He blames himself for delaying rather than complaining that he lacks opportunities. Although he is inclined to the cerebral, in deep shock, and a doubter, he is not ineffectual. What does seem to unequivocally manifest itself through the terminology of the secondary literature—"the problem of delay," "the problem of problems," "mystery"—is that a particular mode of relating to people is brought to collapse through the rhetorical operations of this play.

In this failure, Hamlet's inability to explain himself to himself enables the fictional domain to reflect a real-life response to it. We can now unpack the literature-as-reading-us metaphor, through which literature and self-knowledge are often linked, into a detailed claim. Through structuring a response in which one experiences the disappointment of nonpenetration, this work positions the reader in a similar cognitive and emotive stance as the one articulated by its leading character in his opening lines. Shakespeare introduces Hamlet both as an uncontacted man and as one who understands the limitations of communication. However, this is merely a philosophical position, stemming from awareness of an unbridgeable gap between some dimensions of self and the possibilities of disclosure. The strength of this work is that the attentive reader is not only told something about the limitations of contact but also made to experience them.

King Lear's Hidden Tragedy

"Do your worst, blind Cupid, I shall not love."[1] Lear articulates this dismal sentiment to Gloucester in that moving scene in which the two wronged fathers meet: one at the height of his madness, the other blind and full of self-hatred after his failed suicide attempt. The moment is one of an agonizing realization that the pain of mistrust has gone so deep that one is sealed off from love. After leveling accusations at his daughters, which is what Lear was doing in his previous stage appearance, he reaches the state in which even anger is not experienced.

Lear's "hidden" tragedy involves giving up on this, his parenting. He begins by giving up on Cordelia ("I give her father's heart from her," I.i.120; "let her be thine; for we have no such daughter," I.i.257). But with Cordelia this is mostly talk. He will die loving her, although grasping what such love encompasses in terms of the inner value of parenting will require a process of discovery. Unlike Cordelia, when it comes to Regan and Gonerill, he will succeed in withdrawing from parenting, and this culminates in his ultimate indifference when he sees their dead bodies:

KENT. Your eldest daughters have fordone themselves
And desperately are dead.
LEAR. Ay, so I think.

(V.iii.265–66)

The theme itself is horrifying. When do people give up on their children? A plausible answer is that some wounds elicit more than furious hatred—working deeper, dislodging the affective structure. The tragic movement in *Lear*, the "fall," does not simply consist of articulating the

---

[1] All references, citations, and spelling of names follow the (Folio-based) *The New Cambridge Shakespeare* edition, edited by Jay L. Halio, 1992, Cambridge University Press. Accumulatively, the number of lines that differ between the Folio and the Quarto add up to about an act (Albany's role suffers the most in the move from Quarto to Folio). I shall call attention to textual differences relevant to the reading in the notes. Actually, there are twelve slightly different copies of the 1608 Quarto, and in one case, a difference between these will be pertinent to a detail of the following reading. For a discussion of the problems surrounding the Quarto, see Richard Strier's textual introduction to the Quarto-based *King Lear* (forthcoming from Bedford Books).

consequences of a monstrous case of filial ingratitude, but of letting go of a core attachment. This process will not be evident upon a first reading or watching of the play. Gonerill and Regan are so horrible that readers will disregard any dimension of loss concerning them. The fraudulent and (in Regan's case) sadistic daughters bias us into processing the tragedy primarily in relation to the Lear-Cordelia relations of banishment, reconciliation, and grief whereas Gonerill and Regan are no more than hypocritical vultures who elicit from Lear disappointment, disbelief, and rage. The horror encapsulated in the moment above, Lear's complete detachment from the deaths of Gonerill and Regan, usually escapes us on first readings because of the enormity and terror of Lear's words about Cordelia. But perceiving a loved one's immorality does not preclude loving them. Mere wickedness is not enough. Perceiving one's child's immorality would elicit pain, shame, and anger in a parent, but not a dislodging of parental attachment. Even the terrible Richard III generates some emotion from his mother, who, in contrast to Lear's indifference to the bodies of his dead daughters, remains to the end disappointed, angry, and hoping for her son's death. So the option of dismissing Gonerill and Regan as monsters is easier for a reader than for a loving father, even a superficial one. Moreover, Shakespeare is careful to avoid aiming the more hideous dimensions of his daughters' wickedness directly at Lear. It is we, not Lear, who are presented with Regan's sadism and Gonerill's cold deadliness. It is we who note that when they shut him out in the storm, they do so without conflict—and the alarming moral confidence that they exhibit is, indeed, the first unequivocal point at which their moral hollowness first appears (in terms of moral assessment, their actions in the division scene are more complicated than hypocrisy).

The presentation of the parental in this play consists of exposing the components of parental experience in two contrasting movements: first, through the barriers Lear encounters working himself out of parental attachment in regard to Gonerill and Regan; second, through the fuller understanding of parental meaning he discovers in his relationship with Cordelia. After examining these movements, I shall respond to some objections to the attempt to read *Lear* in this way (these objections include the idea that imposing contemporary notions of parenting on an early-modern context is an obvious anachronism; that "parenting" cannot be discussed in a way that detaches the parental from the paternal—and possibly the monarchial—in this play; as well as the objection according to which Lear does not love his daughters at the beginning of the play). I shall then turn to the philosophical dimensions of the reading: what the reading tells us about parenting and about working oneself into value.

Growing out of Parenting

Lear begins by saying, "Are you our daughter" to Gonerill, a statement that is still laden with affect and attachment, but in the end he is indifferent to her death as well as the death of his "dearest Regan." This withdrawal begins earlier. After his proclamation that he cannot love, Lear's accusations are leveled at the world in general, at his sons-in-law, but no longer at his daughters. His "great rage," as the gentleman tells Cordelia, has been "killed in him" (IV.vi.76–77). He is indifferent to whether or not he will see Gonerill and Regan (Cordelia: "Shall we not see these daughters and these sisters?" Lear: "No, no, no, no! Come, let's away to prison," V.iii.8) and, apart from his detached words upon seeing their bodies, this lack of interest in any grand scene of accusation is his last reference to them in the play.[2] In light of the previous indications of Lear's love for them, his earlier rage at his daughters should strike us as more complex than anger: not merely reciprocating the actions of Gonerill and Regan but an attempt to *maintain love* for them when their actions hurt him enough to threaten his parenthood. Withdrawing from parental attachment is not chosen but forced upon him, resulting from a perspicuous understanding of what the actions of his loved ones imply. This suggests that we can relate to Lear's tragic fall not just through the experiences of pain and offense but also through those involved in the struggle to maintain or forego defining elements of one's identity. We can, for example, read Lear's question whether anyone recognizes him (I.iv.185–89) not merely as reaffirmation of a lost status but also as an experience of disintegration, a feeling that he has ceased to exist, which receding from parental attachment involves. Similarly, losing his identity through the chilling curses he levels at Gonerill is connected to him sensing that he is going mad (I.v.37–38).

Unlike the expulsion of Cordelia and Gonerill from the domain of parental concern, a more hesitant dialectical pattern of entering into and withdrawing from parenting is enacted with his last banished child,

---

[2] The subplot mirrors this when, upon hearing that it was Edmond who implicated him, Gloucester immediately turns his attention to Edgar, never again thinking of Edmond.

Regan. Upon hearing that his messenger was maltreated, he is initially brought to the verge of madness:

> O how this mother swells up toward my heart!
> *Hysterica passio*! Down, thou climbing sorrow,
> Thy element's below. Where is this daughter?
>
> (II.iv.51–53)

But the possibility of true estrangement from Regan, calling her "this daughter," makes him immediately recoil and examine whether or not he prejudged her (II.iv.56).[3] This is the first time he is willing to question the correctness of his own judgments regarding others. He likewise retracts from his anger when Regan and Cornwall refuse to speak to him, all too ready to excuse them since they may be ill (II.iv.98). He becomes unstable and weak, asking the shrewd fool not to follow him to his confrontation with Regan (II.iv.55), and opting to play down his anger when Regan agrees to talk to him. He also avoids confronting Regan for her justification of Gonerill's actions. Such weakness, culminating in him kneeling before Regan in a mock show (which ironically duplicates his actual weakness), is a subliminal choice. The alternative to these concessions is to banish Regan as well. The fear of losing his last child imposes on Lear a weakness that is almost inconceivable to him. As difficult as such concessions are, he is willing to make them rather than withdraw from parenting.

That Lear is preoccupied with losing his role as parent, rather than merely the respect of his children, is anticipated in that poignant exchange when he discovers Kent in the stocks:

> LEAR. What's he that hath so much thy place mistook
> To set thee here?
> KENT. It is both he and she,
> Your son and daughter.

---

[3] The same dialectical pattern is anticipated in Gloucester's relation to Edgar when he alternates between recoiling from fatherhood and maintaining that role by doubting Edgar's alleged treachery (I.ii.52–85). It could be argued that Gonerill anticipates the pattern too. After cursing Gonerill when she drives him out of her house, he tells the fool, "I did her wrong," which according to the reading of D. G. James (1951, pp. 94–96) refers to Gonerill, and he explains this forgiving attitude by saying: "I will forget my nature. So kind a father!" (I.v.20, 27). He immediately returns to anger (line 32), but the "pause" could imply that cursing Gonerill the way he did is to deny ("forget") something relating to his very being as a father. Such a reading is consistent with my interpretation, but I cannot agree with James. Readers persuaded by him that line 20 refers to Gonerill rather than to Cordelia could, however, see the dialectical move out of parenting already there.

LEAR.	No.
KENT.	Yes.
LEAR.	No, I say.
KENT.	I say, yea.
LEAR.	By Jupiter, I swear no.
KENT.	By Juno, I swear ay.
LEAR.	They durst not do't: They could not, would not do't. 'Tis worse than murder, To do upon respect such violent outrage.

(II.iv.11–21)

Lear tries to avoid perceiving the implications of Regan's deeds and the way these threaten his fatherhood. Yet, apart from his shock in his exchange with Kent (which will be acted with meaningful pauses), comes the realization of his fall from power, captured in the move from them not daring, to them being unable, to them not wanting, to perform such an act. But what can be "worse than murder"? Unlike murder, which destroys a person's being, Regan's act leads to the disintegration of not only his present being but his past identity as well. He does not experience her offense merely as a wound he suffers but as an attack that destroys his very identity as a parent. "We note the madness that swells up toward his heart, which, as Adelman reminds us, is itself tellingly referred to as 'mother.'"

Only at this point does he begin to arouse sympathy in the reader/audience. Only now does it dawn on him that disconnecting from a child is not merely a matter of making a declaration but involves a painful struggle. Lear's resistance to cutting himself off from his last child and his accepting weakness create the sort of tension that can draw us to this man, no longer the uncompromising dictator of the previous scenes ("Who stirs?"). And this will make for the strongest moments of the play to follow: he will discover what it means to be a parent whenever he loses this possibility. His first discovery is that parenting overrides fundamental ideals of one's identity, in his case the avoidance of shame, the importance of strength, and his willingness to sacrifice these for a few more moments of preserving parenthood. We can almost miss this process, since the text employs a subtle rhetoric of omissions rather than assertions. Regan excuses Gonerill's actions by telling Lear that he should return to her house, that he is an old man who needs to be looked after, and, strikingly enough, Lear simply refuses to see what she is doing, by *arguing* away her reasons. The Lear of the previous scenes, the Lear who banished Cordelia and assuredly divorced himself from Gonerill, would never argue. He would have immediately taken offense. But this Lear is silencing his inner disposition, thereby conveying a realization of a discovered value.

I said that what elicits our own alienation from the daughters cannot be what is operating in Lear's disconnection from them. We perceive obtuseness, whereas Lear comes up against resistance that he cannot digest. Something altogether different from a perception of wickedness dominates Lear's experience, propelling the process of letting go. To this I now turn.

CHILD THOUGHT

It has been repeatedly noted that Lear is often a child.[4] There are connections between Lear's regression into childish thought and his withdrawal from parenting. Lear's pain relates to his daughters' disregard of his one condition when he resigned from power. It is not the *content* of the unfulfilled condition that torments him. We never see him lamenting the loss of his hundred knights. It is rather that his only condition was not respected, and that his daughters did this not out of wickedness but due to rather ordinary overriding considerations. Unlike the source play in which the daughters explicitly plot in detail Lear's murder, Shakespeare's play gives every indication that Gonerill and Regan would have put up with Lear

[4] Wilson Knight claims that "Lear is mentally a child" (1964, p. 164) referring not only to his uninhibited passion but to his predilection for the imagery of primitive magic manifested in the way he swears by Hecate, the queen of witches (I.i.104), or his use of imagery that discloses the mind of a frightened boy, when he repeatedly alludes to "monsters," "sea monsters," and dragons (W. Knight, p. 185). L. C. Knights noted something "conspicuously infantile" in Lear, manifested in the need for instant gratification, complete endorsement of his self, assuming that he can punish terribly when he can do nothing (II.iv.271–75), and his resorting to rage when this impotence is exposed (1959, p. 101). Rosenberg (1972)—echoing an earlier analysis by L.A.G. Strong (1954)—perceived Lear's childishness in his being "accustomed to dealing" in absolutes *"all or none! Out! Away! Forever! Never!"* (1972, p. 64). We should add to these Lear's regression into childish games (IV.v.193), shouting at his daughters that they will "think" that he will "weep," but "No, I'll not weep" (II.iv.275–76), or his repeated references to the birth-cry (IV.v.170, 172, 174). His moral outrage is also limited to thoughts about punishment, which, interestingly enough, according to Kohlberg's influential theory of moral development, is only the first of six stages of moral development in a child. This, indeed, is the way other characters perceive him too. Lear is chided by his fool for making his daughters his "mothers" (I.iv.133), and he is later blamed by Gonerill for his "pranks" (I.iv.193). In the Quarto she will refer to him as a baby, saying "Old fools are babes again" (I.iii.20).

had he agreed to abide by their rather plausible terms. What remains in *King Lear* of the elaborate plot in the anonymous *King Leir* is an ambivalent remark by Gloucester (III.iv.146), which could easily concern the daughters' attempt to break Lear's stubborn behavior through a didactic stance that children often adopt toward their aging parents ("The injuries that they themselves procure must be their schoolmasters") rather than an explicit plot. Granville-Barker made an ironic apology for Regan and Gonerill, explaining their actions in terms of setting limits for an old, uncompromising parent. I would dispense with the irony. In diminishing the deadly nature of the daughters that he found in the source play, Shakespeare is showing how a reasonable attempt to set such limits can turn into moral obtuseness. This *develops* into the fuller wickedness we see later, but Gonerill and Regan were not that evil to begin with. Gonerill puts up with his difficult behavior for a long time, and Regan says she will receive him "gladly" on his own when he rushes out to the storm. The play gives us no reason to dismiss her statement as insincere.

Lear's discovery, and it is unbearable for him, is that he is accepted only conditionally. That he believed he was loved unconditionally can be perceived in the successful flattery of Gonerill and Regan, who talk of unconditional love. Gonerill tells him that he is loved more than anything that could itself be valued. Regan is content with simply loving him, with no other pleasure able to compete with her love. Both appeal to a love that cannot be compared or superseded by any other consideration. Both succeed, thus not only tapping into but also exposing Lear's need for such love.

Reflecting on the limitations of love will create unease in any parent—indeed, in any loved person. Not everyone will be destroyed by such thoughts. But for a king who enjoyed a life that sustains at least the appearance of unconditional love and who grew to suspect that this was a sham (I argue in an appendix that this suspicion is one of Lear's main underlying motivations), it is precisely such thoughts that can precipitate the disintegration of parental attachment. A philosopher could ask whether genuine love can be conditional, and various answers are possible. But Lear is not worried about the answer: rather he is crushed by the discovery of the question. Parental love—if not generally, at least for Lear—is predicated on the belief in some sort of reciprocal attachment. When this is in doubt, upon discovering that love can be *withheld*, his own love disintegrates and he experiences this as an explosion of his inner being (II.iv.190). (This dependence of love on reciprocal affection may be perceived regarding Cordelia too, his love for her resurfacing only *after* he discovers that she does in fact care for him.)

Being a king who always had his way, Lear is in the rare position of a grown man who has not lost the vulnerability that others, who have to compete for love, generally lose early in life. Through the character of Lear, Shakespeare can thereby highlight one of life's tragedies, the discovery of conditional acceptance by others, which most of us experience (and dismiss) in early formative stages, but that Lear comes to realize only as an adult. By undergoing an infant's tragedy as an adult, Lear forces the tragedy to reach not merely the child within him, but the submerged child in his audience. Apart from possible connections between the play's theme and the Cinderella tale,[5] past commentary gave excellent suggestions regarding the way *Lear* configures infantile response patterns in its audience. For Ella Freeman Sharpe (1947), the play manifests the child's crushing discovery that he is not omnipotent. For J. Stampfer (1960), *Lear* summons and then frustrates the "covenant" that "all men make with society in their earliest infancy." Stampfer referred to our expectation of just retribution, which the tragedy disappoints after not only punishing Lear but going a step further than nemesis requires and breaking this primordial tacit covenant. Rosenberg (1972, pp. 333–34) extracts the psychological pattern the play triggers in terms of response: the archaic fantasy of an enraged child: he saves his parent from catastrophe, after which the parent begs forgiveness, thereupon the child dies, finalizing the parent's tragedy. I add that *King Lear* articulates the painful infantile discovery of conditional acceptance.

The process of withdrawing from the parental intertwines with the infantile, both in terms of thematic motifs and by appealing to archaic thought patterns within the audience. Further examination of these connections requires a return to Lear's progression toward a nonpaternal identity—specifically, the way the child surfaces in this movement.

Fighting Nature

Shakespeare's preoccupation with the difficult idea of the disintegration of parental identity coheres with this tragedy's unique presentation of the tragic experience as a confrontation between the protagonist and nature. Nature is perhaps the most discussed theme in *Lear* scholarship. But there does not seem to be any discussion of it in relation to parenting. Since "nature," for us as for Shakespeare, is so intimately bound up

---

[5] See Jay Halio's introduction to the New Cambridge Shakespeare edition, pp. 10–11.

with parenting, it is intriguing to see how Shakespeare connects these two themes. Saying that parenting is "natural" or "instinctive" is nothing new. Yet the nuanced phenomenology Shakespeare weaves brings out what the "natural" in parental experience may mean.

Shakespeare first turns nature into an inner resistance that Lear tries to overcome:

> . . . and thou all-shaking thunder,
> Strike flat the thick rotundity o'th'world,
> Crack nature's moulds, all germens spill at once
> That make ingrateful man.
>
> (III.ii.6–9)

More than a call for nature's destruction, Lear asks for the annihilation of its creative aspect, thereby repeating and accelerating a theme that structured his horrific reply to Gonerill. Lear is discovering the natural by confronting it as he recedes from parental connection. Shakespeare is interested in this particular confrontation rather than any other. The poetic interest in focusing on encountering nature in particular can be gathered from Shakespeare having his Lear call out to nature rather than following the Lear of his sources, who calls out to Fate, as "he" did in Geoffrey of Monmouth and John Higgins, or to God, as "he" did in William Warner (Bullough, p. 314, 327, 335). Such alterations are consistent with the attempt to focus on parental disconnection.

Note now the last line quoted above from Act III: Lear is harping on people being "ungrateful," thus staging a fascinating retreat to Cordelia's terms of attachment, which had so enraged him before. His descent to a sense of love predicated on repayment ("I return those duties back as are right fit") is not only a further development of his weakness but a willingness to accept conditional love. He no longer expects his daughters to simply love him but to love him *because* of what he has given them. He makes this explicit in his next lines, telling the elements that he has no quarrel with them since, unlike his daughters, he gave them nothing (III.ii.15–17).

It is after this diminishment that Lear can no longer sense his body. He does not feel the storm, invading "to the skin." But the analogy between disconnection from his daughters and detachment from his own body goes even further. Lear's withdrawal from the body is conveyed through his experiencing it as if he perceives it from the outside, watching the organs destroying each other—"Is it not as this mouth should tear this hand For lifting food to't?" The reference to *this* hand and *this* mouth registers a sense of estrangement from his own body, connecting the relation to one's children with the relation to one's own limbs. It is also an internalization of an emblazoning rhetoric that Lear repeatedly deploys in relation to those around him ("that face of hers"; "hated back"; "banished trunk"), an internalization that occurs whenever he is diminished in the play ("Beat at this gate that let thy folly in"; "old fond eyes, beweep this cause again, I'll pluck ye out"), but unlike these self-references, imaging his daughters as a vicious mouth is also to turn them into a part of the same organism of which the metaphorical hand is also a part. This figure of organic self-destruction captures not merely his anger but his sense of a self-consuming inner rapture taking place. Lear says that he will "punish home," which, more than the surface sense of punishing to the full, again signifies violence to something of which he himself is part. It is then, as Granville-Barker notes (1946, p. 292), that the child in him resurfaces: like a boy at bedtime he will "pray" and then "sleep." His next lines (III.iv.27–43), about which Bradley remarked that they belong to those passages that "make one worship Shakespeare," are usually read as his awakened moral sense when he moves out of his solipsism as a result of the humiliation to which he is reduced. But the very last lines, in which he promises to be more compassionate to the poor in the hope of seeming "more just" in the eyes of "the heavens," reveal the childish wish for pain to be alleviated by promising to be good.

Like drifting on a current and realizing its strength only when diverging from it, the natural element in parenting is exposed as a massive force that carries the parent along and is imperceptible until it is opposed. The confrontation itself is experienced as a growing estrangement from one's own body, which is sensed as being in paradoxical, self-destructive turmoil that one can only witness and do nothing about. The confrontation with nature is also experienced as a regression into childish thinking, in which the move away from being a parent is also a move away from adulthood. This will ultimately be felt as a loss of sanity, a swelling *Mother* endangering his heart. When he does begin to lose his sanity and projects his troubles onto Edgar, Lear progresses from these to a desire for decontextualization. Removing his clothes, wishing to owe nothing to anyone, is to turn from focusing on what his daughters owe him (Cordelia's conception of love to which he has been reduced), to a disconnection in which others need never be acknowledged. The specific form of the madness, unclothing, is a refusal of shame, and ignoring others is a return to the solipsism of a baby, a return to the time in which one is not a parent.⁶ It is also, for him, a form of truth, of being true.⁷ When he ignores Gloucester's words, which tell him that his daughters plan to kill him (III.iv.134–35), he is conveying a separation that is almost complete. The process is finalized when he calls for Regan to be anatomized.⁸ This is often acted as Lear himself making carving motions in the air, like some uninterrupted Abraham. After this mock killing, Lear's disconnection from his daughters is complete and from now on we see nothing but his indifference to them.

Lear's Love?

The obvious objection to reading the play in terms of a disintegration of parental sentiment is to deny that Lear loves his daughters at the beginning of the play. The objection is substantial. Although Lear spoke of such love to France (I.i.214), at least regarding Cordelia, the unfeeling way he banishes Cordelia suggests that although old, genuine parental attachment has not yet crystallized in Lear, and that he relates to parenting and parental love through a self-centered perspective. Cordelia is for him no more than a source of joy. A deeply loving parent, even a rash one, would find it at least difficult to banish the child whom he loves most, and he would then forever dwell on the event. Neither aspect can be discerned in Lear, who hardly thinks of Cordelia after banishing her. In the two instances when she does come to his mind (I.iv.221–25;

---

⁶ The relations between shame, self-exposure, and inability to acknowledge the other take on a different form in Cavell's reading of the play. For Cavell (to simplify), Lear will not expose himself due to shame, and this is why he avoids Cordelia's love. I see a somewhat different process, in which withdrawal from perceiving others intertwines with the withdrawal from and disintegration of parenting. Unlike Cavell, I do not see shame as the propelling cause of the tragedy, but as an end state the dramatic force of which relates to the inability to experience it: unclothing means that Lear's "madness" is a loss of the capacity to experience shame.

⁷ The "uncorrected" Quarto version of the line is "come on be true," an addition missing from the "corrected" Quarto as well as the Folio (Richard Strier forthcoming). It is right, I think, to say that the uncorrected Quarto is here more powerful than the other versions.

⁸ For those who wish to preserve it, the Quarto's mock trial could be an intermediate stage in the process of disconnection. Maintaining an accusing attitude will thereby turn into Lear's last attempt to remain a parent. We note that in this mad fantasy the trial *cannot* be completed. The natural conclusion of the fantasy should be execution, but it is interrupted by the escape of one of the daughters (Gonerill). Even at this late stage, Lear cannot follow the fantasy through, at least not with Gonerill. The short fantasy ends with him demanding Regan to be anatomized.

I.v.20) as well as when he recognizes her in Act IV, he is concerned with his regret and his guilt, never with love.

As for Gonerill and Regan, it appears even less likely that Lear loves them at the beginning of the play. Consequently, he should be even less concerned with them as they begin showing their horrific side to him. Lear is cold and mechanical in relation to Gonerill. He is somewhat warmer to Regan ("dearest Regan"), but here too, like the mere joy Cordelia is for him, one suspects a parental sentiment that does not go very deep. Lear is introduced experiencing parenting through self-centered terms. He uses his daughters and their actions as mere possessions that create his own sense of worth (and such deployment of one's children may have been an expected norm for some).[9] And so to claim that Lear withdraws from parenting and that this is a hidden tragic dimension of the play makes little sense if he has nothing much to withdraw from, since he is not a loving parent to begin with.

Yet superficial love is still love. While Lear is not a deeply caring parent at the beginning of the play, he does appear to love all of his daughters. He is prepared to live with Gonerill and Regan, rather than retire to some other place, and this indicates some degree of attachment on his part. He directs terms of emotional endearment to Regan. Most importantly, none of the daughters doubts his love (the jealousy of the older daughters stems from his loving Cordelia more [I.i.282] not from them being unloved). So while such love is superficial, it is difficult to deny that Lear loves all of his daughters at the beginning of the play (and this makes for the dramatic tradition of Lears who kiss their daughters during the opening contest, thus emphasizing paternal love).

Indeed, it is precisely his superficial experience of parenting that discloses the hidden tragic movement I am suggesting. The idea of discov-

---

[9] Dreher (1986, p. 21) cites John Stockwood (1581): "children are worthie to be reckoned among the goodes and substance of their fathers." This, though, compared with her other evidence, as well as evidence given in Houlbrooke (1985), seems an extreme position rather than the convention (see Ben Johnson's poems, "On My First Daughter" and "On My First Son"). In fact, the way by which the terrible D'Amville exemplifies precisely this limited view of parenting in Tourneur's *The Atheist's Tragedy* (V.i.99–100) may even suggest that seeing one's child merely as a means was associated with a limited morality of some sort. Colin Wilcockson (1991) supplies textual evidence for Shakespeare's presentation of parental authority in different plays, adding external evidence culled from the speeches of James I for political manipulation built into paternal status. For some surveys as to the nature and scope of paternal authority, see Rosemary O'day (1994, pp. 52–57) and Lawrence Stone (1979, pp. 116–27). For the transcoding between the monarchial and the paternal, see T. McFarland (1981).

ery and deepening of value only as one loses it is a structural feature in the epistemology of value that many tragedies employ. Lear initially fills the role of parent in a vacuous way. As the play unfolds, Lear will understand the depth of the role as he recedes from it. The desire to remain a parent will reduce him to a conciliatory attitude, it will diminish him to pleading, to endorsing parental sentiments founded on repayment (an idea that he initially despises), it will bring him to his knees—all of which are unbearable to his previous sense of self. He will thereby experience parental attachment as a force that transcends his old personality, a personality he will discard so that he can maintain (or work himself further into) parental sentiments. Madness—the destruction of his identity as such—will ensue only after attachment is finally dislodged in the imagined dismembering of Regan.

Lear's Love

As for the entrance *into* love, Lear's growing attachment to Cordelia involves the operation of visualized religious elements. The confused recollection of biblical visions that surfaces in Lear just before he and Cordelia are imprisoned (V.iii.20–25),[10] coheres with the heavily visual impact of the play, made up from its incisive images,[11] its powerful spectacles,[12] or

---

[10] Including the image of Samson—the hero who was twice betrayed by women and later blinded—and the foxes; the image of Joseph's solving Pharaoh's dream, his treacherous brothers coming to him only after a famine; the possible reference to Jephthah's daughter (the "sacrifices" on which the gods throw incense)—all these biblical stories serve as subtext to the lines above. The first two stories are strongly associated with betrayal. The story of Joseph also reenacts the infantile fantasy Rosenberg attributed to the experience of the entire play: being wronged (this time not by a parent but by one's siblings) and then saving them when one is in a position of power.

[11] The winds that "crack" their "cheeks," which—as Jay Halio, the Cambridge editor, notes—brings to mind the way the winds are drawn in old maps (III.ii.1), the "sheets of fire" Kent alludes to (III.ii.44), the "wheel of fire" on which Lear is bound, scorched by his own tears (IV.vi.43), the "pelican daughters" being nourished on their parent's blood, the mouth tearing at the hand that feeds it, the imagined cliffs of Dover.

[12] Gloucester's blinding, Lear's war with the elements, like Job calling out to God and (unlike Lear) receiving an answer in that ancient biblical storm. One political explanation for this invocation of visual religious elements alludes to Shakespeare's England as still missing the icons of the old religion (C. L. Barber, 1980; M. O'Connell, 2000). Barber and O'Connell have suggested that these needs were channeled from the churches and the biblical-oriented mystery plays to the spectacles of the contemporary Elizabethan theater.

the architectural placing of characters.[13] The other tragedies mostly leave us with memorable lines, not with such vivid religious imagery, the centrality of which may be gathered from past commentary, that reveals repeated invocation of religious spectacle to describe the play's impact.[14]

A reading/viewing experience of this sort, in which visual, religious, and primordial elements interplay, attests to a tragic experience that goes beyond organizing themes, attending to figures, or abstracting to the philosophical. I am referring now to the final inverted pietà scene in which we confront the most memorable religious spectacle this play offers when Lear enters with the dead Cordelia in his arms, lamenting that she will "come no more."[15] Lear now recognizes that some values and some forms of love are not possessed as things that one can have and may potentially lose. Neither are they hidden, waiting to be summoned from a submerged dimension. They are rather met, encountered upon discovering the price one would pay to preserve them.

Lear's newly discovered love for Cordelia supplies an additional fascinating depth to the learning by suffering pattern. Shakespeare is presenting a distilled tragic sense: the realization of value coupled with the recognition that it has been lost forever through one's own actions ("She's gone for ever" [V.iii.233]; "I might have saved her; now she's gone for ever" [V.iii.244]). Lear turns from rage at the injustice of the world, at everything being contaminated and meriting annihilation, to a dawning recognition of the *specifics* of what has been lost. This change

---

[13] Derek Traversi followed Robert Heilman's thorough analysis of the sight pattern in the play, in perceiving architectural constructions in the placing of characters (1969, p. 456).

[14] The play reminded Bradley of the statues at the Medici Chapel (1904, p. 244). Coleridge too recalled Michelangelo (1937, p. 134), as did Lamb and Marvin Rosenberg, the latter citing the former, himself being reminded of the statue *Moses* (1972, p. 24). Mrs. Jameson said that "if Cordelia reminds us of anything on earth, it is of one of the Madonnas in the old Italian pictures, 'with downcast eyes beneath th' almighty dove'" (1893, p. 251).

[15]

> And my poor fool is hanged. No, no, no life?
> Why should a dog, a horse, a rat have life,
> And thou no breath at all? Thou'lt come no more,
> Never, never, never, never, never.
> Pray you, undo this button. Thank you, sir.
> Do you see this? Look on her! Look, her lips.
> Look there, look there.   *Lear dies*
> (V.iii.279–84)

is manifested in moving from the first to the second tragic peak (from the storm to bemoaning Cordelia), but it is also built into the latter—the scene Dr. Johnson could not bring himself to reread. In lamenting Cordelia, he moves from the unfairness of death when the rest of the world goes on, to knowing that she will "come no more." This emphasizes a particularized understanding of parental love for the first time in the play. Lear now realizes that the father's joy of having his child enter his visual field is gone forever. Value appears not as intellectual recognition but as the inner warmth of reperceiving one's child. He now also notes the importance of moments spent together as time, the most expendable of commodities, gains a new significance ("Cordelia, Cordelia, stay a little"). Most importantly, unlike the opening of the play, in which love depended on verbal performance, in which degrees of love could be compared and repaid through quantification, here love for one's child is recognized as unrelated to actions, directed at the child's "thereness," at her being present, with him, in his sight.

❏

What, then, is parenting? *King Lear* closes with the identification of parenting with a relation of need to the very presence of the child. It is not Cordelia's actions or personality but her physical closeness that comes to matter most to Lear. Parenting is not primarily a concern with her words or her views but a relation of need to time spent together, manifested in the wish for her to "stay a little." The play repeatedly shows parenting to be a relation that is much deeper than the parent's personality by exhibiting how formative ideals of the parent's identity are readily exchanged for a few more moments of parental connection. As for parental disconnection, the play portrays the experience of such a process as a complete disintegration of the parent, involving alienation from one's own body, a desire for the world to disappear, and an experience that cannot be contained within the bounds of sanity.

Philosophy and Literature

Some of our most incisive philosophers have been staggeringly dismissive to matters of parenting. Plato seemed utterly obtuse about parenting, suggesting in *Timaeus* that it would be desirable for the sake of the commonwealth to separate parents from their children. More opens his *Utopia* by apologizing to Giles for his slow intellectual output, since:

"when I get home, I have to talk with my wife, chatter with my children, and consult with the servants. All these matters I consider part of my business, since they have to be done unless a man wants to be a stranger in his own house." Grouping wife, children, and servants in the same category, alien as that may appear to us, is still less disturbing than the choice of "business" as the appropriate category for this purpose. Montaigne once remarked that in his younger days "two or three" of his children had died, imparting the kind of indifference that historians of the family such as Aries, Abbot, and Slater thought to be defining of pre-eighteenth-century parenting. Nietzsche probably articulated a sentiment shared by other philosophers when he said that the idea of a philosopher with children is absurd.[16]

I have just claimed that *King Lear* presents important insights about the constitution of parenting. One obvious objection to reading the play in this way is that it is ahistorical: relations to one's children, in Shakespeare's age, are too conceptually remote from ours to facilitate reading the play in terms of a blanket category like "parenting." Lawrence Stone, for example, claims that "in the sixteenth and early seventeenth century very many fathers seem to have looked on their infant children with much the same degree of affection which men today bestow on domestic pets, like cats and dogs" (1979, p. 82). Stone's analysis has been challenged, e.g., by Ralph Houlbrooke (1984, pp. 134–40). Yet several historians still hold that far from the sort of affection and ties we associate with parental attachment today, the meaning of children for Shakespeare's contemporaries was basically to ensure the future of family lineage. They warn us that "in trying to assess parental attitudes toward children it would be wrongheaded to apply modern notions of individuality in a situation where these concepts were barely palpable . . ."[17] If this is so, the conceptual and emotional distance between us and early-moderns should prompt us to regard "parenting" as no more than a cultural construct that is iterated in different ways at different times. Accordingly, we must drop the pretense that we share with early-moderns overlapping parental sentiments that enable us to fruitfully communicate

---

[16] Nietzsche, *On the Genealogy of Morals*, III, 7. For a recent treatment of the child in philosophy, see S. T. Turner and G. B. Matthews (1998). I am obliged to this book's reader for making me aware of changed emphasis and awakened attention regarding parenting in recent philosophy.

[17] For the remark and the evidence, see M. Slater (1984, p. 110). For similar evidence as to the relation and meaning of children in early-modern England, see M. Abbott (1993, p. 47, 81).

with what they may have thought about parenting, as this attempt presupposes a nonexistent transcultural parental essence.

But claims regarding cultural constructs cannot simply be assumed as a priori truths blocking interpretive inquiries that may give us cause to reject them. Imposing the Stone-Abbott-Slater conception of parenting on Shakespeare's plays is (predictably) awkward. Macduff's lament over his dead children (discussed earlier in this book) is only one of several examples in which Shakespeare's treatment of children is at odds with such assessments.[18] The minor consequence of the previous reading is that either Stone and the others are wrong, or employing their framework for the purpose of understanding Shakespeare is erroneous because it underestimates the possibilities of a penetrating insight that goes beyond the conceptual limitations of an age. The interpretation also supported historical continuities and overlap with respect to parenting, thus disagreeing with a relativistic view of parenting.

I avoided aspects of parental meaning that seem to depend on the particularities of the father-daughter relationship. Consequently, the question of Shakespeare's attitude toward patriarchy—whether his plays subvert (Dusinberre, 1975; Dash, 1981), support (Pitt, 1981; McLuskie, 1985), or are ambivalent toward it (Erickson, 1985; Dreher, 1986), as well as questions having to do with his general image of the family (McFarland, 1981)—did not concern me as such. I think that we can justify such insulation of the question of parenting. I do not wish to deny that gender and versions of paternal authority shape in various ways the parenting we see (e.g., Lear's attempt to turn his daughters into his mothers is gendered, a missing dimension in the male-male subplot, as well as probably any adaptation that, like Kurosawa's *Ran*, would replace the daughters with sons). But the constituents of parenting that this examination of the play reveals—the relation to nature, time, presence, weakness—all strike me as shared by both genders, thus portraying "parenting" as such. Denaturalizing supposedly metaphysically given categories like parenting, by exposing the ways in which they are ideologically and historically shaped, is an important achievement of the last two decades of literary studies. But this tool and the part it plays in opposing coercive schemes that rely on systematic effacement of their own contingency can bias us against

---

[18] Shakespeare also deviated from the conception according to which children were imperfect, impure, and naturally evil: see A. Blake (1993) and M. Heberle (1994). L. Boose (1992) also notes the discrepancy between historical accounts regarding parental affection and Shakespeare's plays.

any attempt to respond to experiential overlap between men and women, between our time and Shakespeare's. The very fact of communication, our response to a text written in such a different cultural setting, means that although "us," "our time," "early-moderns," "men," "women," etc., are hopelessly general, they still inform, registering affections and values that can be shared between radically different contexts and that criticism should strive to preserve.

But do such literary insights into the experience of being a parent have anything to do with philosophical method? Have arguments been employed here? Or should the previous discussion be compartmentalized in some different academic department? The philosophical status of describing experiences with values raises its own set of problems. A philosopher can readily agree that parental values are constituted and in fact operate in the ways suggested by the play, yet claim that they *ought* to be formed and function differently. No detailed understanding of actual experiences (assuming that fictional depictions are indicative of actual experiences) can address this normative dimension that distinguishes philosophical reflection from anthropology or psychology. Moreover, nuanced observations of experiences with values are paraphrasable. These can be encountered outside literature and so cannot, on their own, justify a substantial (as opposed to an anecdotal) philosophical appeal to literary works.

Replying to these objections begins with breaking up the discussion into two questions: one pertaining to method, the other to content. The first question is how should one inquire into topics like parenting? The second is what particular beliefs regarding parenting should one cultivate? Starting with method, the moral psychology literature supplies goes beyond detailed understanding of Lear's deepened parental experience. Beyond sharpening or deepening values,[19] literature includes rhetorical forms that create openness and response to propositional content. It thereby informs moral psychology in this further way as well, instructing us how receptive attunement to content is achieved, both in the experience of a fictional character (Lear's opening up to meaning), and in the reader's own modified perception of such content. We can then look for an intellectual method that respects and is sensitive to the need to create an opening up to content. Elsewhere in this book, I argued that the specific connections Shakespeare depicts are contingent true claims, defendable through theories of rationality that encompass patterns of nonvalid

---

[19] Unpacking the metaphors of depth or sharpness (as well as the question of whether we should strive for these) was taken up in the first two chapters.

yet rational reasoning. Such connections—which on their own do not call for literature as such—are then *embedded* within an experience in which responses to the specifically literary dimensions of the work—and these require detailed mapping—enable persuasion to take place.

As for the mapping of experiences of discovery in *King Lear*—that is, the play's fictional moral psychology—the play first particularizes the general tragic formula of discovery according to which the importance and value of things are encountered as they are lost. More than grasping propositional content, values are embedded within experiences that determine the level of understanding. Knowledge is structuralized, meaning that if one does not undergo certain experiences, one never fully understands. *King Lear* also suggests that experiences matter not only epistemologically but also metaphysically. It is not that Lear merely *discovers* the depth of his love through his lived experience but that the growth of the values themselves occurs through and in connection with the process Lear undergoes.[20]

Turning from fictional occurrences to actual response patterns, we see that the insights regarding parenting are imposed on us by embedding them within a carefully constructed viewing/reading experience. Shakespeare's play addresses both the mature personality and, in the five different ways I mentioned above, touches what still remains of the child within us. Through invoking something of the experience of the moments of formative socialization and at the same time repeatedly addressing what is most adult in one—one's parenting—*King Lear* enables the perception of value to occur and at once to touch similar submerged moments. Speaking of a "return" to childhood is absurd. But this should not blind us to rhetorical forms in which the primordial and the critical can both be addressed, thereby accommodating moral insight that transcends systematic ("adult") thought.

But in what sense can an appeal to infantile, precritical aspects of the self be legitimate as part of philosophical discourse? Contemporary

---

[20] I realize that this last contention—according to which the existence of some abstract objects comes in degrees—needs further support given our disposition to think of existence as an all-or-nothing category. Moreover, nothing seems to be able to distinguish convincingly between epistemological as opposed to ontological descriptions of this process. The epistemically phrased "A growing realization of value X" does not seem to differ from the ontological "A growth of X itself." We still speak of love as growing or diminishing, and so I wish to maintain the possible sense of ontological amplification and creation of values through literature rather than just a growing realization of them. But one of these terminologies may be otiose.

ethics is always addressed to the adult. This assumption has hardly been questioned (Kant even made this overcoming of the child the defining element of the Enlightenment). But there has been a subtle attempt, by a mind that cannot be ignored, to show that even this is not sacred in philosophy. Plato's *Phaedo* involves an explicit request by Cebes, the most critical of Socrates' listeners in that dialogue, that Socrates speak as a "charmer" to the child that is in them (77e, 116b). The critical recipient of philosophical meaning asks to be addressed *as* a child. Plato thereby demands his readers to consider nothing less than the value of maturity as part of philosophical communication. Plato is not simply advocating receding from critical thinking but doing this in connection with the issue under discussion: dying and the afterlife—that is, a subject involving an essential agnostic dimension. It is when one wants to avoid the temptation to have no views regarding matters in which certainty is impossible, that there awakens a need, a rational need, to summon the submerged child. Socrates complies with the request in that dialogue, offering a detailed eschatological picture for his childlike hearers.[21] If we resist Hegel's dismissal of such moves as some hopeless prephilosophical confusion of mythical and conceptual thought, we can see that Plato is making a point about philosophical method as such. He is connecting the epistemological status of a claim, the weak degree to which it can be justified, with an enactment of specific response patterns rationally appropriate precisely in such contexts.

The unique experience that *King Lear*'s complex rhetoric creates explains the specific epistemic advantages of literature. If the grasp of value transcends propositional content and requires undergoing specific experiences, then following such processes in insightful fictional occurrences and having similar processes enacted as part of the reading/viewing experience makes moral growth possible. An enhanced moral understanding of this sort does not stem from being persuaded through a conceptual defense but by enriching the regulative themes that govern one's parenting. Parenting is not a given that awaits the correct description. It is, rather, an evolving construct, growing and diminishing through the themes that form it, and the degree of richness or poverty of this interplay largely constitutes what moral thinking on matters like parenting *is*. The suggestive capacities of literature of *King Lear*'s magnitude en-

---

[21] Hebrew readers can examine my detailed analysis of this moment in "Phaedo's Hair" (2002).

able *implanting* new voices within this interplay, thereby broadening moral thought. The depiction of the constituents of parenting in the play can thereby become an aspect of reasoning about parenting, a new coordinate of thought.[22]

The suggestive capacities of literature finesse a built-in resistance that is not always to our advantage. Acknowledging this prevents a rhetorical naiveté according to which intellectual discourse should simply "inform" through truth claims and arguments rather than respect the structuralization of knowledge. Mocking such a simplified outlook at one point in the *Symposium*, Socrates hurls at Agathon that sharp remark I chose as this book's epigraph, that it would have been fine indeed "if wisdom were a sort of thing that could flow out of the one of us who is fuller into him who is emptier, by our mere contact with each other, as water will flow through wool from the fuller cup into the emptier." *King Lear* does not only inform as to experiences with values but tells us something about the *ways* these can be addressed and reshaped. More specifically, a moral psychology according to which recognizing the meaning of parental values partly depends on experiences of pain and regression implies that, short of actually undergoing them, envisaging and following such experiences through a response that allows the submerged child to speak facilitates moral understanding. This is how we can partly duck the most disturbing implication of the play's own epistemology of value. For suppose that, as the play suggests, loss is indeed a condition for perceiving parental value and also for creating and developing it to its fullest capacity. Consequently, one is either in the tragic position that actual loss prescribes or one never fully creates or experiences the meanings that are always potentially there. Literature constitutes a (limited) middle way here by allowing readers to follow the details of the process in others. Do we thereby "learn" the value of

---

[22] Like Stampfer (1960), A. D. Nuttall (1996) thinks that the insight of the audience—*anagnorisis*—in this particular tragedy relates to thwarting the expectation for just retribution and poetic justice, and this, for Nuttall, generates pleasure (p. 102). Unlike Nuttall, for me the play does create insight, but different than the one that Nuttall argues for, and it concerns a deepened sense of the meaning of one's child. The abstract of my own reply to the question that troubles Nuttall ("Why does tragedy give pleasure"?) is: a) tragedy does *not* give pleasure; and b) we watch and read tragedies because they create meaningful experiences for us, and these experiences can, at best, sharpen, amplify, or even create internal meaning and internal value. We look for these meanings, not for pleasure. The latter is merely an epiphenomenal contingency.

parental love? This could seem too crude, no doubt because learning is associated with managing some skill, digesting some piece of knowledge, or grasping some pedantic message, rather than being an experience in which values and voices interlaced with responses that are not limited to analysis. Learning in this latter sense decisively depends on allowing this interplay to occur, by entering and reentering it and choosing this experience as a source of instruction.

Appendix A: A Note on Lear's Motivation

In Geoffrey of Monmouth, in Holinshed, in Higgins, and in Warner, the kingdom is forced out of Lear's hands (Bullough, 1975, p. 313, 318, 326, 335). Shakespeare chose to follow the anonymous *King Leir*—or Spenser's version of the story in *The Faerie Queene* (II.x.-27–32)—in making Lear give it away (Bullough, p.345). Why? The text tells us that Lear divides his kingdom since he wants to retire and announce the dowers so as to avoid future internal war. The verdict of critics has usually been that this initial plan is a mistake obvious to all,[1] though there have been dissenting voices according to which the initial plan shows exquisite political subtlety (e.g., Jaffa, 1964). No one doubts that Lear's actions when he drops his original plan constitute a grave mistake. Indeed, whatever Shakespeare may have intended for his audience to think about the original plan, he takes care to emphasize the implausibility of Lear's revised course of action, through criticisms of it that are mouthed by Cordelia, France, and Kent, and later by Gonerill, Regan, and the Fool. The text thus highlights his actions as implausible as he is taking them (rather than some post factum assessment of a reasonable course of action).

Why does Lear make this error? We could of course say that he is mad or senile. But that Shakespeare was not interested in presenting some foolish old man can be gathered from his employment of his sources. In *King Leir* and in Spenser's version, the old king is truly motivated by the need to know which of his daughters loves him most and seems to sincerely believe that the verbal test could decide this (Bullough, pp.339–41). Shakespeare saves his hero from such a demeaning characterization by making the division itself predecided, and thus the demand for loving oratory no more than a game of verbal pleasing in exchange for presents. Lear is not foolish—so why, again, is he making this error?

Shakespeare supplies a number of hints to suggest an underlying anxiety in Lear that causes him to be so *insistent* on making this error, as well

---

[1] James's *Basilikon Doron* explicitly condemns kings who divide their kingdoms, claiming that such an act creates discord. In his advice to the prince, James says: "make your eldest son Isaac, leaving him all your kingdoms, and provide the rest with private possessions. Otherwise by dividing your kingdoms, ye shall leave the seed of division and discord among your posterity, as befell to this isle by the division and assignment thereof to the three sons of Brutus: Locrine, Albanact, and Camber" (p. 142).

APPENDIX A

as explaining his initial attraction to the division plan and to reversing the relations of dependency between him and his daughters. Lear is occupied with the question of (for lack of better terminology) "self" beyond its determination by the set of roles in which the person is enmeshed. Reversing relations of dependency and control accommodates Lear's desire to find out the true uncontaminated feelings of his daughters. Unlike the tales of kings who put on rags to find out what their subjects truly think of them (*Measure for Measure*, a play contemporary with *King Lear*, explicitly uses something like this theme), here testing the genuine affections of others is not an explicit choice Lear makes but is rather a process he is drawn to. Testing his daughters is not so much a premeditated decision but evolves as part of the actual workings of his interaction with them, as when he runs out into an approaching storm waiting to be stopped by them, or making himself intentionally difficult and uncontrolled at Gonerill's house.[2]

Here are my reasons for attributing to him this motivation:

1. The need itself is an understandable outcome of his predicament. Lear has the problem that troubles anyone who occupies a position of power for too long: surrounding attitudes are always commending and supportive, and so there is no way to know the degree to which they are grounded on dependency. Once mad, Lear will impart the anxieties that flattery creates: "To say 'ay' and 'no' to everything I said 'ay' and 'no' to . . ." (IV.v.96). After a lifetime without the guidance that the resistance of the other provides, the persistent worries of genuine self worth call for some action. This happens upon Lear reaching the point in life where future achievements can no longer motivate present action and not yet entering the mellow numbness of old age that avoids perceiving itself as a form of waiting. Lear's moment—at least on some subliminal level—is one of self-assessment. In highlighting a king's problem with flattery, Shakespeare may even be responding to a particular sensitivity of James I, whose writings on good monarchy include this advice to his son: "Choose then for all these offices men of known wisdom, honesty, and good conscience . . . [who are] specially free of that filthy vice of flattery, the pest of all princes and wrack of republics.

---

[2] This can be challenged by saying that Lear is not being intentionally difficult but is simply acting out the habits of a long life of unconstrained behavior coupled with an egoism that sees no one else. This diminishes Lear, since it will mean that he is so blind to the changed situation and the compromises that it requires of him that he never even contemplates their possibility.

For since in the first part of this treatise I forewarned you to be at war with your own inward flatterer, *philautia*, how much more should ye be at war with outward flatterers, who are nothings so sib to you as your self is, by the selling of such counterfeit wares only pressing to ground their greatness upon your ruins?"[3] The suspicion of flattery as an obstacle to truth recurs in other contemporary drama (see Duke Pietro's lines [I.ii.16–31] in Marston's *The Malcontent*).

2. This motivation is already present in some of the sources. In Geoffrey of Monmouth, Holinshed, and Higgins, Lear's worry that he is loved merely because of his possessions is explicitly ignited by Cordelia in the opening exchange leading to her banishment (Bullough, p. 312, 317, 325). Shakespeare keeps the threat that acceptance and value depend on power as a regulative anxiety operating in Lear, but does not retain the explicit and crude manner in which Cordelia sets it off in these authors.

3. Lear's anxieties are also perceived in his worry that he is nothing but an empty, marvelously attired shell that cannot be loved since there is nothing there to love. Thus, when Lear asks, "Who is it that can tell me who I am?" (I.iv.189) (the Fool answering—or, in Quarto, Lear *himself* saying—"Lear's shadow"), or asks, "Does any here know me?" (I.iv.185), Lear is not merely angry but is giving voice to the fear that his past identity has consisted of no more than his title and power and that nothing now remains. The Fool—the voice of Lear's fears—gives a precise articulation to the anxiety that motivates such a test: "Fathers that wear rags / Do make their children blind, But fathers that bear bags / Shall see their children kind" (II.iv.44–47). It is the examination of the relevance of this piece of folk wisdom to him that worries Lear. Note too how the Fool formulates Lear's precise fears regarding an inner core that may or may not be there. He tells Lear that he is "an O without a figure" and that he is "nothing" (I.iv.152–53). When Regan declares that "he hath ever but slenderly known himself" (I.i.284), she is missing Lear's anxiety that there is *nothing* to know. In this context, the haunting repetition of the word

---

[3] *Basilikon Doron*, p. 135. There are various other intertextual connections between the plays performed by the King's Men and the King's own writings and predilections. *Macbeth* and *Measure for Measure* contain their own echoes of the king's theoretic interests (*Measure for Measure* responds to passages and problems set out in *Basilikon Doron*) or meaningful events in his life (*Macbeth* is often seen as responding both to The Gunpowder Plot and to James's fascination with witchcraft, exhibited in his *Daemonologie*). *King Lear* may be continuing this tacit dialogue with the King's sensitivities.

APPENDIX A

"nothing" in the play gains special significance by enkindling the submerged dread of being a nothing.[4]

4. Attributing this motivation to Lear also explains his otherwise implausible behavior toward Cordelia in the division scene. Lear's outrage at Cordelia is not the reaction of some hysterical old man (Richardson, 1783). He is also not simply reacting angrily to his daughter's breaking the conventional expectation of the obedience of a child, especially a daughter, to parental authority, nor is he simply angry at failing in his attempt to bribe some love out of his daughters one last time (Cavell, 1987). Cordelia incites Lear's anger because her words tap into *the very same* anxiety that partly led him to divide his kingdom in the first place. Lear's outrage on hearing Cordelia's chain of "nothings" in the division scene stems from her repeatedly voicing precisely his own fear of being a nothing, loved only because of the bonds of duty, not more nor less. Cordelia characterizes her filial duty not by alluding to some merit of his but as a form of repayment ("You have begot me, bred me, loved me. I / Return those duties back as are right fit, / Obey you, love you, and most honour you" [91–93]). Anyone can collapse upon learning that a loved one relates to loving them merely as an obligation ("I love your majesty / According to my bond, no more nor less"). The fact that she equates his love with a duty that needs to be returned by her is not only to offend him by manifesting an extremely impoverished and cold experience of the emotions Lear holds dearest. It is also to import into affective relations the economic language of debts that can be repaid and, by implication, ultimately *settled*.

An obvious objection to all this is that attributing to Lear a test implies that he is more frank than most parents, willing to consider possible answers that most will never dare to face. Yet such a reading seems to be flatly contradicted by the surface meaning of the division scene, in which Lear appears to readily fall for the "glib and oily art" of insincere speech. At least, this is what Cordelia and Kent perceive, whereas Regan sees nothing but the instability of an old man who has "ever but slenderly known himself" (I.i.285). But Regan oversimplifies Lear. Lear has a dialectical relation to his regulative anxiety. His is not the story of an unreflective old man, but rather of one who alternates between shunning

---

[4] Rosenberg (1972, p. 69) counts thirty uses of "nothing" and hundreds of uses of other negative words as opposed to only about thirty uses of affirmatives in the entire play.

certain threatening implications and being strongly pulled to examine what they are. We note, for example, how Cordelia and Kent repeatedly ask him to reflect on the untruthfulness of Gonerill and Regan, yet he refuses to consider this. The fact that he is *aware* of dark possibilities rather than simply blind to them is also conveyed through his demand to get Cordelia's banishment over and done with, refusing to hear Kent's insistence that he rethink his decision in a cooler hour. The reluctance to pause manifests a desire to avoid the sort of considerations that, as Lear knows, cool reasoning will inevitably raise. We also see this when the Fool confronts him with a possible truth, and Lear threatens him with the whip. He thereby refuses to acknowledge truth, eliciting from the Fool: "Truth's a dog must to kennel" (I.iv.97). At the same time, Lear tells the Fool that if he lies "we'll have you whipped" (I.iv.142). This is Lear's regulative tension, oscillating between the need to know and the desire to remain "pleased" (I.i.229), which is manifested in threatening the fool with the whip when he says too much (I.iv.96), or in looking for some distraction on first being confronted with the possibility that he is being wronged by Gonerill (I.iv.57–61).

The desire to know is stronger than the need to avoid looking, and so Lear goes on with the test. The results of the test are, of course, sad. But one way to connect with Lear's experience is to note that *not* going on with the test carries its own price. Note that the tragedy closes not with a statement regarding reestablished order, but with the wish that "we that are young shall never *see so much* . . ."

Appendix B: A Note on Shakespeare and Rhetoric

SHAKESPEARE did not read deeply books of rhetoric or dialectic, nor did he participate in thematic advancement of this or that general conception of rhetoric. But it is still reasonable to ask in this book's context what version of rhetoric Shakespeare would most probably have encountered, living as he did in a cultural and educational milieu that placed such a high value on rhetoric.

Beginning with education, studies of Renaissance rhetorical training in Shakespeare's England inform us that the curriculum was basically limited to Cicero, Quintilian and Aphthonius. Baldwin (1944) gives evidence of Shakespeare's familiarity with Cicero's *Topics*, the *Ad Herrenium*, Erasmus's *De Copia*, as well as Quintilian. A similarity between Don Armado's letter in *Love's Labor Lost* and an example in Wilson's *The Art of Rhetoric* (Plimpton, 1933, pp. 117–18) suggests Shakespeare's familiarity with Wilson—which was in any case probably the most popular textbook of rhetoric—whose book was primarily inspired by the great Latin rhetoricians. Although it was known to specialists, Aristotle's *Rhetoric* was translated and began to circulate only in 1619. The significance of this is that it was probably not the argument-oriented conception of rhetoric that Aristotle emphasized but rather the figurative, embellishment-oriented one that would have reached Shakespeare (Skinner, 1996, pp. 36–37). One possible qualification of this claim is the popularity of *in utramque partem* exercises—arguing for both sides of a question—as part of the rhetorical education of the time, a tradition that presupposes an Isocratean version of probable argumentation and Protagorean skepticism regarding monologic truth. Though there is no reason to suppose that the deeper framework that underlies this practice, even if Shakespeare was exposed to it, had a lasting effect on him at his age.

The centrality of Cicero and Quintilian suggests that the integrative ideal of combining reason and eloquence may have reached Shakespeare directly or by paraphrase. The integrative ideal is advocated by Cicero in his *On Invention* or *The Orator*, and it is more instrumentally expressed in book twelve of Quintilian's *Institutio Oratoria*. This speculation is strengthened if we suppose that he would have practiced exercises of elaborate writing, as these were presented in Erasmus's *De Copia*, a text that presupposes the Ciceronian ideal of copious wisdom and Cicero's rejection of a distinction between wisdom and its expression.

One should not, however, overemphasize the significance of Shakespeare's education regarding this matter, as he left school when he was about fifteen and we have no reason to suppose that theoretical matters underlying the curriculum would have reached him or that he cared deeply about them. Controversies over Ramism, too, probably never touched Shakespeare in any significant way. Harvey and Fenner, who imported Ramism into England, published their work only in 1574 (Harvey) and 1584 (Fenner), which makes it difficult to guess whether and to what extent Ramism infiltrated into education in the 1570s. The counter-Ramist sentiment of Vossius was published in England through Farnaby only in 1625, and so my own guess is that the theoretical implications of the Ramist reforms, which involved an ongoing Oxford-Cambridge controversy, would have hardly interested Shakespeare in its theoretical form. Marlowe's familiarity with Ramus—dramatizing his murder in *The Massacre at Paris*, or putting the first line of the *Dialectic* into the mouth of Dr. Faustus (Miller, 1939, p. 118)—suggests a different connection of these issues with Shakespeare (not through his education but through Marlowe), though once again we are guessing.

Works Cited

Abbott, M. *Family Ties: English Families, 1540–1920*. London: Routledge, 1993.

Adamson, J. Othello *as Tragedy: Some Problems of Judgment and Feeling*. Cambridge, NY: Cambridge UP, 1980.

Adelman, J. *The Common Liar: An Essay on* Antony and Cleopatra. New Haven/London: Yale UP, 1973.

——— "Iago's Alter Ego: Race as Projection in *Othello*." *Shakespeare Quarterly* 48.2 (1997): 125–44.

——— *Suffocating Mothers: Fantasies of Maternal Origin in Shakespeare's Plays*, Hamlet *to* The Tempest. New York: Routledge, 1992.

Adler, C. A. "Richard III—His Significance as a Study in Criminal Life-Style." *International Journal of Individual Psychology* 2.3 (1936): 55–60.

Anderson, M. "Hamlet: The Dialectic between Eye and Ear." *Renaissance and Reformation* 27.4 (1991): 299–313.

Aristotle. *On the Parts of Animals*. Trans. A. I. Peck. Cambridge: Harvard UP, 1937.

Babb, L. *The Elizabethan Malady: A Study of Melancholia in English Literature from 1580 to 1642*. East Lansing: Michigan State College Press, 1951.

Bacon, F. "Of Deformity." In *The Essays of Francis Bacon*. Ed. Mary A. Scott. New York: C. Scribner's Sons, 1908.

——— *Sylva Sylvarum. Works*. Eds. J. Spedding, R. L. Ellis, and D. D. Heath. London: 1857.

Baldwin, T. W. *William Shakespeare's Small Latine & Lesse Greeke*, Vol. 2. Urbana: University of Illinois Press, 1944.

Barber, C. L. "The Family in Shakespeare's Development: Tragedy and Sacredness." In *Representing Shakespeare: New Psychoanalytic Essays*. Eds. Murray M. Schwartz and Coppélia Kahn. Baltimore and London: The John Hopkins UP, 1980, pp. 188–202.

Bartels, E. C. "*Othello* and Africa: Postcolonialism Reconsidered." *William and Mary Quarterly* 3rd ser. 54 (1997): 45–64.

Barthelemy, A. G. *Critical Essays on Shakespeare's* Othello. New York: G. K. Hall & Co., 1994.

Beardsley, M. C. *Aesthetics: Problems in the Philosophy of Criticism*. New York: Harcourt Brace, 1958.

Blake, A. "Children and Suffering in Shakespeare's Plays." *Yearbook of English Studies* 23 (1933): 293–304.

Boethius, Anicius Manlius Severinus. *Fundamentals of Music*. Bk. 1. Trans. Calvin M. Bower. New Haven: Yale UP, 1989.

Boose, L. E. "The Father and the Bride in Shakespeare." In *Ideological Approaches to Shakespeare: The Practice of Theory.* Eds. R. P. Merrix and N. Ranson. New York: The Edwin Mellen Press, 1992, pp. 3–38.

Booth, W. C. *Modern Dogma and the Rhetoric of Assent.* Indiana: Notre Dame UP, 1974.

——— *The Company We Keep: An Ethics of Fiction*, Berkeley: University of California Press, 1988.

——— "Why Ethical Criticism Can Never be Simple." *Style* 32.2 (1998): 351–65.

Bradley, A. C. *Shakespearean Tragedy: Lectures on* Hamlet, Othello, King Lear, Macbeth. London: Macmillan, 1904.

——— "Shakespeare's *Antony and Cleopatra*." In *Oxford Lectures on Poetry.* London: Macmillan, 1941.

Brooke, A. *The Tragicall Historye of Romeus and Juliet.* Edited version of Brooke's translation supplied in the Arden edition of Shakespeare's *Romeo and Juliet*, 1562.

Brown, J. R. *Shakespeare,* Antony and Cleopatra: *A Casebook.* London: Macmillan, 1991.

Brudney, D. "Knowledge and Silence: *The Golden Bowl* and Moral Philosophy." *Critical Inquiry* 16.2 (1990): 397–437.

——— "*Lord Jim* and Moral Judgment: Literature and Moral Philosophy." *The Journal of Aesthetics and Art Criticism* 56.3 (1998): 265–81.

Brümmer, V. *The Model of Love: A Study in Philosophical Theology.* Cambridge/New York: Cambridge UP, 1993.

Bullough, G. *Narrative and Dramatic Sources of Shakespeare*, Vol. VII. New York: Columbia UP.

Burnett, C., M. Fend, and P. Gouk. *The Second Sense: Studies in Hearing and Musical Judgment from Antiquity to the Seventeenth Century.* London: Warburg Institute, 1991.

Burton, D. M. *Shakespeare's Grammatical Style.* London: University of Texas Press, 1973.

——— "Discourse and Decorum in the First Act of *Richard III.*" *Shakespeare Studies* 14 (1981): 55–84.

Burton, R. *The Anatomy of Melancholy*, Vol. II. Kessinger Publishing, 1991.

Calderwood, L. J. *Shakespearean Metadrama.* Minneapolis: University of Minnesota Press, 1971.

——— *To Be and Not To Be: Negation and Metadrama in Hamlet.* New York: Columbia UP, 1983.

Campbell, G. *The Philosophy of Rhetoric.* Carbondale: S. Illinois UP, 1963 (orig. 1776).

Carroll, N. "Art, Narrative, and Moral Understanding." In *Aesthetics and Ethics: Essays at the Intersection.* J. Levinson (ed.). Cambridge/New York: Cambridge UP, 1998, pp. 126–60.

Cavell, S. *Disowning Knowledge in Six Plays of Shakespeare.* Cambridge: Cambridge UP, 1987.

Charney, M. *Shakespeare's Roman Plays.* Cambridge: Harvard UP, 1961.

Clemen, W. H. *The Development of Shakespeare's Imagery.* New York: Hill and Wang, 1962.

Coleridge, S. T. *Lectures on Shakespeare, Etc.* London: Dent, 1937.

——— *Shakespearean Criticism*, Vol. I. London: J. M. Dent & Sons, 1960.

Cooper, H. M, A. A. Munich, and S. M. Squire, eds. *Arms and the Woman: War, Gender, and Literary Representation.* Chapel Hill: University of North Carolina Press, 1989.

Cope, J. I. *The Theater and the Dream: From Metaphor to Form in Renaissance Drama.* Baltimore/London: The John Hopkins UP, 1973.

Copenhaver, B. P, and C. B. Schmitt. *Renaissance Philosophy*, Oxford: Oxford UP, 1992.

Crombie, A. C. *Science, Optics and Music in Medieval and Early Modern Thought.* London: Hambledon, 1990.

Currie, G. "Realism of Character and the Value of Fiction." In *Aesthetics and Ethics: Essays at the Intersection.* Ed. J. Levinson. Cambridge/New York: Cambridge UP, 1998, pp. 161–81.

Curtis, J.R. "The 'Speculative and the Offic'd Instrument.'" *Shakespeare Quarterly* 24.2 (1973): 188–97.

Danto, A.C. Introduction to *The Philosophy of (Erotic) Love.* Eds. Robert Solomon and Kathleen Higgins. Lawrence: University Press of Kansas, 1991.

Dash, I. *Wooing, Wedding, and Power.* New York: Columbia UP, 1981.

Day, G. M. "'Determine'd to Prove a Villain': Theatricality in *Richard III*." *Critical Survey* 3.2 (1991): 149–56.

De Man, P. "The Epistemology of Metaphor." *Critical Inquiry* 5.1 (1978): 13–30.

de Rougemont, D. *Love in the Western World.* Trans. M. Belgion. New York: Pantheon, 1956.

Diamond, C. *The Realistic Spirit: Wittgenstein, Philosophy, and the Mind*, Cambridge: MIT Press, 1991.

——— "Martha Nussbaum and the Need for Novels." *Philosophical Investigations* 16.2 (1993): 128–53.

Dickey, F. M. *Not Wisely But Too Well: Shakespeare's Love Tragedies.* California: Braun & Alhambra, 1966.

Dollimore, J. *Radical Tragedy: Religion, Ideology and Power in the Drama of Shakespeare and his Contemporaries*, 2nd ed. Durham: Duke UP, 1993.

Draper, J. W. *The Othello of Shakespeare's Audience.* New York: Octagon Books, 1966.

Dreher, D. E. *Domination and Defiance: Fathers and Daughters in Shakespeare.* Lexington: The University Press of Kentucky, 1986.

Dusinberre, J. *Shakespeare and the Nature of Women*. New York: Barnes and Noble, 1975.

Duska, R. "Philosophy, Literature and Views of the Good Life." *Proceedings of the American Catholic Philosophical Association* 54 (1980): 181–88.

Eldridge, R. *On Moral Personhood: Philosophy, Literature, Criticism, and Self-Understanding*. Chicago: The University of Chicago Press, 1989.

Eliot, G. *Middlemarch*. London: Penguin Books Ltd., 1970.

Empson, W. *Essays on Shakespeare*. D. B. Pirie, Ed. Cambridge: Cambridge University Press, 1986.

Erickson, P. *Patriarchal Structures in Shakespeare's Drama*. Berkeley: University of California Press, 1985.

Evans, G. L. *The Upstart Crow: An Introduction to Shakespeare's Plays*. London: Dent, 1982.

Evans, I. *The Language of Shakespeare's Plays*. London: Methuen & Co., 1959.

Evans, R.O. *The Osier Cage: Rhetorical Devices in "Romeo and Juliet."* Lexington: University of Kentucky Press, 1966.

Falck, C. *Myth, Truth, and Literature: Toward a True Post-Modernism*. Cambridge/New York: Cambridge UP, 1989.

Febvre, L. *The Problem of Unbelief in the Sixteenth Century: The Religion of Rabelais*. Trans. Beatrice Gottlieb. Cambridge: Harvard UP, 1982.

Feldman, A. B. "Othello's Obsessions." *American Imago* 9.1 (1952): 147–64.

Fernie, E. "Shame in *Othello*." *The Cambridge Quarterly* 28.1 (1999): 19–45.

Ferry, A. *The "Inward" Language: Sonnets of Wyatt, Sidney, Shakespeare, Donne*. Chicago and London: The University of Chicago Press, 1983.

Foakes, R. A. "Images of Death: Ambition in *Macbeth*." In *Focus on Macbeth*. Ed. J. R. Brown. London: Routledge & Kegan Paul, 1982, pp. 7–29.

Foster, D. W. "Macbeth's War on Time." *English Literary Renaissance* 16.2 (1986): 319–42.

Frankfurt, G. H. *The Reasons of Love*. Princeton: Princeton UP, 2004.

Freud, S. "Those Wrecked by Success." In *The Standard Edition of the Complete Psychological Works of Sigmund Freud*. Ed. James Strachey. London: The Hogarth Press and the Institute of Psychoanalysis, Vol. 14, 1957, pp. 316–32.

Gallagher, C. "Marxism and the New Historicism." In *The New Historicism*. Ed. H. Aram Veeser. New York/London: Routledge, 1989.

Garber, M. B. *Dream in Shakespeare: From Metaphor to Metamorphosis*. New Haven and London: Yale University Press, 1974.

Gibbons, B. Introduction to the Arden edition of *Romeo and Juliet*. London: Methuen & Co., 1980.

Gosson, S. *The Schoole of Abuse: Containing a Pleasant Invective against Poets, Pipers, Players, Jesters, & C*. Elibron Classics: n.p., 2003 [1579].

Gouk, P. "Some English Theories of Hearing in the Seventeenth Century: Before and After Descartes." In *The Second Sense: Studies in Hearing and Musical*

Judgment from Antiquity to the Seventeenth Century. Eds. C. Burnett, M. Fend, and P. Gouk. London: Warburg Institute, 1991, pp. 95–114.
Graff, G. "Cooptation." In *The New Historicism*. Ed. H. Aram Veeser. New York/London: Routledge, 1989, pp. 168–81.
Granville-Barker, H. *Prefaces to Shakespeare*, Vol. 1. Princeton: Princeton UP, 1946.
Greenblatt, S. *Renaissance Self-Fashioning: From More to Shakespeare.* Chicago: The University of Chicago Press, 1980.
—— *Marvelous Possessions: The Wonder of the New World.* Oxford: Clarendon Press, 1988.
—— *Learning to Curse: Essays in Early Modern Culture.* New York/London: Routledge, 1990.
Greenblatt, S. and C. Gallagher. *Practicing New Historicism.* Chicago: The University of Chicago Press, 2001.
Gross, K. *Shakespeare's Noise.* Chicago: The University of Chicago Press, 2001.
Guj, L. "*Macbeth* and the Seeds of Time." *Shakespeare Studies* 18 (1986): 175–88.
Gurr, A. *Playgoing in Shakespeare's London.* Cambridge: Cambridge University Press, 1994.
Hallstead, R. N. "Idolatrous Love: A New Approach to *Othello*." *Shakespeare Quarterly* 19.2 (1968): 107–24.
Hammond, A. Introduction to the Arden edition of *King Richard III*. New York: Routledge, 1981.
Hampshire, S. *Morality and Conflict.* Cambridge, Mass.: Harvard UP, 1983.
Harbage, A. *As They Like It: An Essay on Shakespeare and Morality.* New York: Macmillan Company, 1947.
Hassel, R. C., Jr. "Last Words and Last Things: St. John, Apocalypse, and Eschatology in *Richard III*." *Shakespeare Studies* 18 (1986): 25–40.
Hazlitt, W. *Characters of Shakespeare's Plays.* London: Oxford UP, 1962 [1817].
Heberle, M. A. "'Innocent Prate': *King John* and Shakespeare's Children." In *Infant Tongues: The Voice of the Child in Literature.* Eds. E. Goodenough and M. A. Herberle. Detroit: Wayne State UP, 1994.
Heilman, R. B. *This Great Stage.* Baton Rouge: Louisiana State UP, 1948.
—— *Magic in the Web: Action and Language in* Othello. Lexington: University of Kentucky Press, 1956.
—— "Satiety and Conscience: Aspects of *Richard III*." *The Antioch Review* 24 (1964): 57–73.
Hendricks, M. and P. Parker. *Women, "Race," and Writing in the Early Modern Period.* London/New York: Routledge, 1994.
Heywood, T. *An Apology for Actors.* Elibron Classics (unabridged facsimile of the edition published in 1841 by The Shakespeare Society): n.p., 2003 [1612].

Hillman, D. "Visceral Knowledge." In *The Body in Parts: Fantasies of Corporeality in Early Modern Europe*. Eds. D. Hillman and C. Mazzio. London: Routledge, 1997, pp. 81–106.

Holland. N. N. "The Dumb-Show Revisited." *Notes and Queries* 203.5 (1958): 191.

——— "Romeo's Dream and the Paradox of Literary Realism." In M.D. Faber's *The Design Within: Psychoanalytic Approaches to Shakespeare*. New York: Science House, 1970.

Hollingdale, P. "Othello and Desdemona." *Critical Survey* 1.1 (1989): 43–52.

Honigmann, E. A. J. *Shakespeare: Seven Tragedies: The Dramatist's Manipulation of Response*. London/Basingstoke: The Macmillan Press, 1976.

Hospers, J. "Implied Truths in Literature." *Journal of Aesthetics and Art Criticism* 19.1 (1960): 37–46.

Houlbrooke, A. R. *The English Family: 1450–1700*. London: Longman, 1984.

Jaffa, H. V. "The Limits of Politics: *King Lear*, Act I, Scene I." In *Shakespeare's Politics*. Eds. Allan Bloom with Harry Jaffa. Chicago: Chicago UP, 1964, pp. 113–45.

(King) James I. *Basilikon Doron*. In *The True Law of Free Monarchies and Basilikon Doron*. Eds. D. Fischlin and M. Fortier. Toronto: CRRS, 1996 [1599].

James, D. G. *The Dream of Learning: An Essay on the Advancement of Learning, Hamlet, and King Lear*. Oxford: Clarendon Press, 1951.

James, S. *Passion and Action: The Emotions in Seventeenth-Century Philosophy*. Oxford: Clarendon Press, 1997.

Jameson, (Mrs.) A. B. *Shakespeare's Heroines: Characteristics of Woman, Moral, Poetical, and Historical*. London: George Bell & Sons, 1893.

Jones, E. *Scenic Form in Shakespeare*. Oxford: Clarendon Press, 1971.

——— "Richard III's Disfigurement: A Medical Postscript." *Folklore* 91.2 (1980): 211–27.

Joughin, J. J. and S. Malpas. *The New Aestheticism*. Manchester: Manchester UP, 2003.

Kalin, J. "Philosophy Needs Literature: John Barth and Moral Nihilism." *Philosophy and Literature* 1.1 (1976): 170–182.

——— "How Wide the Gulf?" (A Rejoinder to H. M. Curtler). *Philosophy and Literature* 2.1 (1978): 116–23.

Keats, J. *Selected Poems and Letters*. Ed. D. Bush. Boston: Houghton Mifflin, 1959.

Kerrigan, W. "*Macbeth* and the History of Ambition." In John O'Neill, ed. *Freud and the Passions*. University Park, Penn. State UP, 1996, pp. 13–24.

Kertzer, J. *Poetic Argument: Studies in Modern Poetry*. Kingston/London/Montreal: McGill-Queen's UP, 1989.

Kirsch, A. "The Polarization of Erotic Love in *Othello*." *The Modern Language Review* 73.4 (1978): 721–40.

―――. "Macbeth's Suicide." *ELH* 51.2 (1984): 269–96.

Kirschbaum, L. *English Literary History II*, 1944. From *A Casebook on Othello*, Ed. L. F. Dean. New York: Thomas Y. Crowell Company, 1962.

Knight, W. *The Imperial Theme*. London: Methuen, 1951.

―――. *The Wheel of Fire: Interpretation of Shakespeare's Tragedy*. New York: Meridian Books, 1964.

Knights, L. C. *Some Shakespearean Themes*. Stanford, 1959, or London: Chatto & Windus, 1957.

Kott, J. *Shakespeare: Our Contemporary*. Trans. B. Taborski. New York: Anchor Books, 1966 [1964].

Lamarque, P. and S. H. Olsen. *Truth, Fiction, and Literature: A Philosophical Perspective*. Oxford: Clarendon Press, 1994.

Leavis, F. R. *The Common Pursuit*. London: Chatto and Windus, 1952.

Lehmann, C. "Strictly Shakespeare? Dead Letters, Ghostly Fathers, and the Cultural Pathology of Authorship in Baz Luhrmann's *William Shakespeare's Romeo and Juliet*." *Shakespeare Quarterly* 52.2 (2001): 189–221.

Levine, G. "Reclaiming the Aesthetic." In *Aesthetics and Ideology*. Ed. G. Levine. New Jersey: Rutgers UP, (1995): 1–28.

―――. "Saving Disinterest: Aesthetics, Contingency, and Mixed Conditions." *New Literary History* 32.4 (2001): 907–31.

Levin, R. *New Readings vs. Old Plays*. Chicago: The University of Chicago Press, 1982.

Loomba, A. "Sexuality and Racial Difference." In Barthelemy, 1994, pp. 162–86.

Loomba, A. and M. Orkin. *Post-Colonial Shakespeares*. London/New York: Routledge, 1998.

Lucking, D. " 'And All Things Change them to the Contrary': *Romeo and Juliet* and the Metaphysics of Language." *English Studies* 78.1 (1997): 8–18.

Lyotard, J. F. *The Differend: Phrases in Dispute*. Trans. G. van den Abbeele. Minneapolis: University of Minnesota Press, 1988.

Mahood, M. M. *Shakespeare's Wordplay*. London: Methuen & Co., 1968.

Mason, J. *Philosophical Rhetoric: The Function of Indirection in Philosophical Writings*. London/New York: Routledge, 1989.

Maus, K. E. *Inwardness and Theater in the English Renaissance*. Chicago/London: The University of Chicago Press, 1995.

McCormick, P. "Moral Knowledge and Fiction." *The Journal of Aesthetics and Arts Criticism* 41.4 (1983): 399–410.

McFarland, T. "The Image of the Family in *King Lear*." In *On King Lear*. Ed. Lawrence Danson. Princeton: Princeton UP, 1981, pp. 21–118.

McGann, J. J. *The Romantic Ideology: A Critical Investigation*. Chicago: The University of Chicago Press, 1983.

McGuire, P. C. "*Othello* as an 'Assay of Reason.' " *Shakespeare Quarterly* 24.2 (1973): 199–209.

McKeon, Z. K. *Novels and Arguments: Inventing Rhetorical Criticism.* Chicago/London: The University of Chicago Press, 1982.

McLuskie, K. "The Patriarchal Bard: Feminist Criticism and Shakespeare—*King Lear* and *Measure for Measure.*" In *Political Shakespeare: New Essays in Cultural Materialism.* Eds. J. Dollimore and A. Sinfield. Ithaca: Cornell UP, 1985, pp. 88–108.

Melville, H. *Moby Dick.* London: Penguin, 1994 [1851].

Mew, P. "Facts in Fiction." *The Journal of Aesthetics and Arts Criticism* 31.3 (1973): 329–37.

Miller, P. *The New England Mind: The Seventeenth Century.* New York: The Macmillan Company, 1939.

Mills, L. J. "Cleopatra's Tragedy." *Shakespeare Quarterly* 11 (1960): 147–62.

Milo, R. D. *Immorality.* Princeton: Princeton UP, 1984.

Montrose, L. "Professing the Renaissance: The Poetics and Politics of Culture." In *The New Historicism.* Ed. H. Aram Veeser. New York/London: Routledge, 1989.

Morrison, T. *Beloved.* London: Vintage, 1987 [1977].

Moulton, R. G. *Shakespeare as a Dramatic Artist.* New York: Dover, 1966 [1885].

——— *The Moral System of Shakespeare: A Popular Illustration of Fiction as the Experimental Side of Philosophy.* New York, 1903.

Murry, J. M. "Antony and Cleopatra." In *Shakespeare.* New York: Harcourt, Brace, & Co., 1936.

Neil, M. "'Mulattos,' 'Blacks,' and 'Indian Moors': *Othello* and Early Modern Constructions of Human Difference." *Shakespeare Quarterly* 49.4 (1998): 361–74.

Newman, K. "'And Wash the Ethiop White': Femininity and the Monstrous in *Othello*," in Barthelemy, 1994, pp. 124–43.

Northcote, B. "The Background to the Liebestod Plot in the Works of Thomas Mann." *The Germanic Review* 59.1 (1984): 11–18.

Novitz, D. "Learning from Fiction." *Philosophical Papers* 9 (1980): 60–73.

——— *Knowledge, Fiction, and Imagination.* Philadelphia: Temple University Press, 1987.

Nussbaum, M. *The Fragility of Goodness.* Cambridge/New York: Cambridge UP, 1986.

——— *Love's Knowledge: Essays on Philosophy and Literature.* New York: Oxford UP, 1990.

——— *The Therapy of Desire: Theory and Practice in Hellenistic Ethics.* Princeton: Princeton UP, 1994.

——— *Poetic Justice: The Literary Imagination and Public Life.* Boston: Beacon Press, 1995.

——— "Exactly and Responsibly: A Defense of Ethical Criticism." *Philosophy and Literature* 22.2 (1998): 343–65.

―――. "Literature and Ethical Theory: Allies or Adversaries?" *Yale Journal of Ethics* 9.1 (2000).

Nuttall, A. D. *Why Does Tragedy Give Pleasure?* Oxford: Oxford UP, 1996.

O'Connell, M. *The Idolatrous Eye: Iconoclasm and Theater in Early-Modern England.* Oxford: Oxford UP, 2000.

O'day, R. *The Family and Family Relationships, 1500–1900: England, France and the United States of America.* London: Macmillan, 1994.

Ornstein, R. "Love and Art in Antony and Cleopatra," in *Later Shakespeare*. Eds. J. R. Brown and B. Harris. London/New York: Edward Arnold, 1966.

―――. *A Kingdom for a Stage.* Cambridge, Mass.: Harvard UP, 1972.

Ophir, A. *The Order of Evil: Chapters in the Ontology of Morals.* Tel-Aviv: Am-Oved [Heb.], 2000.

Palmer, F. *Literature and Moral Understanding: A Philosophical Essay on Ethics, Aesthetics, Education, and Culture.* Oxford: Clarendon Press, 1992.

Parker, P. "Fantasies of 'Race' and 'Gender': Africa, *Othello*, and Bringing to Light." In Hendricks and Parker, 1994, pp. 84–100.

Pearlman, E. "The Invention of Richard of Gloucester." *Shakespeare Quarterly* 43.4 (1992): 410–29.

Phillips, D. Z. *Through a Darkening Glass: Philosophy, Literature, and Cultural Change.* Indiana: University of Notre Dame Press, 1982.

Pitt, A. *Shakespeare's Women.* London: David and Charles, 1981.

Plimpton, G. A. *The Education of Shakespeare: Illustrated from the Schoolbooks in Use in His Time.* London/NY: Oxford UP, 1933.

Pollard, D. E. B. "M. J. Sirridge, Fiction, and Truth." *Philosophy and Phenomenological Research* 38.2 (1977): 251–56.

Posner, R. A. "Against Ethical Criticism." *Philosophy and Literature* 21.1 (1997): 1–27.

Putnam, H. "Literature, Science, and Reflection." *New Literary History* 7.3 (1976): 483–92.

Reid, L. A. *Ways of Knowledge and Experience.* London: George Allen & Unwin, 1961.

Richardson, W. *A Philosophical Analysis and Illustration of Some of Shakespeare's Remarkable Characters.* London, 1774; rpt. New York: AMS Press, 1966.

Riemer, A. P. *A Reading of Shakespeare's "Antony and Cleopatra."* Sydney: Sydney UP, 1968.

Rivers, I. *Classical and Christian Ideas in English Renaissance Poetry: A Student Guide*, 2nd ed. London: Routledge, 1994 [1979].

Rorty, R. "Texts and Lumps." *New Literary History* 17.1 (1985): 3–16.

Rose, M. *Heroic Love: Studies in Sidney and Spenser.* Cambridge: Harvard UP, 1968.

Rosenberg, M. *The Masks of King Lear.* Berkeley: University of California Press, 1972.

Rossiter, A. P. *Angel with Horns, and Other Shakespeare Lectures.* London: Longmans, 1961.

Rozik, E. "The Common Roots of Dreams and the Theatre: A Revision of the Rhetoric Terminology in Freud's *The Interpretation of Dreams.*" *Assaph* 7 (1991): 75–102.

Rupprecht, C. S., ed. *The Dream and the Text: Essays on Literature and Language.* New York: State University of New York Press, 1993.

Schlegel, A. W. *Course of Lectures on Dramatic Art and Literature.* Trans. John Black. New York: AMS Press, 1965.

Sharpe, E. F. "From *King Lear* to *The Tempest.*" In *Collected Papers on Psycho-Analysis.* Ed. Marjorie Brierley. The International Psycho-Analytical Library, No. 36. London: Hogarth Press, 1947, pp. 214–41.

Shell, M. *Money, Language, and Thought: Literary and Philosophic Economies from the Medieval to the Modern Era.* London: The Johns Hopkins UP, 1982.

Shelley, M. W. *Frankenstein.* Indianapolis: The Bobbs-Merrill Company, 1974 [1818].

Sidney, P. *An Apologie for Poetrie* [*Sidney's Apologie for Poetrie*]. Ed. J. C. Collins. Oxford: Oxford UP, 1941 [1907].

Simmons, J. L. *Shakespeare's Pagan World: The Roman Tragedies.* Charlottesville: UP of Virginia, 1973.

Singh, J. "Othello's Identity, Postcolonial Theory, and Contemporary African Rewritings of *Othello.*" In Hendricks and Parker, 1994, pp. 287–99.

Sirridge, M. J. "Truth from Fiction." *Philosophy and Phenomenological Research* 35 (1975): 453–71.

Skinner, Q. *Reason and Rhetoric in the Philosophy of Hobbes.* Cambridge: Cambridge UP, 1996.

Slater, M. *Family Life in the Seventeenth Century: The Verneys of Claydon House.* London: Routledge, 1984.

Slights, C. W. "Slaves and Subjects in *Othello.*" *Shakespeare Quarterly* 48.4 (1997): 377–90.

Slights, J. "Rape and the Romanticization of Shakespeare's Miranda." *Studies in English Literature, 1500–1900* 41.2 (2001): 357–80.

Smidt K. "Two Aspects of Ambition in Elizabethan Tragedy: *Doctor Faustus* and *Macbeth.*" *English Studies* 50 (1969): 235–48.

Snow, E. A. "Sexual Anxiety and the Male Order of Things in *Othello.*" *English Literary Renaissance* 10.3 (1980): 384–412.

Solomon, C. R. *The Passions.* New York: Anchor Press, 1976.

Spivack, B. *Shakespeare and the Allegory of Evil.* New York: Columbia UP, 1958.

Stampfer, J. "The Catharsis of *King Lear.*" *Shakespeare Survey* 13 (1960): 1–10.

States, O. B. *The Rhetoric of Dreams.* Ithaca/London: Cornell UP, 1989.

——— *Dreaming and Storytelling.* Ithaca/London: Cornell UP, 1993.

Statman, D. "Literature, Law and Mercy." *Studies in Law* 18 (2002): 53–85, (Hebrew).

Stavropoulos, J. C. "Love and Age in *Othello*." *Shakespeare Studies* 19 (1987): 125–41.

Stempel, D. "The Transmigration of the Crocodile." *Shakespeare Quarterly* 7 (1956): 56–72.

Stewart, G. "Shakespearean Dreamplay." *English Literary Renaissance* 11.1 (1981): 44–69.

Stone, L. *The Family, Sex and Marriage: In England, 1500–1800*. New York: Harper Torch Books, 1979.

Strong, L. A. G. "Shakespeare and the Psychologists." In *Talking of Shakespeare*. Ed. John Garrett. London: Hodder and Stoughton, 1954, pp. 187–208.

Tatarkiewicz, W. *A History of Six Ideas: An Essay in Aesthetics*. Trans. C. Kasparek. The Hague: Nijhoff- PWN/Polish Scientific Publishers, 1980.

Tomlinson, G. *Music in Renaissance Magic: Toward a Historiography of Others*. Chicago: University of Chicago Press, 1993.

Tourneur, C. *The Atheists Tragedy*. From *Four Revenge Tragedies*, Ed. K. E. Maus. New York: Oxford UP, 1995.

Tracy, P. J. *The Love Play of Antony and Cleopatra: A Critical Study of Shakespeare's Play*. The Hague-Paris: Mouton, 1970.

Traversi, D. *Shakespeare: The Roman Plays*. London: Holis & Carter, 1963.

—— *Shakespeare: The Last Phase*. Stanford: Stanford UP, 1965.

—— *An Approach to Shakespeare*, third ed. New York: Doubleday, 1969.

Turner, S. T. and G. B. Matthews. *The Philosopher's Child: Critical Perspectives in the Western Tradition*. Rochester: University of Rochester Press, 1998.

Van De Vate, D. *Romantic Love: A Philosophical Inquiry*. University Park: Pennsylvania State UP, 1981.

Van Laan, T. F. *Role-Playing in Shakespeare*. Toronto/Buffalo: University of Toronto Press, 1978.

Van Peer, W. "Canon Formation: Ideology or Aesthetic Quality." *The British Journal of Aesthetics* 36.2 (1996): 97–108.

Vaughan, V. M. *Othello: A Contextual History*. Cambridge/N.Y.: Cambridge UP, 1994.

Vitkus, D. J. "Turning Turk in *Othello*: The Conversion and Damnation of the Moor." *Shakespeare Quarterly* 48.2 (1997): 145–76.

Walker, D. P. "Ficino's *Spiritus* and Music." In *Music, Spirit and Language in the Renaissance*. Ed. P. Gouk. London: Variorum Reprints, 1985, pp. 129–50.

Walsh, D. "The Cognitive Content of Art." *The Philosophical Review* 52.311 (1943): 433–51.

—— *Literature and Knowledge*. Middletown, Conn.: Wesleyan UP, 1969.

Warner, M. *Philosophical Finesse: Studies in the Art of Rational Persuasion*. Oxford: Clarendon Press, 1989.

―――― "Literature, Truth, and Logic." *Philosophy* 74.287 (1999): 29–54.
West, R. *Narrative, Authority, and Law.* Ann Arbor: University of Michigan Press, 1993.
White, J. B. *When Words Lose Their Meaning: Constitutions and Reconstitutions of Language, Character, and Community.* Chicago/London: The University of Chicago Press, 1984.
Wilcockson, C. "Father-Directors, Daughter-Performers in Shakespeare." *Critical Survey* 3.2 (1991): 134–41.
Williams, R. *Marxism and Literature.* Oxford: Oxford UP, 1977.
―――― *Problems in Materialism and Culture.* London: Verso, 1980.
Wilson, C. "Literature and Knowledge." *Philosophy* 58.226 (1983): 480–96.
Yehoshua, A. B. *The Terrible Power of a Minor Guilt: Literary Essays.* Syracuse: Syracuse UP, 2001.
Zamir, T. "Seeing Truths." *Journal of Nietzsche Studies* 15 (1998): 80–87.
―――― "The Face Of Truth." *Metaphilosophy* 30.1/2 (1999): 79–94.
―――― "Phaedo's Hair." *Iyyun* 51 (2002): 139–54.
Zemach, E. *Real Beauty.* University Park: The Pennsylvania State UP, 1997.

Index

Page references in italics indicate illustrations.

Abbot, M., 198, 199
Adamson, Jane, 157–58
Adelman, J., 141–42
Ad Herrenium, 211
Adlerian psychology, 74, 74n.18
aesthetic experience/response, xiv, 14, 28, 29–35, *30–31,* 109–11
aesthetics, 59–61
amoralism, 66, 85–86, 88n. See also under *Richard III*
anatomy, Renaissance, 168–69, 168–69n.1
The Antiquities of the Jews (Josephus), 141
Antony (historical figure), 141n.12
Antony and Cleopatra (Shakespeare): Adelman on, 141–42; Antony's death, 145; Antony's protectiveness, 139–40; Antony's weakness, 143–44; Cavell on, 144n.17; Charney on, 141–42; Cleopatra's beauty, 134–35, 135n; Cleopatra's love, 137–40, 143–46, 144n.18, 159; Cleopatra's violence toward the messenger, 140; on cost of vice, 130n; doubts about love in, 135–38, 136–37n.9; embodiment in, 138–39; exhibitionistic love in, 136–37n.9; knowledge from exemplification of mature love in, 146–50; love as withdrawal from masculinity in, 133, 133n.6; mature love/passion in, 129, 130–32, 133, 136, 137, 142–43, 156; naming in, 136–37n.9, 137; performative conception of love in, 132–33nn.4–6, 132–35, 136–37, 137n.10; readers' responses to the affair, 130n, 140–46, 142n, 149; seduction in, 134; sources for, 131, 135n, 141, 141n.12; Traversi on, 124n, 141–42
arguments: abductive vs. paraductive, 8n.15; examples/enthymemes in, 7–8, 8nn.14–15, 23n.4, 36–37; inductive, 8–9, 9n.16; invalid/nondeductive practical reasoning, 9–10, 9n.17, 14, 24, 146; particular vs. categorical propositions in, 8, 8n.15; rhetorical analysis of, 7–10, 8n.14; and rhetorical means of justifying beliefs, 9–10, 14. *See also* beliefs; rationality
Aries, Phillippe, 198
Aristotle: on emotional purging, 55; on hearing vs. sight, 169n.2; on invalid practical reasoning regarding first-truths, 9n.17; on literature-as-example, 7–8, 8n.14, 23n.4, 36–37, 146; *Poetics,* 5n.6; *Rhetoric,* 7–8, 23n.4, 211; on sound, 177
art: as character-forming, 35; class-dependent idealization of, 32; enhanced realness through, *30–31,* 31–32; mimetic view of, *57–58,* 58n; pleasure as primal function of, 59; and symbol, 166
articulation, aesthetic, 29, 33
The Art of Rhetoric (Wilson), 211
Ascham, Roger, 23n.3
The Atheist's Tragedy (Tourneur), 67, 115, 170, 170n, 194n
Avicenna, 168n

Babb, Lawrence, 130n, 160n
Bacon, Francis, 71n, 169n.2
Barber, C. L., 195n.12
Basilikon Doron (James I), 163n.13, 205n, 206–7, 207n
Beauregard, David, 45
beauty, 71n
beliefs: acceptance of vs. justification for, 14–15, 14n.25; and contexts of discovery/justification, 24, 128; empathic, 6–7; error theory based on coherence among, 38; formation through aesthetic response, 109–10; imagination's role in formation of, 6, 6n.11; normative vs. descriptive formation of, 10, 10n.19; rhetorical means of justifying, 9–10, 14. *See also* arguments

INDEX

Beloved (Morrison), 32
Bèrubè, Michael, 60
Bloom, Harold, 66
Bodkin, Maud, 152n.1
body, as a form of the soul, 71n
Boethius, 169n.2
Boose, L., 199n
Booth, Edwin, 154
Booth, Wayne, 23n.4, 38, 44, 46
Bradford, Gamaliel, 142n
Bradley, A. C., 46, 79n.20, 97n, 192, 196n.14
Brooke, A.: *The Tragicall Historye of Romeus and Juliet,* 114, 114n.5, 116, 118, 124
Brooks, Cleanth, 45
Brudney, D., 46, 90n
Brümmer, Vincent, 132n
Bullough, G., 135n
Burke, Kenneth, 44
Burton, Dolores, 70n.11, 73–74n.16, 139–40

Calderwood, James, 121n
carpe diem vs. staleness, 129
Cavell, Stanley: on blindness of readers, 123n.15; on existential concerns as epistemological problems, 4n; on *Hamlet,* 172; influence of, 45; on *King Lear,* 26, 96n.6, 123n.15, 193n.6; on *Othello,* 37, 151, 152n.1, 163n.14; on perception/misperception of characters, 90n; on philosophical criticism, xiii; on *Richard III,* 79, 79n.21, 88n; on skepticism in Shakespeare's work, 67n.5, 88n
Chapman, George: *The Revenge of Bussy D'Ambois,* 170, 170n
character analysis, categories for, 52, 53
Charney, M., 141–42
child, overcoming of, 201–2
children, 199, 199n
Cicero: *On Invention,* 211; *The Orator,* 211; on rhetoric, 23n.3, 211; on wisdom, 211–12
Cleopatra (historical figure), 131, 141, 141n.12
cognitive experience, 65, 180

cognitive feeling, 6n.10
Coiter, Volcher, 168n
Coleridge, S. T., 112–13, 116, 196n.14
concrete universals, 33, 45
consciousness, actual vs. possible, 49
consequentialism, 15
contemporary literary studies. *See* literary studies
context, appeals to, 11, 11n.22, 36, 37–38
contractarianism, 55
conversationalist reasoning, 25
conveying vs. describing, 13–14n.24, 147–48
Crooke, Helkiah, 168–69nn.1–2
cultural materialism, 49, 56

Daniel, Samuel: *The Tragedy of Cleopatra,* 135n, 144
Danto, Arthur, 112n
David (historical figure), 30
David (Michelangelo), 27, 27–28, 30, 43
The Day the Swallows Spoke (Matthee), 126
deconstruction, 4n
dehumanization of characters, 78–79, 79n.20
Dekker, Thomas: *The Shoemaker's Holiday,* 115
de Rougemont, D., 164n
Derrida, Jacques, 44
Descartes, René, 88n
describing vs. conveying, 13–14n.24, 147–48
despair literature, 173
Diamond, Cora: on coherence-based error theory, 38; on empathy, 166; on literature as yielding knowledge through coherence, 5n.3; on literature's particularity, 6n.9; moral interest of reading, 46; neoromanticism of, 44; on philosophy as an imaginative response to life, 4n
Dickey, Franklin M., 19, 130n
didactic vs. philosophical criticism, 18–19, 19n
Dido, Queen of Carthage (Marlowe), 160n
Disoi Logoi (need to bring out many sides of an issue), 25n

226

INDEX

Dowden, Edward, 136
Ducasse, C. J., 28, 31

Eagleton, Terry, 53
ears, Renaissance conceptions of, 168–69, 168–69n.1
Ecclesiastes, 93
Edward II (Marlowe), 42
Eldridge, R., 6n.9, 146
Eliot, George: *Middlemarch*, 39–41, 43
Eliot, T. S., 181
empathy/empathic beliefs, 6–7, 33, 66, 86, 166
empiricism and innate essences, 33–34
Empson, William, 172n
Enlightenment, 165, 202
Epicureans, 16n
epistemological basis of philosophical criticism, 3–19; and aesthetic experience, 14; epistemological roles of literary experiences, 11–12nn.21–22, 11–14, 13–14n.24; and literary arguments, 7–10, 8nn.14–15, 9–10nn.17–19, 14–15; and literary experience, 6–7, 6n.11, 147–48, 147n; and literary language, 4–6, 5–6nn.6–9, 5n.3; methods of analyzing reader response, 17–18, 18n; and philosophical vs. didactic criticism, 18–19, 19n; structuralization of knowledge, 16–17
Erasmus, 72–73n.15; *De Copia*, 211–12
error theory, 35–38
ethics: developing moral reasoning, 24–25, 25n; and literary studies, 54–56; and literature (*see* moral basis of philosophical criticism); moral action as grounded in avoiding pain/punishment, 84; and rhetoric, 21, 24–25; and truth, 15. *See also* moral basis of philosophical criticism
ethos, 165
Euripides: *Medea*, 36, 57; *Trojan Women*, 36
Evans, Robert, 122n.11
examples/enthymemes in arguments, 7–8, 8nn.14–15, 23n.4, 36–37

The Faerie Queene (Spenser), 20, 29, 98, 115, 173, 205
Falck, Colin, 6, 6n.11, 44
Fathers and Sons (Turgenev), 98
Fenner, Dudley, 212
Ferry, Anne, 58–59
Ficino, Marsilio, 169n.2
Foster, D. W., 95n
Foucault, Michel, 44
Frankenstein (Shelley), 89n
Freud, Sigmund, 99, 99n.10

Gadamer, Hans-Georg, 55, 166
Gallagher, C., 59–60
Garnier, Robert: *The Tragedie of Antonie*, 134–35, 135n
Geoffrey of Monmouth, 205, 207
Gibbons, Brian, 113n.2, 121n, 124, 124n
Goldmann, Lucien, 49
Goodheart, Eugene, 60
Gosson, Stephen, 169n.2
Granville-Barker, H., 189, 192
Greenblatt, Stephen, 55, 58–60, 58n, 148, 152n.1, 155n
Gross, Kenneth, 153n, 176n.7
Guj, Luisa, 95n

Halio, Jay, 195n.11
Halstead, R. N., 152n.1
Hamann, Johann Georg: antirationalism of, 44
Hamlet (Shakespeare), 168–82; Cavell on, 172; ears/hearing/audibility in, 168, 169–70, 174–76, 175–76nn.6–7; embodiment in, 99, 180; eyes/sight in, 168, 178; Gertrude's self-knowledge, 176–77, 176n.9; Gertrude's sight, 178, 178n; Hamlet on mature love, 129n; Hamlet's antilife speeches, 98; Hamlet's delayed revenge, 170–71, 170n, 180–81; and *Othello*, 179; Pyrrhus and Priam story, 173, 175n; readers' responses to, 171, 181; self and action/playacting in, 168, 171–75, 172–73nn.4–5; "to be or not to be" soliloquy, 172–73
Hammond, A., 79n.20
Hanmer, Thomas, 181

227

happiness, 136, 161n.10
Harvey, Gabriel, 212
Hazlitt, W., 97n, 112–13, 114n.4, 116, 123
hearing, Renaissance conceptions of, 168–69, 168–69nn.1–2
heart, sound heard in, 177, 177n
Hegel, G. W. F., 174, 202
Heidegger, Martin, 44, 55
Heilman, Robert B., 46, 72n.14, 83n, 152n.1, 196n.13
Heywood, Thomas, 41n
Higgins, John, 207
Hillman, D., 176n.9
Holinshed, Raphael, 205, 207
Holland, Norman, 124, 124n, 168
Honigmann, E. A. J., 18n
Houlbrooke, Ralph, 198
humanists/humanistic culture, 23n.3, 47–48n.3
Hymn in Honor of Beauty (Spenser), 71n
hyperbole, 122

ideological/conceptual networks, 50–51
ideology, as language abstracted from material conditions, 32
individuality, birth of, 173n
innate essences, 33–34
Institutio Oratoria (Quintilian), 211
in utramque partem exercises, 211
Isocrates, 25n

James, D. G., 186n
James I, king of England, 194n; *Basilikon Doron,* 163n.13, 205n, 206–7, 207n
Jameson, Mrs., 196n.14
The Jew of Malta (Marlowe), 42
Johnson, Ben: *Sejanus,* 29
Johnson, Samuel, 46, 97n, 197
Jones, Emrys, 70n.11, 110, 110n
Joseph (biblical figure), 195n.10
Josephus, Flavius: *The Antiquities of the Jews,* 141
Julius Caesar (Shakespeare), 17
justification, truth as practices of, 25

Kalin, Jesse, 9n.17, 107n
Kant, Immanuel, 202

Kantianism, 55
Keats, J., 6n.8
Kerrigan, William, 92n.3
Kertzer, Jonathan, 10n.19
King Henry VI, Part III (Shakespeare), 69, 69n.9, 70n.11
King Lear (Shakespeare), 183–204; biblical/incisive visions in, 195–96, 195–96nn.10–14; Cavell on, 26, 96n.6, 123n.15, 193n.6; conditional acceptance/love in, 190, 191; deaths of Gonerill and Regan, 183–84; Edmond's villainy, 70, 79n.20, 185n; experiences of discovery in, 201, 201n; Gloucester's relation to Edgar, 186n; and *King Leir,* 189, 205; Lear's childishness, 188–90, 188n, 192, 195n.10; Lear's love, 183, 193–97; Lear's motivation for dividing his kingdom, 205–9, 206n; Lear's need for love, 189; Lear's shame/madness, 192–93, 193n.6, 193n.8, 195; Lear's war with the elements/nature, 190–93, 195n.12; Lear's withdrawal from parenting, 183–84, 185–88, 186n, 191, 193, 193n.6, 193n.8, 197; Lear's withdrawal from the body, 191–92; readers' response to, 190, 201, 203n; repetition in, 72; sources for, 205, 207; tragic movement in, 183–84, 194–97; villainy as love deprivation in, 79n.20
King Leir, 189, 205
King Richard the Third. See *Richard III*
Kirsch, Arthur, 110, 110n, 151
Kirschbaum, Leo, 151, 152n.1
Knight, Wilson, 17, 103n, 188n
Knights, L. C., 188n
knowledge: and contingency, 146, 147–49; and experience, 12–13, 27–28, 127 (*see also* epistemological basis of philosophical criticism); functional/didactic view of, 4; knowing how vs. knowing that, 129, 149–50; knowing the shape that things may take, 149–50; knowing what it is like, 149; and public verification, 17; as reducible to behavior, 13, 13n.23; structuralization of, 16–17, 34. *See also*

epistemological basis of philosophical criticism
Kohlberg, Lawrence, 188n
Kott, J., 152n.1
Kyd, Thomas: *The Spanish Tragedy,* 115, 170, 170n

Lamarque, P., 6n.8, 14n.25
Lamb, Charles, 196n.14
Leavis, F. R., 151, 152nn.1–2
Levine, George, 60
literary studies, 45–61; and aesthetics, 59–61; arguments against philosophical criticism from, 50–54; culturally oriented, xiii–xiv, 46–49, 47–48n.2–3; and cultural materialism, 49, 56; and ethics, 54–56; formalism within, 45; and mimetic criticism, 57–58, 58n; and New Historicism, 47, 49, 55; and New/Old Criticism, 45; vs. philosophical criticism, 45, 47–48, 47–48n.3; and political criticism, 48–49, 52–56, 54n, 58, 59, 61; and romanticism, 55–56; and self-experience/culture, 52, 53–54; and tradition, 50, 52–53, 54; and truth, 56–59, 58n
literature: arguments in, 7–10, 8nn.14–15, 9–10nn.17–19, 14–15; as character-forming, 35; and cognitive experience, 65, 180; describing/conveying and telling/showing oppositions in, 13–14n.24, 147–48; despair, 173; as educational, 27, 27–29; as example, 7–8, 8n.14, 23n.4, 36–37, 146; and identity completion, 166–67; as imaginative response to social networks, 48–49; instrumentalization of, 19, 19n, 49, 111; knowledge through, 7n.12; language of, 4–6, 5–6nn.6–9, 5n.3; literary experiences, epistemological roles of, 11–12nn.21–22, 11–14, 13–14n.24; literary experiences, generally, 6–7, 6n.11, 147–48, 147n; logos vs. pathos in, 10n.19; moral growth through (*see* moral basis of philosophical criticism); particularity of, 6, 6n.9; philosophical reflection on (*see* philosophical criticism); repetition in, 72–73nn.14–15; rhetorical capacities of, 22–24, 22n; suggestive capacities of (suspending disbelief), 11, 11n.21, 34, 60; uniqueness of, 59–60; as yielding knowledge (*see* epistemological basis of philosophical criticism). *See also* philosophy, and literature

logos, 10n.19, 165
Lolita (Nabokov), 86
Loomba, Ania, 153n
love: action-oriented aspects of, 132n; as blindness, 127–28; courtly, 160n; and death, 163–64, 164n; early-modern conventions of, 147; as ennobling, 130n; happiness in, 136; idealization of, 160, 160n, 163; *Liebestod,* 163–64, 164n; as malady/folly, 115, 130n, 160n; mature, 129, 130–32, 133, 136, 137, 142–43; as performance, 132–33nn.4–6, 132–35, 136–37, 137n.10; and philosophy, 112, 112n, 125–27 (see also *Romeo and Juliet*); vs. rationality, 40–41, 129, 130n; religious undertones of, 160n, 163; theory of, 126; as two that become one, 163, 163n.13. See also *Antony and Cleopatra; Othello; Romeo and Juliet*
Love's Labor Lost (Shakespeare), 211
Luhrmann, Baz, 123

Macbeth (Shakespeare), 92–111; ambition/motivation of Macbeth, 92–93n.3; belief-formation from reading, 109–10; blood/embodiment in, 99–102; collapse of Lady Macbeth, 99, 99n.10; emotion in Malcolm–Macduff–Ross scene, 103–6, 103n, 105n; Freud on, 99, 99n.10; gender in, 106n.14; guilt in, 101–2; James I's influence on, 207n; Lady Macbeth's tempting of Macbeth, 97n; masculinity in, 105–6, 106n.15, 133n.6; Moulton on, 97n; nihilism of Macbeth, 93–96, 96n.6, 98–99, 102–3, 107–9; postponement in, 94–98; rhetorical contrast in, 108–9; Rossiter on, 99n.10; success/emptiness of Macbeth, 98–99, 99n.10; temporality in, 95–98, 95n; values of characters, 17, 109

229

Macpherson, Crawford, 58–59
Magnus, Albertus, 168n
Marlowe, Christopher: *Dido, Queen of Carthage,* 160n; *Edward II,* 42; *The Jew of Malta,* 42; *The Massacre at Paris,* 3, 212; *The Tragical History of Doctor Faustus,* 42
marriage, 39–41, 43
Marx, Karl, 44
Marxism, 32–33, 50, 51
The Massacre at Paris (Marlowe), 3, 212
Maternity (Picasso), 30, 30–31
Matthee, Delene: *The Day the Swallows Spoke,* 126
Maus, Katharine Eisaman, 58–59
McKellen, Ian, 95
McKeon, Zahava Karl, 10n.19
Measure for Measure (Shakespeare), 98, 173, 206, 207n
Medea (Euripides), 36, 57
Melville, Herman: *Moby Dick,* 56–58
The Merchant of Venice: Bassanio and Antonio's friendship, xi; hatred's purity in, xi; justice in, xii; law in, xi–xii; religious values in, xii; Shylock's confrontation with Portia, xi; Shylock's hatred/alienation, xi–xii
Metamorphoses (Ovid), 57
Michelangelo: *David,* 27, 27–28, 30, 43; *Moses,* 196n.14
Middlemarch (G. Eliot), 39–41, 43
Middleton, Thomas: *The Revenger's Tragedy,* 170, 170n
A Midsummer Night's Dream (Shakespeare), 124n, 129n
Mills, L. J., 142n
Milo, Ronald D., 66–67n.3
Milton, John, 20
mimetic criticism, 57–58, 58n
Moby Dick (Melville), 56–58
modernism, 54n, 55
Mondino dei Lucci, 168n
Montaigne, Michel de, 198
Montrose, L., 50
moral basis of philosophical criticism, 20–43; and aesthetic response/sense of reality/self-experiences, 29–35, 30–31;
and didactic/moralistic literature, generally, 20–21; and enrichment through drama, 41–42, 41n; and error theory, 35–38; and literature as educational, 27, 27–29; and marriage, 39–41, 43; and moral contributions of literature, 21–24, 22–23nn.2–3, 24n.6; and philosophy as inquiry vs. education, 26–27; and rhetorical capacities of literature, 22–24, 22n
moral development, 188n
moral motivation, Humean accounts of, 23–24, 24n.5
More, St. Thomas: *Utopia,* 197–98
Morrison, Toni: *Beloved,* 32
Moses (Michelangelo), 196n.14
Mother and Child (Picasso), 30–31, *31*
Moulton, R. G., 46, 67n.6, 68–69n.8, 69–70n.10, 80, 97n
Murry, J. M., 138, 150
musicology, Renaissance, 168–69, 169n.2
mythos, 165

Nabokov, Vladimir: *Lolita,* 86
nature as mother, 70, 70n.12
new aestheticism, 60
New Historicism, 47, 49, 55
Newman, Karen, 153n
New/Old Criticism, 45
Nietzsche, Friedrich, 88, 198
nihilism: vs. aesthetic experience, 111; descriptive vs. normative, 107n; of Macbeth, 93–96, 96n.6, 98–99, 102–3, 107–9; and the value of rationality, 93, 107
North, Thomas: *Plutarch's Lives of the Noble Grecians and Romans,* 131, 134–35, 141, 141n.12, 143n.15, 144
Novitz, David: on aesthetic views of literature, 19n; on coherence-based error theory, 38; on functional/didactic view of knowledge, 4; on the imagination, 6n.11; on inductivism, 9n.16; on literature as yielding knowledge through coherence, 5n.3; neoromanticism of, 44
Nussbaum, Martha: on aesthetic views of literature, 19n; on coherence-based error theory, 38; on empathy, 166; on inte-

grating formation/assessment of beliefs, 7; on learning from literature, 146; on literary experience, 6; on literature as yielding knowledge through coherence, 5n.3; on literature's particularity, 6n.9; on living through art, 31; neoromanticism of, 44; on perception/misperception of characters, 90n; on philosophical criticism, xiii; on philosophy and love, 112n; on reflection through literature, 44n
Nuttall, A. D., 203n

O'Connell, M., 195n.12
Olsen, S. H., 6n.8, 14n.25
On Invention (Cicero), 211
The Orator (Cicero), 211
Ornstein, Robert, 69–70n.10
Othello (Shakespeare), 151–67; Cavell on, 37, 151, 152n.1, 163n.14; as a critique, 165–66; Desdemona's beauty, 155–56; Desdemona's love/sexuality, 152n.1, 156–60, 157–57nn.7–8; and *Hamlet*, 179; Heilman on, 152n.1; Iago's vengeance, 70; Iago's villainy, 151; knowledge and resistance in, 161–62, 162n.11; love as death in, 163–64, 164n; love as war/violence in, 161–62, 162n.12, 163, 164–67; Othello's erotic refusal/temptation scene, 151–53, 152nn.1–2, 161n.10; Othello's instrumentalization, 154–55, 154n.5, 158–59; Othello's jealousy, 151–52, 152n.1, 160n; Othello's love, 119n.8, 152nn.1–2, 154–56; Othello's murder of Desdemona, 86–87, 152–54, 153n, 159, 163n.14, 164; Othello's status, 154, 154n.4; Othello's suicide, 162–63; Othello's tragedy, 159, 160–61n.9, 160–64; readers' response to, 163–64; selfhood/subjectivity in, 154–55, 155n.6; truth in, 57
Ovid: *Metamorphoses*, 57

parenting, 194n, 197–200, 199n, 202–3. See also *King Lear*
patriarchy, 199

Peirceian abduction, 8n.15
Pembroke, Countess of: *The Tragedie of Antonie*, 134–35, 135n
perception/misperception of characters, 89–90, 90n
Perelman, Chaim, 23n.4, 44
Petrarch, 23n.3
Phaedo (Plato), 202
Phaedrus (Plato), 57, 133, 160n
Phèdre (Racine), 42
Phillips, D. Z., 6n.9
philosophical criticism: vs. abstract philosophical thought, 45; adherents/viability of, 44–46, 44n; and aesthetic experience, xiv; Cavell on, xiii; and contemporary literary studies (*see* literary studies); vs. didactic criticism, 18–19, 19n; epistemological basis of (*see* epistemological basis of philosophical criticism); faulty morality of, 51–52; formalist, xiv; vs. modernism, 48n.3; moral basis of (*see* moral basis of philosophical criticism); Nussbaum on, xiii; reductive, xiii; usefulness of, xii–xiii
philosophy: vs. education, 26–27, 35; and foundational questions of value, 93; and literature, 86–91, 107–11, 125–28, 146–50, 163–67, 179–82, 197–204; and love, 112, 112n, 125–27 (see also *Romeo and Juliet*); vs. rhetoric, 44
The Phoenix and the Turtle (Shakespeare), 161n.9
Picasso, Pablo: *Maternity*, 30, 30–31; *Mother and Child*, 30–31, 31
Plato: on beauty as a condition for intellectual responsiveness, 29; on dying/afterlife, 197; idealism of, 55; on innate essences, 33–34; myths as expressing the ineffable, 5–6n.7; on parenting, 197; *Phaedo*, 202; *Phaedrus*, 57, 133, 160n; on poets, 11n.21; on reaons/needs, 88; *Symposium*, 163, 203
Plotinus, 29, 55
Plutarch's Lives of the Noble Grecians and Romans (North), 131, 134–35, 141, 141n.12, 143n.15, 144
Poetics (Aristotle), 5n.6

INDEX

political criticism, 48–49, 52–56, 54n, 58, 59, 61
Pollard, D. E. B., 146
Posner, Richard, 19n, 33
postmodernism, 44, 47n.2, 54n
poststructuralism, 57
propositional content, 72
Puritanism, 160n
Putnam, Hilary, 7n.12

Quintilian, 23n.3; *Institutio Oratoria*, 211

Racine, Jean: *Phèdre*, 42
Ramism, xv, 212
Ramsay, Frank, 108
Ransom, John, 45
The Rape of Lucrece (Shakespeare), 13–14n.24, 46–49, 47n.2, 58–59, 71n, 162n.12
rationality: and conversationalist reasoning, 25; and error theory, 11–12n.22; invalid/nondeductive practical reasoning, 9–10, 9n.17, 14, 24, 146, 200–1; vs. love, 40–41, 129, 130n; and nihilism, 93; rhetorical theory of, 7–10, 8n.14, 22–23, 23n.3; validity/certainty, identification with, 23, 23n.4; value of, 93, 107. *See also* arguments
realness/self-experiences, 29–35, *30–31*
Reid, L. A., 6n.10
repetition, 72–73nn.14–15
revenge, 170–71, 170n, 172n
The Revenge of Bussy D'Ambois (Chapman), 170, 170n
The Revenger's Tragedy (Middleton), 170, 170n
rhetoric: antirationalism promoted by, 25; and Cartesian ideals, xv, 23n.4; and Cicero, xv; Cicero on, 23n.3, 211; effectiveness of vs. justification in, xv; and ethics, 21, 24–25; *in utramque partem* exercises, 211; literature's rhetorical capacities, 22–24, 22n; vs. philosophy, 44; and Quintilian, xv; Quintilian on, 23n.3, 211; and Ramism, xv, 212; relativism promoted by, 25; Shakespeare's education in, 211–12; Thomas Wilson on, 211

Rhetoric (Aristotle), 7–8, 23n.4, 211
Richard III (historical figure), 65
Richard III (Shakespeare), 65–91; alienation of Richard, 69, 71–72, 73, 74, 83, 89, 89n; amoralism/evil of Richard, 65–66, 67n.6, 75, 78–79, 87, 88, 90, 93–94; Anne rejected by Richard, 79, 79n.21, 83, 84; Anne's response to/ spitting at Richard, 78–82, 115; aposiopesis in, 73–74n.16, 74; barking dogs in, 71–73, 73–74n.16; beauty in, 70–71; Bloom on, 66; Burton on, 73–74n.16; Cavell on, 79, 79n.21, 88n; Elizabeth vs. Anne in, 82n; embodiment in, 99; empathic understanding of Richard, 66; impotency of Richard, 70, 70n.11; infanticide by Richard, 84; justification of evil by Richard, 67–69, 68–69n.8; misperceptions by Richard, 89–90, 90n; moral skepticism in, 84–86, 88, 89–90, 93; Moulton on, 80; nature in, 70, 70n.12; nemesis in, 83–84; regret lacking in Richard, 83–84, 83n; repetition in, 72–73; responses to, 87–88, 87n; self-hatred by Richard, 71, 73, 74; split in/shadow of Richard, 73–78, 75–76n; as a tragedy, 88–89; ugliness/deformity of Richard, 69–70n.10, 69–72, 73, 74
Richards, Ivor Armstrong, 45
Richardson, William, 13n.24
romanticism, 55–56
Romeo and Juliet (Shakespeare), 112–28, 113n.2; blindness of characters/readers, 123–25, 123n.15, 128, 137; and Brooke's *Tragicall Historye of Romeus and Juliet*, 114, 114n.5, 116, 118, 124; Coleridge on, 112–13, 116; dreamlike response to, 124–25, 124n; embodiment in, 138–39; evasive quality of, 112–15; first love/erotic expression in, 112–13; Gibbons on, 113n.2, 121n, 124, 124n; Hazlitt on, 112–13, 114n.4, 116, 123; Holland on, 124, 124n; hyperbole in, 122, 130; Juliet's beauty, 125, 134; Juliet's erotic gaze, 119–20, 120n; Juliet vs. Romeo, 119–20, 120n; love and death in, 164n; and love as laughable

malady, 115; love at first sight in, 122–23, 155–56; love vs. reason in, 119, 119n.8, 129n; oxymoron in, 122, 122n.11; Romeo's dismissal of philosophy, 118; Romeo's love as suspending doubt, 116–20, 123, 136, 137; Romeo's love as suspending reality, 120–22, 121n; Romeo's switch from Rosaline to Juliet, 113–16, 114nn.4–5, 117, 123–24, 129n; Romeo's unreflectiveness/shallowness, 116–18; and shared structure of feeling, 57; youthful love/passion in, 130–32, 133
Rorty, Richard, 5n.3, 38
Rosenberg, Marvin, 188n, 190, 195n.10, 196n.14, 208n
Rossiter, A. P., 67n.6, 99n.10
Ryle, Gilbert, 129, 149
Rymer, Thomas, 46

Samson (biblical figure), 195n.10
Scaliger, J. C., 169n.2
Schlegel, A. W., 112–13
scientific vs. poetic discourse, 45
scientism, 48n.3
seeming/being gap, 173
Sejanus (B. Johnson), 29
self: and action, in *Hamlet*, 168, 171–75, 172–73nn.4–5; birth of, 173n; and disclosure, 179–80, 182; infantile aspects of, 201–2
self-completion, 55
Shakespeare, William: children in works of, 199, 199n; on dehumanization, 79n.20; describing/conveying and telling/showing oppositions in works, 13–14n.24, 147–48; didactic goals of, 20–21; dreamlike quality of works, 124n; education in rhetoric, 211–12; insights in works, xiii; literary excellence of works, xiii; methods of analyzing reader response to, 17–18, 18n; moral views of, xv; oppositions of love/reason, romance/reflection, and passion/marriage in works, 129, 129n (*see also* love; *Romeo and Juliet*); parenting in works of, 194n (*see also King Lear*); repetition used by, 72, 72n.14; skepticism addressed by, 67, 67n.5; works (see also *Antony and Cleopatra; Hamlet; King Lear; Macbeth; Othello; Richard III; Romeo and Juliet*); *Julius Caesar*, 17; *King Henry VI, Part III*, 69, 69n.9, 70n.11; *Love's Labor Lost*, 211; *Measure for Measure*, 98, 173, 206, 207n; *A Midsummer Night's Dream*, 124n, 129n; *The Phoenix and the Turtle*, 161n.9; *The Rape of Lucrece*, 13–14n.24, 46–49, 47n.2, 58–59, 71n, 162n.12; *Timon of Athens*, 29; *Titus Andronicus*, 34, 36; *Troilus and Cressida*, 129n; *The Two Gentlemen of Verona*, 115, 129n
Sharpe, Ella Freeman, 190
Shell, Marc, 161n.9
Shelley, Mary: *Frankenstein*, 89n
The Shoemaker's Holiday (Dekker), 115
Sidney, Philip, 23n.3, 24n.6
sight vs. sound, 168–69, 169n.2
Singh, Jyotsna, 153n
Sirridge, M. J., 146
skepticism: classical, 67, 67n.5; epistemological, 88n; moral, 84–86, 88, 88n, 89–90, 93
Skeptics, 16n
Slater, M., 198, 199
Slights, Camille Wells, 152n.1, 155n
Smidt, Kristian, 93n.3
Snow, E. A., 152n.1
Solomon, Robert, 112n
sound, 168–69, 169n.2, 174, 177
The Spanish Tragedy (Kyd), 115, 170, 170n
Spenser, Edmund: *The Faerie Queene*, 20, 29, 98, 115, 173, 205; *Hymn in Honor of Beauty*, 71n
Spivack, Bernard, 69n.8, 79n.20
Stampfer, J., 190, 203n
Stempel, Daniel, 130n
Stewart, Garret, 124n
Stockwood, John, 194n
Stoics, 16n
Stone, Lawrence, 198, 199
structures of feeling, 52, 53
symbolic thought, 166
Symposium (Plato), 163, 203

233

Tamora, 28–29
Taylor, Charles, 58–59
thematic categories, 51
thematic criticism, 49–50
Theyestes, 28–29
Timon of Athens (Shakespeare), 29
Titus Andronicus (Shakespeare), 34, 36
Tourneur, Cyril: *The Atheist's Tragedy,* 67, 115, 170, 170n, 194n
tradition, 50, 52–53, 54
The Tragedie of Antonie (Garnier), 144
The Tragedie of Antonie (Garnier-Pembroke), 134–35, 135n, 144
The Tragedy of Cleopatra (Daniel), 135n, 144
The Tragical History of Doctor Faustus (Marlowe), 42
The Tragicall Historye of Romeus and Juliet (Brooke), 114, 114n.5, 116, 118, 124
Traversi, Derek, 124n, 141–42, 196n.13
Troilus and Cressida (Shakespeare), 129n
Trojan Women (Euripides), 36
truth: and ethics, 15; and literary studies, 56–59, 58n; vs. necessary truth, 146; poststructuralism on, 57; as practices of justification, 25

Turgenev, Ivan: *Fathers and Sons,* 98
The Two Gentlemen of Verona (Shakespeare), 115, 129n

understanding, conceptions of, 15–16, 149
utilitarianism, 55
Utopia (More), 197–98

value, metaphysics/ontology of, 109
Van De Vate, D., 132n
van Peer, Willie, 123
Vossius, Gerhard Johann, 212

Walsh, D., 149
Warner, Martin, 8n.15, 10n.19, 205
Weitz, Morris, 45
Wilcockson, Colin, 194n
Williams, Bernard, 85, 87
Williams, Raymond, 48–49, 50, 51, 53, 55–56, 59–60
Willis, Thomas, 169n.1
Wilson, Thomas: *The Art of Rhetoric,* 211
Wimsatt, William Kurtz, Jr., 33, 45
world disclosure, 55
Wright, T., 177n

Yehoshua, A. B., 11n.21